Stories from the '64 Alaska Earthquake

The Day Trees Bent To The Ground

Compiled by Janet Boylan
Edited by Dolores Roguszka
Photographs by Dolores Roguszka

Publication Consultants — Since 1978

PO Box 221974 Anchorage, Alaska 99522-1974

ISBN 1-59433-021-2

Library of Congress Catalog Card Number: 2004115634

Copyright 2004
Anchor-Age Center
1300 E. 19th Avenue
Anchorage, AK 99501
(907) 258-7823
FAX (907) 278-2454
Website: www.anchorageseniorcenter.org
E-Mail: asc-admin@ak.net

—First Printing November 2004—
—Second Printing February 2005—
—Third Printing September 2005—
—Fourth Printing September 2006—
—Fifth Printing April 2008—
—Sixth Printing July 2012—
—Seventh Printing June 2015—

Front cover photo by Dolores Roguszka: *A spectacular sandwich*!
Sport car smashed between a concrete floor and a bathroom, with
the rest of the house precariously balanced on top! Home of Richard R. W. "Dick" Fischer , at 2035 Linn Place. Located in Turnagain,
from Susitna View Parkway south one block (between Foraker and
Dall Boulevards).

The photographer expected great sales to various publications of this
view. However, *Life Magazine* got there first and published almost an
identical view, in color, on the cover of their earthquake issue!

Manufactured in the United States of America.

Dedication

This book is dedicated to all those who were shocked into a new respect for nature on March 27, 1964, and especially to the 151 of them who contributed their stories to this collection.

Contents

Foreword

This book was conceived for two purposes. First, as a way to preserve some of the history of the Alaska Earthquake of 1964, before it is lost forever. The second purpose was a means of making money for the Anchor-Age Center, a nonprofit corporation that is always in need of funds to provide services through the Anchorage Senior Center.

It is the mission of the Anchor-Age Center to "enhance the quality of life for people 55 years old and older in the Anchorage Bowl and to serve as a resource."

We endeavor to "encourage independence through socialization and the promotion of healthy lifestyles; to assure that all seniors in the Community are aware of the various services for seniors at the Center and in the community; and to provide a central meeting place for senior organizations and others."

In purchasing this book, you are helping the Seniors of Anchorage live a fuller, more productive life.

Our Gratitude

Thanks to those who helped put this book together.

Jean Paal was a most talented Assistant Editor.

Gene Roguszka for acting as our Research Assistant.

Roberta Ward and Arlene Glassner helped gather the stories.

The Staff at the Anchorage Senior Center were invaluable.

Don and Dana Anderson, Andrew Lukaszevich, of Software North LLC, lent Technical Assistance to get us underway.

Castleton Enterprises, in their usual competent fashion, kindly rushed our "scan the negatives" order. We value their services.

This exciting book would not have been possible without those who contributed stories. Many, many thanks to you all.

And, finally, we appreciate the expert advice of Evan Swensen, Publication Consultants, who put it all together for us.

We couldn't have done it without you.

We apologize for any errors, but take responsibility for any we've overlooked.

Janet Boylan
Dolores Roguszka

Dolores Roguszka

As It Was

Good Friday, March 27, 1964, 5:36 PM

As the face of the earth in and around Anchorage rolled, rumbled, and ripped apart; as the bluffs along the shore churned, heaved and jolted free, sliding into Cook Inlet, taking with them some 100 homes of this cities' elite … now but broken, twisted shreds; as portions of the downtown business district dropped into a hole fifteen feet below street level; as buildings danced weirdly; as a small child sobbed, "Mommy, Mommy, make it stop!"; the terror of a world gone berserk was felt elsewhere too.

I was driving to my home some 15 miles south of Anchorage. Until now it had been a pleasant day. Clara McCutcheon and I had had lunch together and, since Gene and I were planning to buy a truck and camper, she and I had gone to see what was available in campers. In late afternoon we decided to call it a day and I drove her home, then headed for O'Malley Road.

Rural O'Malley Road was empty of any other traffic. I hardly had a moment for my mind to register the fact that trees on either side of the road were behaving oddly as they bent and bowed, touching their tops to the ground, when I felt that something had gone wrong with the car. It shook, jumped and wrested the steering wheel from my hands. It felt as if all four wheels had fallen off. I finally managed to stop in a snowdrift alongside the road, opened the door, and stepped outside. Immediately I was thrown to the ground. Even from a prone position, I could see the earth moving like sea waves. I tried to stand and was thrown back to the ground. After the third or fourth attempt I finally managed to get a grip on the wildly dancing car and crawled inside, filled with nausea and terror. Either the world had gone insane, or I had definitely "flipped my wig!"

A few feet in front of the car I watched a crack appear, almost in slow motion as it crossed the road. The ground opened and then closed again. It seemed an eternity when eventually the nightmare was over and all around me was an eerie silence. Still not another person or car in sight. Just silence. I had managed to stop in the area near where the Alaska Baptist Convention Building is today, just west of the only home in the area then, Dr. Ralston 's house.

Still shaking with fear I started the car and continued on my way home. I was a professional photographer and the only thought I had was "I've got to get home, pick up my camera gear, and come back to photograph that crack!" It was hours later when I realized my cameras were in the back seat of the car all along! Nor did I realize just how many "cracks" I would eventually photograph!

A real "mess" greeted me when I got home! Gene and the five dogs were shaken, but okay. The little log cabin still stood, minus the chimneys. The fireplace facing had detached from the wall and crushed the two new chairs sitting in front of it. Cabinet doors had been wrenched open but the Melmac (plastic dinner ware we used for every day dining) was safe. It hadn't moved. The good china was now only chips and chunks. The homemade jelly, jam and catsup cabinets had disgorged their contents over the winding stair-well and had splattered onto adjoining walls. The mint jelly stuck like glue to every surface it touched. It was months before I could get it all scraped away. The smell of mint became so obnoxious to me that I can't stand it, even today, some 40 years later.

As the aftershocks began, we were terrorized again and again. We watched the five Cocker Springer type dogs, Tina and her pups Mac, Phyllis, Cecil and Otto. Apparently they could pick up the vibrations before we felt them, and would head for the door. Every time they ran for the door, we ran too. We managed to pack some essentials, like food, water, bedding, changes of clothing, etc. into the car and parked it away from the house and out of range of any trees that might fall on it and waited for whatever was going to happen.

Power was out. Our kitchen stove used bottled propane so we could cook and use the oven to heat the place. With no power we had no water from our well, but we could melt snow. Clean up began. My antique pump organ had danced to the middle of the room. It had to be pushed back to its normal place. Gene's 4-inch jointer had jumped up and down and gouged holes in the concrete basement floor. No major damage here. This proved to be true of most log houses. The logs could move and shift as the quake did its damage. Conventional construction fell down.

In Kodiak, local Civil Defense head Frank Irick watched television with his teenaged children while his wife Helen worked the evening shift at their business establishment. The family had, only a month prior, moved into their new home, high on a hill. At 5:36 PM dishes began to rattle. A "pull-down" lighting fixture over the dining room table swung to and fro. Water sloshed over the top of the huge aquarium. Within minutes the "quake" was over ... no destruction at the Irick home. The City of Kodiak suffered only minor damage as a result of the tremor. But the worse was yet to come.

Miles away, in Prince William Sound, death and destruction were headed for the King Crab Capital of the world. Seismic waves raced along at 500 miles per hour towards Kodiak Island.

A towering wall of seawater struck the island community, carrying fishing boats from the harbor inland and depositing them throughout the city. When the wave smashed into the Irick place of business, Helen was fortunate enough to escape with only a serious drenching.

When the waves receded, Frank Irick's unpleasant duty began. To State Civil Defense headquarters he had to report nineteen dead or missing and presumed dead.

Of a fishing fleet of about 100 boats, Kodiak reported thirteen missing and presumed lost from the seismic waves; one sunk and four other destroyed in the eighty mph winds, which lashed the island a few days following. Fourteen other boats were beached or blown onto a breakwater, with four counted as total losses. Others of the fleet suffered light to heavy damage.

In the harbor the 131-ton crab boat *Selief*, captained by Bill Cuthbert, was anchored. The tsunami battered other boats into the *Selief* but the 80 ft. boat stayed afloat and rode the waves. At one point Captain Cuthbert remembers the breather between waves, when he ran a mooring line to the nearest thing at hand ... a telephone pole. He finally came aground. "About that time the marine operator was calling boats on the radio," he reported. "When she got to me, she says, "Where are you, captain." "So I told her ... "By dead reckoning, in the schoolhouse yard."

Another crab fisherman managed to anchor his boat in the harbor, but found himself harassed by debris coming out on the backwash. "I didn't mind the little stuff," he said, "but then I got hit by the Standard Oil Company Building. Lousy thing, she cracked my bow."

Nearly seventy firms in Kodiak lost business inventories and places of business. One was the Irick venture. In the downtown area, 157 dwelling units were destroyed.

Prior to 1960 this community faced serious economic difficulties as it had only one industry, that of salmon fishing and canning. The king crab industry since that date had boomed the area. But now, three of the four crab processing plants had been wiped out.

The gigantic wave smashed docks and waterfront, completely destroying the small boat harbor. I visited, on assignment for the Elks

Crab boat *Selief* was propelled by the seismic sea wave onto the schoolhouse yard.

Club, the stricken community a few days following Black Friday. Photographs were needed to help in assessing damages to the Elks Club Building. Already the Civil Defense group was busy with a "cleanup" operation. Wreckage was being "dozed" into piles and huge bonfires lighted the snowy evening skies as they consumed the debris.

Grimy faces and dark-circled eyes plainly showed the fatigue of the men as they toiled. Fishermen … without boats. Longshoremen … without docks. Cannery workers … without canneries. Clerks …

without stores. All of them, working twelve to eighteen hours a day, without pay. Why? "Because the 'cleanup' has to be finished before we can start to build again."

Somehow, through the efforts of the City, the Civil Defense, and many others, everyone was being fed. Everyone had a place to sleep.

Though uncertain of the future, these Alaskans hadn't given up, and they hadn't lost their sense of humor. The story was told in Kodiak of the first meeting of two fishermen after the tidal wave. One said to the other ... "Say, Joe, have you found your wife yet?" "Hell no", replied the other, "I've been too busy looking for my boat!"

Afognak, which dates back to Russian occupation of Alaska, lost fifteen homes, the village store, post office and community hall. The entire village area sank several feet, and for safety's sake the villagers decided to move to higher ground. All 170 residents of Afognak managed to reach the safety of the mountain behind their village before the tidal wave struck. Only one injury was reported.

As a result of the March 27th disaster, Alaska gained a new Aleut community. In gratitude to the Lions Clubs of District Forty-nine for assistance, the residents named the new village Port Lions. It was located some twenty-four miles south of their old home at Afognak. Lion's Clubs throughout the world assisted with relocation to the tune of approximately $650,000. They plan to construct forty new homes and a community hall. The U. S. Bureau of Indian Affairs will arrange for water, sewer systems and other public facilities.

Information has been sketchy from some areas, Anvik, on the Lower Yukon, reported four dead or missing and presumed dead.

Coast Guardsman Frank O. Reed died at Cape St. Elias.

In Craig, one family is homeless as a result of the seismic wave.

Six hundred miles west of Anchorage, and twelve miles inland from the Bering Sea, the village of Emmonak reported that the earthquake cracked the walls of the schoolhouse.

At Halibut Cove, where nearly everyone lives on the waters edge, a number of warehouses have been jacked up as protection from the tidal rise of some four and a half feet.

The Kake cannery, in Southeastern Alaska, suffered damage from higher tides.

A resident of Kotlik, on the north mouth of the Yukon, said their area "got shook up", while Kwiguk, on the south mouth of the Yukon, "got shook up and the ground cracked."

In Northwestern Alaska, Nome reported that the quake wasn't

felt there, although one old-timer noted that new cracks appeared in the ice of the Bering Sea.

At Ouzinkie, on Kodiak Island, the Spruce Island Fisheries king crab plant was destroyed. Chris T. Johnson, superintendent of the Ouzinkie Packing Corp. king crab plant said his companies' losses may be as much as $500,000 and that they had no insurance. Johnson reported the Ouzinkie Packing Corp. payroll had been about $5,000 every two weeks. It employed mainly Aleuts.

Port Ashton, Port White Shed and Lowell Point (near Seward), each reported one death.

Minor damage was reported at Port Baily, as well as at Port Graham, on Cook Inlet. Port Nellie Juan suffered three casualties.

The Chugach foothills community of Basher had a building loss of thirty-five per cent according to "Mayor" Maynard Taylor. Taylor said the loss "Will be total unless earth fill can be obtained to shore up foundations."

The small fishing village of English Bay situated on Cook Inlet a few miles south of Seldovia , suffered minor quake damage. Damage was expected on the gravel landing strip at the village, as it is only one to two feet above normal high tides.

One of the hardest hit of Alaska's villages was that of Chenega. The entire village, with the exception of the school, was swept out to sea by the ninety-foot seismic wave. Civil Air Patrol planes evacuated residents of this small community to Cordova, where they were housed in a church building until new homes could be made at Tatitlek or Ellemar.

Of the seventy to seventy-five inhabitants of Chenega, only fifty-six survived the gigantic wave. Among those dead or missing and presumed dead were most of the village fishermen and seal hunters.

Most of the Kenai Peninsula noted only minor damage after the strongest earthquake ever recorded in North America. While no shortage of essentials has yet been felt, the Kenai-Soldotna-Ninilchik and other nearby communities may note an absence of some items for a while. The entire area is isolated except by air. Merchants are making tentative plans to consolidate deliveries by barge, which could be brought into Kenai River to the Kenai City Dock or could land their loads at the Arness Terminal at Nikiski, near the new Standard Oil Refinery, some eighteen miles north of Kenai.

The Kenai Chamber of Commerce recently adopted a resolution asking that local, state and federal agencies act in all urgency to aid

Seward and that Seward be rebuilt to the exclusion of facilities at Whittier. Chamber members, according to President James E. Fisher, believe that the entire Kenai Peninsula might be damaged more by emphasis in rebuilding Whittier than it was by the earthquake.

The Office of Emergency Planning, through Civil Defense, announced that Homer sustained a loss of approximately $1,280,000.

A spokesman in Homer stated that crab pot losses were two out of three. A good pot costs over $200.

Stores lost stock; the Inlet Hotel was badly damaged and abandoned; a portion of land at the end of the spit sloughed away, sending a log house into a hole; the Bootlegger's Cove small boat harbor drained dry during the quake and the protective rock jetty of the basin disappeared.

With the threat of high tides, Lands End Resort, located at the end of the Homer Spit, was elevated to avoid the possibility of flooding.

While substantial property damage was sustained, there were no reports from this community of any loss of lives or injuries.

A compilation of facts from Southcentral Alaska reveals interesting sidelights.

The poultry industry marked the first flight of its kind with the shipment of 3,000 ready-to-lay chickens to R. C. Collins of Palmer, via a charter C46. A hatchery operator in Bellingham, Washington shipped the fowl from Seattle to Collins, who has about 10,000 laying hens. Collins, it was reported, suffered small quake damages. Other poultry farmers in the area were hard-hit.

Officials announced that the Nikolski School suffered no damage in the quake. Villagers were evacuated to the nearby military site but have now returned to the village. From Alitak, False Pass, Sand Point, Cold Bay and Pauloff Harbor also came word that "The school is in good shape." Schools on St. Paul Island and St. George Island are "fine", according to word received. An additional report from these Pribilof Islands noted that the rolling motion of the quake made numerous persons dizzy and ill but there were no casualties or damage.

Reports from Port Wakefield indicate that land in that area may have sunk as much as four feet. The high tides of mid-April put four inches of water on the floor of the Wakefield King Crab Plant. Employees are now dismantling machinery and equipment of the Wakefield plant and moving it to higher ground, in anticipation of still higher tides in May. The installation suffered only minor quake damage.

The waterfront community of Seldovia escaped major damage from the March 27th quake and seismic waves. However, the land level has dropped and some flooding has occurred during mid-April high tides. The lowest portions of the two-mile stretch of boardwalks went awash during the high tides and serious flood damage is still a possibility.

The Alaska quake was felt around the world. Scientists in Sweden, during the first seventy-two hours following the quake, measured more than 100 after shocks. Seismic sea waves caused several deaths in Crescent City, California. Tidal rises were recorded in Texas gulf ports, the Hawaiian Islands and Japan. Surprisingly enough, some Alaska communities felt nothing. Hooper Bay, on the Bering Sea shore of the Yukon Delta, didn't feel a tremor.

How many times can one community face oblivion and come back, time after time, to plan and work for the future? We marveled, in our story about Cordova, featured in the March 1964 issue of *Alaska Sportsman*, at the resiliency of these people. And now, catastrophe has struck again.

The latest report shows one casualty in Cordova.

Property damage was substantial. According to the Office of Emergency Planning, this community suffered approximately $1,775,000 in losses.

The damage has proved to be far greater than was first thought; canneries, boat yards and razor clam beds were left high and dry by massive land uplift. The Port of Cordova is now at least six feet more shallow than it was before the quake.

On the highway from the City of Cordova to the airport, thirteen miles distant, nearly every bridge was severely damaged and the earth nearby settled from one to five feet.

The devastating earthquake could very well have sounded the death knell for the Copper River Highway. Damages have been estimated at $34.6 million. Nine bridges were either completely smashed or were wrecked in some degree. Scores of rockslides and avalanches tore at the roadbed. Spring breakup could destroy more of the damaged structures. Increased erosion due to quake cracks will probably wreck more of the road.

The dream of a road from Cordova to Chitina may be erased forever. Present losses are so substantial that, in the face of greater priority needs of other state highways; even repairs may not be considered for many years to come.

The port city of Valdez, however, had staggering losses.

The town lost forty per cent of its business district. Ten to twenty per cent of the residential area was wiped out. Sewer and water systems completely demolished. Thirty persons dead or missing and presumed dead. Docks were swept away. Oil storage tanks burst and fires cut away at the heart of the town.

The Alaska Steamship Company's *Chena* was unloading at the Valdez dock when the tidal wave struck. The Captain reported that the vessel surged over the top of the dock, rolling violently. The force of the wave drove the stern of the ship inshore, permitting engines to be started immediately. As the water receded the *Chena* steamed back into the bay, barely scraping the top of a warehouse as it passed over it.

Below decks two longshoremen were killed outright as steel hatch covers lurched down upon them ... another had feet so crushed that they both had to be amputated half way to the knee.

One ships' officer reported seeing a man with two children racing for the city along the dock causeway. One child couldn't keep up so the father scooped her into his arms and continued to run. Suddenly the earth sunk out of sight beneath them ... in the maelstrom that swirled over the position only a spring straw hat for a little girl spun on the roily waters ... "Then the wave hit us and I nearly went over when the ship listed more than thirty-five degrees...."

A survey conducted by the U. S. Coast and Geodetic Group shows the Valdez harbor now forty-eight to 150 deeper than before the quake. The harbor had been 222 to 600 feet deep.

The seaport town of Seward was deeply involved with plans for a celebration. The announcement had just been made that Seward had been named "All-America City". Because of the happenings of March 27th, another citywide observance was held ... the first Seward Memorial Sunday, which is observed each year on the first Sunday after Easter. The All-America awards were not cancelled in 1964, only postponed.

The plight of Seward was serious. It suffered the complete destruction of the industrial area; an estimated $1.8 million loss to its' fishing fleet; total destruction of at least eighty-three homes. Thirteen persons missing and presumed dead and three known dead.

The quake caused a fire at the Standard Oil Company tank farm. The City light plant was lost in the flames. Six seismic waves, one following another, spread burning oil throughout the area. All docks were wiped out. Railroad equipment was overturned, rails twisted and broken. The waves pounded an Alaska Railroad diesel some 300 feet away from the track. As wave after wave surged over Seward, fishing craft were flung from the harbor area for a distance of a half a mile or more. Some homes floated from their foundations, others were pushed.

The old cannery at Lowell Point slid into Resurrection Bay. A new barite plant, due to open the following month, disappeared. A radio station, located approximately 1,000 feet from the beach prior to the gigantic waves, was seen later floating in the lagoon. The small boat harbor with sixty small craft completely vanished.

U. S. Coast and Geodetic Survey reports showed that the Seward port is now 390 to 450 deep in the dock area, compared with pre-quake depths of twenty to 120 feet.

At Old Harbor, Kodiak Island, the fourth seismic wave took all but a few of the thirty-nine houses of the village out to sea. According to Herman Androwvitch, the bay almost went dry. He saw the rocks on the bottom as the wave receded. All residents of this little Aleut village survived the disaster.

Aleut Roger Williams, a former U. S. Marine, related the happenings in his village of Kaguyak. "The quake itself did little damage to the community which sheltered thirty-two persons on Good Friday. The first seismic wave did not cause much damage. Before the second wave struck, some twenty minutes later, men of the village obtained sleeping bags from the village and raced back up the hill.

The third wave, which crested at fifty feet, devastated the twelve homes of the village. Two thirty-six foot fishing boats in the bay disappeared. Others belonging to the village and stored along the shore were also lost.

St. Nicholas Russian Orthodox Church had just been completed. When hit by the third wave, the church was ripped from its' foundations and deposited a mile from the village, totally wrecked. Only the cross, holy pictures and flags with religious pictures on them were salvaged. Tears were openly shed at the loss. Completely surrounded by water, the villagers spent the night atop the little hill. The next morning the discovery was made that two of their number were missing. One body was found. "Chief Simmie Alexandroff is presumed dead." Roger Williams assumed the responsibility of leadership of his people.

A story reported by the *Anchorage Daily News*, and one which has become a legend, is repeated here. The sixty-two year-old care-taker of St. Nicholas Church, Nick Rastopsoff, relates ... " a friend of mine from Egegik said he talked to a man of the Kuskokwim country. Last October month this man died. He began to get stiff. After two days he came alive again. He warned of the earthquake. He had been up there (pointing upward) and had talked to God. God told him."

Said young Chief Roger Williams, "I really would like to talk to that man."

And so would a number of others who have attempted to predict earthquakes!

Part Two

A short time after the earthquake and seismic waves, which struck Southcentral Alaska, had subsided, we were cruising at 11,600 feet in our Cessna, past the face of Mount Witherspoon headed for Harriman and College Fiords.

Geologists had indicated that the center of the earth's slippage radiated outward from College Fiord. This slippage had caused nearly $800 million damage to Alaskans and their property.

Our aerial excursion was to see what nature had done in the wilderness areas as well as the population centers.

Over Knik Glacier, the barrier ice that creates Lake George, in the midsection of the twenty-mile long river of ice, everything was a shambles. The three mile wide glacier was pulverized. It looked like shaved ice served at a bar.

The face of Surprise Glacier, which heads in the high pass of the Chugach Mountains, had receded in smashed fragments some two hundred yards. A portion of the glacier, which also drops into Harriman Fiord, gave mute evidence of massive icefalls.

In the distant south the entrance to Whittier Harbor was evident and enroute there we noted that huge avalanches had raced down steep gullies from the 7,000 foot level. Elsewhere great stone masses had broken away from the vertical cliff sides plunging recklessly down the steep mountain slopes, creating new irregularities on the already rugged mountain faces.

At one juncture we circled a gaping maw in solid rock. It swal-lowed up completely several avalanches while we watched. How deep those new stone crevasses were, only the maker knew.

Port of Whittier, about seventy-five miles from Anchorage, hove into view and we dropped the nose of the Cessna to lose altitude and could see that the oil docks were gone. The sawmill of the Columbia Lumber Company was smeared to rubble. Cabins and small houses adjacent just didn't exist ... nor some of their occupants. The oil storage facilities had burned out. Many had collapsed, whether from heat of fire or seismic wave force we could not determine. Part of the equipment of Whittier's huge docks had been swallowed up in the sea, yet a portion of the port was still usable. Many barges loaded with freight cars and vans were moored there and as we circled we could see two tiny tugs wrestling a huge Hydro-Train barge some ten miles down the bay. Rail facilities had been severely damaged. Observations concluded that Whittier had sunk six and one half feet.

When the wracking subsided the death toll stood at eleven dead or missing and presumed to be dead.

In the pass over Portage Glacier we turned the dogleg at about 1,000 feet. The face of this "tourist glacier" lay in the same shambles we saw at Knik Glacier. Portage Lake, which is over 600 feet deep, had heaved and slopped until massive pressure ridges of its ice covering were piled high here and there, particularly near the ledge area. Yet no open water showed on the lake.

The U. S. Forest Service reported that their tourist rest and view facility had been substantially damaged. Portage Glacier Lodge, owned and operated by Keith and Peggy Keathley, looked okay from the air as we circled at about 100 feet altitude.

We flew over Portage Pass to look at the Seward-Homer-Anchorage Highway. It was wrecked. The rearrangement of the crust of the earth literally tore the roadways apart, smashed bridges of the Alaska Railroad as well as the highways.

At least one fissure as much as five feet wide ran for a thousand yards down the yellow centerline of the road. In places the stripe was neatly halved. Due to the settlement of the landmasses, otherwise innocuous tides raced like a tiger through the crevices in the highway embankment ... ripping and tearing. Huge slabs of asphalt cement lay at crazy angles.

In a short seventy-five mile stretch of road, nineteen bridges were gone. The seven-mile Portage Cut-Off Road was fractured and ripped in a regular pattern. The whole valley, including the road, looked like a waffle. Many pressure ridges were twelve feet high, others a mere three feet.

At Portage Junction the Alaska Railroad Station still stood, though rather drunkenly. The tracks passing the station were waved as if a giant curling iron had passed down the rails, permanently kinking them.

The 110 pound steel rails at the bridgehead of the Twenty Mile River were sprung outward fifteen feet and the rail spikes had been snapped out of the ties for 200 feet by the sinking, wracking motion of the earth. The rail bridge stood though it had been heaved up (or the grade sunk) on the north end ... the highway bridge just a few feet west lay in the bed of the river, huge chunks of sea ice sprawled over the cement decking.

Enroute back to Anchorage we passed over the community of Girdwood. We noted a gaping black scar where Joe and Alice Danich's Little Dipper Inn once stood. Most ludicrous was sea ice covering the Girdwood airport and standing in chunks in the front yards of the remaining homes. Girdwood was a mournful view, yet it didn't suffer so much from shock as flood. Looking further up the valley toward Mt. Alyeska, Alaska's internationally famous ski resort, we noted a huge avalanche had crossed in front of the new lodge. Some few still skied.

Winging across Turnagain Arm we passed over the old village of Sunrise and on to the village of Hope. It was in this area that gold was first discovered in Alaska in the 1850s. Again sea ice was everywhere among the houses. Ominous watermarks on the sides of structures bore mute evidence of new tidal levels. The land had sunk. Even moderate tides ranged through the village. One house sat alone on a new island in the middle of the creek passing through the small community. Canoes and boats were tethered to front doors.

Approaching Anchorage, avalanches on the mountain sides were frequent ... a rockslide occasionally left a more serious mark on the slopes. Flying over this small metropolitan city of 88,000 population we could see huge rifts along Fourth Avenue southwest through L and M Streets to Eleventh Avenue. The same fault line seemed to run into the Turnagain residential area, Anchorage's newest. Here the escarpments slid. Slid into the sea. More than a hundred homes were smashed beyond comprehension as the earth writhed.

It was here in the Turnagain residential area that I had come face to face with the horrible consequences of March 27th. Shortly after the earthquake, a group of geologists formed a committee to assess the damages and potential future damages in this area. With continuing aftershocks, there was every possibility that other bluff areas and homes could slide into the sea. The area had been evacuated and no one permitted to go near. These geologists needed complete photographic coverage of the damage, and their leader, Dr. Ruth Schmidt, called to ask if I'd do the job. She noted, "I don't know if you will

A new cliff is formed when ground, houses and trees were hurtled towards the Inlet. This house is left hanging over the new cliff, and fears were that the next aftershock would cause it to join the jumble on the ground, which had subsided at the time of the big shock.

ever get paid, at the moment there is no money, but if there ever should be appropriations made you can submit a bill." I agreed to go into the area with the geologists, do what photographs they needed, would give them prints to use, and would retain all rights to the negatives and their future use. I also agreed that if money were ever available, I would submit a bill. If not, so be it. We made an appointment to meet near Turnagain and to walk into the area.

It was not an easy walk. Wreckage was strewn everywhere. Houses, in various stages of destruction, were in places they should not have been. Jumbled piles of earth blocked normal walkways. At last we stood on the newly formed bluff, where I began my work. Photos were made from all angles. We moved further inland to capture additional damage on film. We walked up and down, around crevasses, picking our way over wreckage that had once been a part of a home. Personal belongings scattered the landscape. We reached one home that now hung precariously over a bluff. The geologists wanted a photograph of the overhang. The only way to get the angle they wanted was to find a piece of packing crate, place it over a crevasse, lay down on my stomach and shoot back towards the bluff. The geologists stood at the top of the embankment while I balanced over the crevasse. About ready to depress the shutter, I felt the beginning of an aftershock. With visions of disappearing forever into the crevasse, I scrambled to my feet, headed for the embankment and shouted, "I quit!" Dr. Ruth looked at me and said, "Why, Dolores, if something happened, at least you are with people who could describe it technically!" That struck me as so ludicrous that I went back to work when the aftershock was over!

We managed to complete the work they wanted done and I supplied a number of prints for their use. I recognize some of my photographs in various U. S. government publications regarding earthquakes, credited to various government agencies. There never was any money available, and so I never submitted a bill. It wasn't important then, and it never became important. The importance was in the recording of this event, and a pride in being able to do so.

In our flying excursion we could plainly see that downtown Anchorage also suffered severely. Nearly three blocks of the main business district just east of the fourteen story Anchorage-Westward Hotel settled from eight to fifteen feet. There was such a shambles it was difficult to separate one building from another. Had I been in my usual place on that memorable day, I too would have perished. My darkroom at home was in process of being built, and in the meantime I used the darkroom at Mac's Foto, on Fourth Avenue. In return for the use of the darkroom I also did work for the owner, Steve McCutcheon. Normally on a Friday afternoon I would have been sitting at the enlarger. On that day the earthquake demolished the building, tilting it in such a fashion as to send heavy file cabinets full of eight x ten photographic prints crashing through the walls, taking everything in their paths ahead of them. The cabinets and their contents were buried in the rubble. Had it been a usual day, I would have also been buried.

At least three lives were lost in the Fourth Avenue holocaust. But no one knows how many really died. For part of this area was the land of the wino ... the range of the drunks. No one will ever know how many of these poor unknowns ... no address, no relatives, no "nothing" ... bodies known often only by a nickname, were swallowed up in the vortex of grinding gravel, concrete and timbers, that went smashing to perdition at 5:36 PM Good Friday of 1964.

Banking, we turned over the Government Hill Elementary School ... half of it lay in a canyon thirty-five feet deep ... torn, the roofs smashed, pieces of shattered glass stuck in the walls ... had it been in session at the time of the quake, 300 children would have perished in less than five and one half minutes.

Gliding for a landing on Lake Hood ice the curt voice of the air traffic controller warned that the pilot landed at his own discretion. Lake Hood, the worlds' most populous seaplane base, too had suffered damage.

Alaska's airports had come in for their shellacking. At Anchorage, the International Control Tower collapsed, killing one Federal Aviation Administration traffic controller. Anchorage's international jet flights now responded to orders from nearby Lake Hood seaplane base control center. The main international administration building and terminal lost its smoke pipe while floor and ceilings were contorted.

At least a dozen small planes were damaged either from falling debris or heaving of the ice on lakes where they parked during the flying season of skis. The tail section of one Cessna 180 fell into a huge fissure as the ice opened along the Lake Hood shore. That same ice clamped back together with malefic force, and gobbled up the complete rear controls area of the aircraft.

Fortunately, the airport at Valdez suffered relatively minor damage and continued to be used for relief and rescue operations of the quake, fire and tidal wave ravished Prince William Sound community. Large cracks appeared in the aprons and taxiways but the main runway held solid.

English Bay, on lower Cook Inlet, whose airport was normally only a few feet above high tide mark was gutted and washed is now so frequently under water as to be unusable for any aircraft, including amphibious types.

The airstrip on Fire Island, a military installation adjacent to Anchorage, sunk as the land in that area tilted (this is in line with the fault that slumped Anchorage business district and caused the huge slide in the residential area). It is now covered with debris and tidal pools rendering it useless to anything but helicopters.

One aviation official, who did not wish to be quoted, said that the State's airports probably suffered somewhere between one and a half and four million dollars in damage. The full import will not be realized until the frost has gone completely out of the ground sometime in July.

In Anchorage there was no tidal wave. Yet the port area suffered nearly four million in damage because the earths crust sank nearly four feet. Waves now erode areas that have not been under water for hundreds of years. In the Turnagain residential area "sea wavelets" lap the edges of bathtubs as a vagrant bottle of bubble bath dings persistently against the porcelain.

One bard succinctly observed, "Over in Turnagain the haves, have not ....and down in the flats (slum area), the have nots still ain't got nothin".

Governor of Alaska William A. Egan estimated that the fury of the elements cost the state nearly thirty million dollars in INCOME revenue this year.

The American Red Cross said that nearly 3,500 families have been directly affected by the quake, earth slides and seismic or tidal waves. More than 550 Alaska homes have been wiped out forever and more than 1,300 others suffered major structural damage. School systems alone in the stricken area lost ten million dollars of capacity. More than half of Western Alaska fishing industry was lost or materially damaged in the amount of twenty-five million dollars.

In five and one half minutes Nature totaled up a loss of between $750 and $800 million. To a state with 586,000 square miles of area, roughly 240,000 population, 50,000 of them taxpayers ... a state legislative budget recently concluded calling for nearly eighty million dollars in appropriations, the thirty million dollars of income loss in taxes will place Alaska's financial situation in precarious balance.

Part Three

The Alaska shock of March 27, 1964 was one of the greatest

earthquakes on record. It lasted some five minutes. Initial reports were of an 8.4 to 8.6 reading on the Richter Scale. It was later determined to be a 9.2 on the Richter Scale. It caused a loss of life of 115 people; left 4,500 homeless and caused damages of over $750,000,000, more than 100 times the cost to buy Alaska from Russia in 1867.

Alaska and Alaskans have long experienced earthquake activity. It is estimated that over a million earthquakes occur each year throughout the world. Many of these earthquakes are in unpopulated areas or under vast oceans, causing little or no concern.

There are, however, specific geographic locations where the majority of these earthquakes occur. These are along various belts of seismic activity, one of which includes the west coast of the United States, Canada and a large part of Southern Alaska. In the Aleutian Islands many submarine shocks are recorded which originate usually on the landward side of the great Aleutian Trench that runs parallel to and just south of the Island chain.

There are many active fault lines that constantly threaten Alaska with tremors. Four of these lines, the Lake Clark, Cook Inlet, Seldovia and Fairweather Faults, converge near Anchorage.

As pressures build in the earth's crust, the underground rocks bend and fold until a point is reached when the strain becomes intolerable, then the rock gives way at some weak point, often far beneath the surface. As the pressure is released, the pent-up energy reverberates in enormously powerful waves. Large areas are thrust upward, and mountains are built.

However, it was not the mountain building process itself that caused the major damage in the 1964 Alaska earthquake. The vibration, sliding and settling of loose glacial-alluvial deposits together with the shaking of water logged clays and silts, was responsible.

The quake itself was horrifying enough, but it was only the beginning of the devastation. Somewhere off Alaska's southern coast, the sea bottom had heaved and plunged violently, setting millions of tons of water in motion. The tsunamis, seismic sea waves (and commonly, but mistakenly, called tidal waves), were on their way to the coastal towns and villages of Alaska. They lashed the beaches of Hawaii; rolled over Crescent City, California, and rammed the coasts of North America. Major damage resulted in many areas from the tsunamis, not the quake which preceded.

Will man ever be able to predict earthquakes? Prevent them? Scientists have proposed theories, but as yet none have been tested nor proven. Perhaps some day in the not too distant future we will find a way to make use of the knowledge gained through the studies of the Alaska and other earthquakes throughout the world. Let us hope so.

A street in Turnagain totally broken into pieces. Many streets were thus damaged as the fault line tore through the area.

This manuscript is the result of a call from the late Robert Henning, publisher of *Alaska Sportsman*, who requested an article covering the earthquake, just a few days following the catastrophic event. It didn't arrive in Seattle soon enough, and the Sportsman went to press with other material. Written at that time, it has been reposing in my file cabinet all these years. It is a privilege to have it included in this book for the benefit of the Anchorage Senior Center.

Kathryn Alio

Refugees at Providence

Dorothy Hill and I were working at Northern Commercial Company on Fifth Avenue in the lingerie department, right by the front door, when we felt the first tremors. The big cash register crashed against the wall. People were trying on clothes. They began to get hysterical, screaming and rushing to the front door to get out. I had heard you shouldn't go outside for fear of electrocution, so I remained in the entrance until the big glass door and plate glass windows fell out on the sidewalks.

From the street you could hear the building creaking as if in great agony. My outdoor clothes were still in the building. After it stopped shaking, men went to the basement to bring coats up so we could go home. I was wearing mules for work, and my boots were lost. A nice lady came in a car and asked if she could take me somewhere. I was living on N Street by the inlet. She took me as far as she could, but couldn't get to "N" street so she let me off at the Knik Arms Apartment. Another nice woman standing outside brought me some boots.

When I got home I found the bookcase had fallen over, the bed askew and the grand piano lifted out of its casters and moved. It looked impossible to stay there. A neighbor, Mr. Ayerst, had cooked pork chops for dinner and baked a cake for Easter. The pork chops were on the floor, but the cake didn't move off the table.

A kid ran down the street yelling "tidal wave coming," so we decided to leave. Mrs. Ayerst, who was a violinist in the symphony, took her violin and dog but the car was too small, there was no room for me.

My daughter lived in Palmer. I remember thinking, "I have to take a clean girdle," but I left my purse. The ground was all rolled. I managed to get up to "L" Street on my way to Palmer. (I wouldn't have made it; the Knik River Bridge had dropped six feet.) There I ran into some friends who couldn't get to their home in Turnagain, so we went to Providence Hospital.

Big Army flat bed trucks were there putting lights into the hospital. The hospital put out big vats of food for people. Many, many people were at the hospital. I spent the whole weekend there. Mattresses were placed on the floor in the basement. Medical records were strewn out all over the floors. There was chaos.

On Sunday morning we were sitting with everybody else with no place to go. Service men came to the hospital and asked people if

The house shown is at 612 K Street, tilted by a pressure ridge. Large building in the background is the Knik Arms Apartments at 1110 Sixth Avenue.

they wanted to send messages to the states. My fifteen-year-old niece rushed to tell people Anchorage had been flattened. I wrote a letter and the Air Force took it outside. On Tuesday my family got it and learned I was all right.

When the road was cleared and Romig Hill was passable, I went with friends to their home in Turnagain.

Leroy N. Allinger

Bump Up, Bump Down

I was working at Air Power Overhaul on International Airport Road and Jewel Lake Road at the time of the earthquake. I got off work at four o'clock and went to town to get some supplies and

A rubble that was the beginning of a new Alaska Sales and Service Building at 1300 East Fifth Avenue. Under construction, the concrete beams cracked and fell.

prices on lumber at B & R Building Supply Company on Medfra Street. This was just behind what was going to be the new home of Alaska Sales and Service. I was in the office when the earthquake hit. I looked out in the yard and things were starting to fly around and falling off shelves so I decided to stay inside. I thought about getting under a desk for protection. I remember we all thought it was over and then it really hit again. I don't remember the duration of time, but it was pretty severe. I looked over at the Alaska Sales and Service new building. The dust was a big cloud over the unfinished concrete beams. The crew that had been working had just left for the day so no one was injured. Later they took the building down and started over.

I started for home down the Seward Highway to O'Malley. The road had a lot of pavement breaks. You bumped up a foot and then you bumped down a foot. You could see the bump ups but the bumps down were a surprise.

I got home and looked over our place. My wife, Phyllis, and children were all okay.

Phyllis L. Allinger

Birch Road

We lived on Birch Road north of O'Malley. I was in the living room. My daughters Linda, age twelve, and Bonny, then two, were playing on the floor in the kitchen. Beverly, who was ten, was sitting on the couch when the earthquake began.

Things started to come out of the cabinets and the refrigerator. Linda grabbed Bonny and brought her into the living room. I told Beverly to stay on the couch, and about that time a bowling trophy fell from a shelf and grazed her on the head.

Our oldest daughter, Diana, was babysitting down on Dogwood Road, which is now 104th Street. I was quite concerned for Diana's safety, and as soon as my husband, Leroy came home, I sent him out to find her. What a relief when he came back and said she was fine. She had managed to get all the children outside and to a neighbors' place, when a large stone fireplace fell into the house where she had been staying.

We had a water tank full or half full, but we wanted to reserve it. We had no idea when the electricity would be on again. We had a wood stove in the basement on which we cooked and melted snow to make water to flush toilets. We were amazed at what little water that all that snow made. There were a lot of trips out to get snow to melt.

We made out okay. I had a good friend, Phyllis Day, who told me she was chased out of her kitchen by a portable dishwasher.

Ahmad and Eldiene Amer

Spenard Road

We were living in a four plex at 1300 Twenty-ninth Place in Spenard (now Benson Boulevard). We were getting ready to have our dinner, as we usually did at about 5:30 when the building started to shake. We had been through earthquakes before and did not get too excited at first.

When it kept shaking we decided maybe we should leave the building. The building was two stories high and we were on the top floor. We heard some of the canned goods roll out of a cupboard in the kitchen. We put on our coats and went down stairs but when we got to the outside one could not stand up so we were on the ground till it was over with. We could see our car bouncing all up and down (afterward we learned that going outside could have been the worse thing to do, but we did not have any earth openings as we learned what happened to other people).

It was a long five minutes to be sure and seemed much longer. We went upstairs to the apartment and when we opened the door we could see that the TV set was off the table and other furniture moved about. The bedroom furniture was moved about, and it was not light furniture. When we went to the kitchen we expected to see dishes and pots and pans all over the place, but to our surprise not a cupboard door was open except the one we heard the canned goods rolling from. The reason was that all the doors faced south and the one opened faced to the west and the earth rolled east and west. The only thing we lost was one glass in the bathroom that fell into the washbasin. So we were very thankful for that.

It did not dawn upon us what the damage could be because there was nothing along Twenty-ninth Place.

We spent most of that night near the car where we had a radio and they were talking about tidal waves. So we wanted to hear if it came, but didn't. Thank goodness.

About the middle of the week a radio ham operator contacted Ahmad that some one from Tripoli, Lebanon was trying to find out if his son was all right, and it was his father. Then we knew it was all over the world to be sure. We were just lucky not to have any damage or loss, as so many of our friends and people we knew did. Just hope that one has not to have to go through anything like it again.

No bulldozer created these jumbled masses of earth. One of history's greatest earthquakes, the strongest ever recorded in North America, hit with a force of 10,000,000 times greater than the A-bomb which devastated Hiroshima.

Cea Anderson

Earthquake Glass

I was eleven years old. Everyone was anticipating the upcoming Easter. I was left at our house in Spenard with my two younger siblings, Richard, one-year, and Polly a three-year old while mother went shopping. Richard, Polly and I were sitting under Dad's gun rack watching a puppet show on TV called Space Robbers. That's when the whole house started to move and sway. I got to the window and peered out. I saw the ground rolling like an ocean. I opened the front door and saw two neighbors, Tommy and Duane, coming into their house. I heard Duane yelling, "Don't drop that Gibson!!!" referring to his new guitar.

My mother, Connie Anderson, was shopping at the S and F Foodland two blocks away. She had my two other siblings, Allen and Amelia, with her. The store began to move and sway. She grabbed for the two children and stated, "God is right here!" Allen was the first one out the door. He got hit on the head with a two pound package of Velveeta cheese on the way, but no harm done. My sister Amelia escaped too.

Mother was trying to get out when she fell to the floor onto glass from the pickle and other jars. She had lacerated her knees. She was on the floor when " Moose", a bagger, came and picked her up and helped her out of the store.

Mother arrived at our house. I helped her in and got my baton to help make a tourniquet to stop the bleeding.

My father, John H. Anderson , was at his shop, Anderson Equipment, at East Ninth Avenue and Orca. He tried to get home, but many of the roads were split open.

Mother was taken to the Community Hospital at 825 L St. by a neighbor from North Carolina to have her knees looked at. Personnel in the Emergency Room poured iodine in and butterfly bandaged them. She was returned home and during the course of the evening the North Carolina neighbors brought her soup made by candlelight. I never will forget that.

For years the glass came out of my mother's knees. She kept it in a jar and called it her earthquake glass.

Looking west, toward Cook Inlet on Ninth Avenue between L and M Streets. Curious residents inspect the offset in the road caused by the fault line running through the street and Ninth Avenue Park.

George Arcand

O'Malley Road

I just arrived home from work. My wife, Ruth, was preparing the evening meal. Just as I reached the door in the house, and greeted her, the earthquake hit.

I grew up in California, and I learned about earthquakes when I was just a small child. I was told what to do. You're not supposed to go outside, and you're not supposed to stay inside because things might fall on you. If you go outside the ground may crack open. So you're supposed to go to an outside entry door and put your back to one of the verticals and stay right there. The strongest place in the house is the doorframe.

Anyway, that is where I went.

The stove started shaking and utensils started sliding. Ruth tried keeping them on the stove. Finally the shaking became so violent that she couldn't handle all the pots and they all came crashing onto the cabinet and floor. The kitchen cabinet doors were swinging open. Dishes and things were flying out. Ruth tried to keep the cabinet doors closed so that wouldn't happen and finally she gave up and came running by me because she was trying to get out of the house. She had no earthquake briefing as a child. So when she ran by me, and stepped out in the yard, I told her, I says, "You come back, the earth may open up." So she came back and I told her to stand right in the door with her back against the doorframe.

Our place, on O'Malley Road, is in the middle of five acres and there are big birch and spruce. I noticed that those trees weren't swinging like they would in a high wind; they would all go in unison in more or less the same direction. During the earthquake the earth was moving in various ways and the trees were just whipping back and forth in every direction, each individual tree. That earthquake lasted just a few seconds over four minutes. I could see the ground rolling, just like waves in the water.

Gene Roguszka measures the split in a tree torn apart by a tension fracture.

Another thing I observed was that the room I was in had some shelves. We had a few things displayed on the shelves. On the north-south wall everything on the shelves came crashing down. But anything on the east-west wall stayed intact. Then it quit, and there was complete silence. There wasn't a sound of a car traveling, a door opening, or a dog barking. It wasn't like anything I heard before or afterward. Eventually sounds got back to normal.

At that time we contacted neighbors and asked if they were okay. Our heating system didn't require electricity. Our neighbors didn't have electricity, and they didn't have any heat. We just had one bedroom, and I said, "Well just bring your air mattresses and sleeping bags, we have heat, so you can come over and spend the night on the floor." So we had four neighbor families that came over. It wasn't until the next day that we had electricity restored. We had propane bottles for our cooking so we didn't need electricity. We had a couple of Coleman lanterns, so we had light, and heat, and food.

As soon as daylight came, we all had breakfast, and our friends all went back to their homes to see what damage there was, and what had to be fixed.

I had to have my well deepened about five feet.

Betty Arnett

Iliamna Avenue

An excerpt from Betty Arnett's true story, Lady, You Ain't Seen Nothin Yet. *Permission to use given to Jan Boylan. 12/29/03 by B. Arnett (346-1781)*

It was close to five minutes of sheer terror. Down on the floor on all fours were all four of us. April, who was seven years old, had obeyed me and crawled under her bed in the adjoining room. Heather, my six year old, had crawled under the crib by her brother, who was three years old, and was nestled against my body. Had the walls come down, only April would have been protected because Hans' crib would have crushed us with the weight of the wall. The floor jerked unceasingly up and down and back and forth.

I felt helpless to protect my children further and so I cried out, "Pray! Children pray!" And in the next breath I prayed aloud over and over again, "Oh, God, please stop it! Please stop it! Please!"

The noise was such that it sounded as though the walls were falling in. In the midst of all of this movement and horrendous noise my young son was yelling, "It's stopped, Mommy. It's stopped!" I realize now that he had never seen his mother in such an emotional state. Perhaps that was his way of trying to bring this 9.2 earthquake to a halt. But it didn't stop. It continued for another two, long, interminable minutes.

With the house dancing up and down, I feared it was the end of all of us. At long last the shaking subsided but the noise continued. We crawled out from under the beds and with great relief I saw that the walls were still standing. I was puzzled as to the source of the loud noise and didn't realize it at the time but the basement walls had fallen in.

April called from the other room, "Mommy, come look! There's a lot of people out in the street and they are staring at our house." We joined her at the windows and I said, "Something awful must have happened to our house! We'd better get out of here!" As we ran down the hall and rounded the corner into the kitchen I glanced out the window and saw my neighbor's two-story house sinking into the ground.

I knew there wasn't time to grab coats, boots, shoes or

Many homes in the Turnagain area were completely destroyed. A very few were intact enough to be moved to new locations. Wayland Lipscomb moves his house from 2124 McKenzie Drive past the intersection of McKenzie and Clay Products Road to a new location just off O'Malley Road. No road existed into his property but he was permitted to use the Gene and Dolores Roguszka driveway and move across their property to reach the final destination. After the house was situated on it's new foundation, a road was built and named Lipscomb Lane. The house remains at that location. Betty and Russ Arnett were able to move their home to a new location after the earthquake. Bluff property was no longer a big attraction.

anything! I opened the carport door and saw two huge cracks in the concrete slab where the car was usually parked. It was March 27, and a light snowfall was on the ground. Hans and April were fully dressed but April had no shoes on. Heather's feet were bare and she was wearing only a housecoat. I carried Heather in my arms and told April to grab her little brother's hand.

In the driveway we came upon two crevasses. I told April and Hans to jump and I attempted to do so myself but Heather's weight threw me off balance and I landed on my tailbone. Fortunately, Heather's feet never touched the ground. After successfully jumping the next crevasse, we reached the neighbors standing in the middle of the street.

"What is it?" I asked. "What has happened to my house?"

"Turn around and look," replied one of them. When I turned to look I saw that the yard on the other side of my house had fallen into the earth forty feet and all of the houses between ours and the bluff (a block and a half away) had fallen into the earth and were all tilted in all directions.

The earth had stopped sliding into Turnagain Arm under one corner of our house. *(Copyright pending.)*

Dorothy L. Arnold

Kodiak

Our home in Kodiak was built high on a bank, two blocks from the water's edge, along a busy street. There was only enough room for Ray's vehicle to be parked between the street and the back of the house.

Only part of the building was built on the rocky ground. The rest of the floor sat on enclosed pilings that were placed on solid rock. Beneath part of the house was a one-bedroom apartment. To reach the only door to the house one walked on a four-foot wide wooden walkway with no railing, also on open pilings.

As I sat typing, working on my Master's thesis, the house suddenly began to shake. I thought, "Gee, the wind has come up." Then as the shaking became stronger, I looked out the window. I noticed the light and telephone wires dancing a jig.

Earthquake! I dashed toward the door and opened it and was hit by a blast of cold air. I ran back into the house, turned off the electric typewriter and grabbed my coat with the thought: "I must get out of here because the house may collapse and fall down the steep cliff."

I ran for my Volkswagen Beetle that was jumping up and down on the bank like a jumping jack and moved it away from the bank before it tumbled over the twenty-foot cliff. I did not pay any attention to the violently swaying light and telephone wires above me, nor to the wildly tilting telephone poles holding up those dancing wires.

My husband, Ray, had gone to pick up tires at Clark's Garage. When the shaking began, he quickly paid for the tires, threw them into his carry all, and headed home. When he reached home and found me sitting in the VW beneath the telephone wires, he laughed. It was then I realized the danger I had put myself into, if a wire broke or a pole snapped.

Our renters came up from the apartment and all of us got into Ray's vehicle and headed toward town and the Navy base. We hoped to find information on the epicenter. As we drove along the waterfront through town toward the base, we came to a stream. I said, " Let's get out of here and go to higher ground. A tsunami is coming. I know for I was told about them while in Hawaii."

Ray's reply was, "Don't worry for I was by here yesterday and noticed the water had dropped." We left the water's edge and drove a bit further. We saw dirt falling down the steep bank on the way to the base. We headed for home. Ray turned on the radio, and when we were a little over half way there, we heard: "Everyone get to higher ground. Everyone get to higher ground immediately, a tsunami is coming. I repeat, go now to higher ground." The radio went blank just before we reached home. Ray looked at me and said, "You were right."

By this time the shaking had subsided. We all went into the house. Suddenly the lights went out. We heard a low roar that became louder and louder. The house shook and below us the water rose. As it receded, it almost took Bob Hall's floatplane dock.

All was quiet, when suddenly the roar, as if a large hailstorm was coming, began again. The water rose higher. A man on Bob Hall's dock tried desperately to get a floatplane readied. In the end he hopped onto a float and began climbing into the plane as the tsunami struck, taking the plane, Bob Hall's dock, and a part of the nearby cannery to sea.

As before all was quiet for about thirty minutes and then came the roaring of the water and the shaking of the house. The water rose higher, and as it receded, the cannery disappeared. Now we saw houses with flickering lights in attics and people clinging to rooftops floating out to sea.

After the third and last wave, Ray said, "I had better go see if someone needs a place to stay tonight." He returned with a man, his wife, and their four-year old son.

As we were eating, the lights came on for we were on the emergency line to the hospital and a school. There still was no water, but we were not concerned as across the street from our house was a spring containing pure water.

The family Ray brought home spent the night and after breakfast, thanked us and returned home to find their house intact. The water had reached only to the edge of our visitor's yard.

Most of Kodiak was without water or electricity. Stores at the water's edge were gone. A few boats that had been in the harbor were not to be seen. One boat was found in the schoolyard four blocks from the water.

Clark's Garage was entirely gone. Mr. Clark had heeded the warning as had so many others and had fled up Pillar Mountain. The

Kodiak's loss in public and private property was estimated at twenty-seven million dollars. Damage was caused by ten seismic sea waves that battered the low-lying areas of the community during the evening hours of March 27 and the morning hours of March 28.

bakery and paper publishing building were gone. The store that still stood after the quake had to throw away the soggy contents left behind by the angry waters. The area outside of town where we went camping and gathered fossilized clamshells had dropped about three feet.

Only those who worked at a given job in the town of Kodiak or on base were allowed to go through where flooded areas had caused havoc. Service men were assigned to prevent looting. The sad part, however, was that some who were assigned to protect items were dishonest and looted. I am not sure whether they were caught.

Cleanup began and by the end of the following week, water and electricity was available. People returned to their homes and schools reopened. The high school had been used as a place of refuge.

It was lucky that on the day of the big shake the fishing fleet was at sea for they rescued Bob Hall's plane and the man who had gone to sea with it. One of the fishing boats had towed it to a safe cove. Various boats from the fishing fleet rescued all the people who had gone to sea on floating houses.

The day after the quake a typical windstorm swept through Kodiak wrecking much of the fishing fleet for they had no safe place to dock. The only casualties were a father and son who left their car and went to higher ground, but returned to the car to retrieve an item and were caught in the second big wave.

According to the radio reports received by those living elsewhere, Kodiak was washed away. My sister, Rachel, from Fairbanks and her husband, Don, tried to reach us unsuccessfully by phone. Don finally went to a White Alice site and learned that Kodiak had not been devastated by a tsunami. They then felt we were all right.

Lois "Stevie" Arnold

First Baby

I had been in Alaska for twelve years before the big quake. Gone through a lot of little quakes with no disaster. I was always noticing small earthquakes and would ask the kids if they felt it, and they always said, "no." On this evening I had bathed the kids, waiting for Dad's arrival for dinner. At the first quiver, I said to them "Sit still so you feel this. This is an earthquake."

Then, it sounded like a freight train coming through the house. The lawn looked like it was waving, like water. We had three china cupboards. There was a TV on top of one. It swayed back and forth, back and forth, and the doors in the cupboards opened and shut, opened and shut, but nothing fell out. I had been cleaning in the bathroom and there were many fancy things on a shelf. These were the only things that fell and broke. I had area rugs on the floor, so I asked the kids to lay on the floor and I covered them with rugs to protect them from flying glass shards from the breaking windows that went all across one wall of the living room.

My husband had stopped at the little grocery store on East Ninth Avenue. Everything was flying off the shelves. The guy at the register said, "Take what you want and go." So he did, and came home.

We had only lived in the house for a year, and had never had gas heat before, so we were worried about the danger and drove to the gas company to see what we should do. After much difficulty we eventually made it. They said not to worry; they had turned the gas off at the inlet.

It was at this point that I started having my first labor pains. The radio had said, don't go to the hospital unless it's an emergency. A neighbor and a nurse down the street were preparing to help me, but a policeman who lived down the street said, "Oh no, go to the hospital, I'll take her." My husband said he could take me. We went downtown to the hospital on "L" Street, but it had been evacuated because of a gas break, so we went to the new Providence Hospital. When you went in the door it was eerie because military gear was lined up in the halls and it smelled terrible from gas. I was so afraid, but I had a normal labor and delivered by candlelight. My pediatrician, Dr. John Tower, delivered her. It was the first baby born in Anchorage after the earthquake. I said I was so frightened I would have had a baby even if I weren't pregnant.

Everything in the hospital was on emergency. I had no bath. Sandwiches instead of meals. They didn't change the beds. I didn't have a private room; they put me in a room with all the oxygen tanks. The service was not the greatest. But the charge was just the same.

Norma Arnold

Try To Have Sex

It is impossible to put into writing what can go through your mind in just a matter of seconds. Things you see and do and don't think about it until later. Some of them humorous after the crisis are over.

I was employed at Safeway in the meat department. Our job was to wrap and weigh the meat and maintain the meat case. We had carts full and ready to go into the coolers for the next day's shoppers and hundreds of cases of hams stacked in every available space ready for Easter.

The carts began to roll a little and I actually felt a little excited because I'd felt my first tremor. There had been plenty of others and everyone else had experienced them and talked about them and I was a little envious.

The little rumble I felt with my feet began to move back and forth. And in seconds the floor was coming up to meet my knees. I bent down to keep my balance and was slammed against the meat case. I saw my coworker crawl toward the cutting room door and pulled her back as cases and cases of hams fell, blocking the door.

The noise was deafening, walls were rolling like waves in the ocean. But each wall rolling in a different direction. It crossed my mind that the ceiling can't stay up there with walls moving like that. We climbed over the meat case and into ankle deep eggs, slippery, slimy, broken eggs. Up the aisle holding onto shelves into mayo, syrup and glass. A woman was crawling through trying to get to the front, hands and legs cut and bleeding. I backed up to take another aisle.

I began to choke, my eyes were burning, and I couldn't

breathe. I put my apron over my nose and mouth and noticed the bleach and ammonia causing gases and knew we had to move fast, but I couldn't see. Wiping my eyes I saw a bag boy in front of me grabbing a baby that had been left alone in panic. The boy ran forward. I followed where I knew he had gone, slipping and sliding in glass. We finally made it to the front. There were cash registers turned over, money laying everywhere mixed in with groceries of all kinds. It crossed my mind that I could pick up the money and just as quick decided, "Who needs it?" My life was more important. Once outside my baby crossed my mind and I headed toward my car. Panic finally getting the better of me.

I then remembered my husband had taken me to work that morning and had my car. His shop was only a few blocks away and I started running. After what seemed like hours my husband pulled along beside me and called for me to get in. We began telling each other the destruction we had seen and headed home to our son. That ride home was agony. I pictured everything but good in my mind. There was a large crevasse across Seward Highway and not caring and not really thinking clearly, my husband jumped it and we kept going. Thinking back I get frightened even thinking of what we did but it was our only route home, and nothing was going to stop us from getting there.

We arrived home and saw our babysitter outside sweeping off the porch. I knew then that everything was all right. I jumped out of the car and asked her if she knew how bad things were in town. All the destruction. No water, no electric. She said no, but it was pretty bad there. She had looked over at the cemetery to see if the dead were rising.

Now, I want to tell you what I was told weeks after the quake, when we could laugh a little.

My co-worker, all of five feet and 100 pounds says I saved her life when I pulled her back and kept her from being buried in cases of hams. She laughs when she tells everyone, that I held her hand after climbing over the meat case. I took time to caution her and tell her not to break any eggs lying on the floor.

I don't remember telling my boss to send someone back in to get all the money lying on the floor. He says he told us all to be back in one hour to help clean up, and I told him he was crazy and I quit my job.

We laugh at my sister and her husband who was driving her

home from work. Got angry because he had a flat tire, then decided the power steering was going out, opened the car door and put one foot out and yelled, "Earthquake!" Closed the door, locked it, and waited while the power poles hit the ground and popped back up again. My sister hit the floorboard on her knees to pray.

My husband coming to the store to get me and sees all the liquor from the liquor store running down the sidewalk into the gutter, and thought "what a waste. I could lie down and let all that booze run into my mouth." Says he saw all the jewelry from the jewelry store laying in the booze and glass from the window display. Didn't think to get me a diamond ring.

And later told by our sitter, how our children who decided all the shaking and rolling was a space ship under attack from some unknown alien and trying to stay on the bed (control center) without falling into outer space. Later said it was a real fun game.

Then there were the aftershocks!

Every little shake I'd grab my husband (asleep or not) and make him sit with me until I'd finally fall asleep from sheer exhaustion. Or when I begged him to take us up into the mountains to run from the tidal wave.

Or when I'd turn on the washer and the vibration when spinning would send us all, including the dog, out the door. The dog being the first one to the door, almost always.

And last, but not least your equilibrium! Try to work, forget it for 48 hours.

Try to eat. You can't find your mouth.

Try to sleep. You can manage if you like spinning around while lying down.

Try to walk. Like a drunk taking a DUI test, you know you're not under the influence, but your head doesn't.

Try to have sex. Well that's good anytime, but we can do without the ground party!

Marjory Bailey

The Chafing Dish

Here it was, Good Friday, and I was fixing dinner and dying Easter eggs for the neighbor children; then came the earthquake. First a roll, then stronger and my husband and I got in the doorway with the dog between us. Here we rode out the quake watching dishes fly out of the cupboards and the ground roll. Needless to say the hard-boiled eggs and dye were on the floor with everything else. At one time I told my husband that the whole house was going to roll over, but then it subsided a bit and we were able to get outside.

Then we were with no electricity, no heat and no water. We checked with the neighbors to see if all were okay. Back home and what to do about dinner? Whatever was already cooked. Since the house was beginning to cool down it seemed wise to go to bed to keep warm, putting our boots, coats and other heavy clothing nearby in case we had to evacuate. Then the aftershocks came, some quite strong, and continued through the night. The dog could hear them and she would bound into the bedroom and we'd roll together. Towards morning she went to her bed and I heard her give a big sigh because neither one of us got much sleep.

Sometime during the night the power came on and since we had a well I jumped up and put the plug in the bath tub, then ran to the kitchen and started filling very container that I could get my hands on before the power went off again, not to return until the next afternoon. The next challenge was what to cook and what in. I had been given a chafing dish and found this to be the answer. I brewed coffee, probably not the best, but it was hot. We invited the neighbors in and I prepared scrambled eggs with bread—no toast. The chafing dish was kept busy as the power kept going off and on. We ate the thawing food from the freezer, one course at a time, of course. To this day I keep the chaffing dish, canned heat and water on hand.

After the power came on my husband used his ham radio to send messages for people to let family in the states know they were okay. At one time a radio contact in Antarctica was used to relay messages back to the states. As calls came in inquiring about people, I would sometimes have to go to the address and check on them and take a message to send back to their family. It was a busy time for us but we were able to help a lot of people

Anchorage's newest and finest; the Turnagain By the Sea housing development suffered the greatest damage for a residential area. More than one hundred homes were lost.

Dr. Helen Beirne

Fifteenth and L

At the time of the earthquake my husband and I lived in a home at the corner of Fifteenth and L on the south side, in the south addition. It was a frame structure. We had just finished dinner.

The first thing I did was rush into the bedroom to look at the L Street Apartments. I had lived in those apartments when I first came to Alaska in 1956, and we had been in an earthquake. The building actually swayed enough that the water sloshed out of the toilet bowl.

I was up on the eleventh floor and it was a frightening experience. I thought an earthquake would really do something to this building, so I went into the back bedroom to look and see if you could see the sway. I have been told that it could have been as much as a ten to fifteen feet. It was enough of a sway that on the first floor level there were cracks around the building. I understand that in both the McKinley and the L Street that is where the greatest amount of sway must have come.

Our furniture started moving in the bedroom and I had an awful time getting out of there. It slid back and forth and I had to push it out of the way to get out. It kept blocking the door. There were some very frightening things happening. Quite a few wires snapped because the telephone poles moved and swished around. You could see some movement of the land and you didn't know if it was your own dizziness from the movement, so we just plunked ourselves in the chair and sort of sat there and watched things happen. We could see out of our windows down into the L Street area.

At our house the basement was damaged quite a bit. There was a big fireplace down there and it was cracked enough that afterward when the rains came the water shot up through the cracks and into the basement. We sold our house shortly afterward and moved into the Knik Arms. Later we moved to the hill but our place wasn't built at that time.

My brother in law, Dr. Michael Beirne lived up on Tenth Avenue. We had to evacuate our area so we went up to his place thinking it

The 1200 L Street Apartments, a fourteen-story building suffered damage but remained standing.

would be higher, and found that he had taken his family and gone out to some people on Lake Otis Parkway.

Shortly afterward I went over to the Teamster's Hospital. I thought I could be of some help. That's where the health department is now. They had evacuated their people so rapidly it was just unbelievable. Then across the street was the old Providence Hospital, which had become more of a senior home and those people had been evacuated. They just did it in no time at all. The movement was just extraordinary. They didn't need me. I went to the new Providence but they didn't need me either.

A week later when we had the aftershock we were at Club Paris, and our friend went all to pieces. We were still so jumpy.

Several of our friends lived in the L Street Apartments because that was one of the few places to rent when you first came to the city. One of our friends was alone with her two children, and one of them was in a wheeled device. It kept going past her and she tried to get a hold of it. It sounded like it went by four or five times, and I'm sure it felt like that.

Bud Berkin

515 Club

It was 1964. I was working as a bartender at the 515 Club in downtown Anchorage. About two weeks before the earthquake I had a date with a young lady to meet me at the bar on Saturday night about 9 PM. For some ungodly reason I was so sick behind the bar that night that I had to take off early. When my date arrived, I told her, "Well, this is not over, our date is still on."

We set up another date for later, and lo and behold, she called over to the 515 to let me know that she was home and sick in bed. She lived in one of the trailer parks here in town. So, when I got off, I took over some hot soup, and left. Some of these days we are going to go out on a date.

We set it up for Friday.

All of a sudden we had the big earthquake.

When the earthquake hit, I was serving cocktails at the 515. My first customers were sitting together at one table. I had served one round of drinks and was on the verge of taking the second round of drinks to the table. I heard a little noise, but didn't pay much attention. I served up the drinks, got them on the table, and was walking away with five empty glasses on the tray. All of a sudden you could hear the ground rumbling. I turned around and looked at the customers and said, "Hey man, I'm standing here balancing glasses and I look like I'm dancing over here." About the time the last syllable came out of my mouth it was like somebody took two corners of the building and just started jerking them around cause everything started flying. The lights started flickering on and off. It blacked out. In the meantime was a woman apparently not from Anchorage yelled out, "Oh my God, we have just been bombed by the Russians."

Old Carl, about eighty-seven years old at the time, always drank his pinch bottle scotch, two drinks every day. He yelled out, "No, you dumb son-of-a-bitch, it's only an earthquake."

Everything is swinging. You can hear bottles and things breaking. I yelled out to the people, "Whatever you do get under the table or something that's solid in case the building caves in." I proceeded to go out toward the front of the store.

We had a foyer area where we had two pinball machines. I walked by those and got in the little alcove area. I got out the first door and as I go to push the second door I realized I'm still balancing five empty glasses on a tray. So instead of dropping them I go back in the 515 and proceed to put them down so they won't get broken.

There was a ladies dress shop next door with large windows. As I got out half way to the street I could see the cars are bumping and

Anchorage Hardware and Sporting Goods, 347 Fourth Avenue.

jumping. All of a sudden I saw that glass expanding, and it expanded to where the pressure just blew it out into smithereens.

In the meantime, out toward the street, this young lady started running hysterically, and I said "Hey, hey." She's yelling and screaming, and I thought, well, in the San Francisco movie, they showed where you have to slap them in the puss, so that's what I did. I slapped her in the puss, and it worked. I told her "You just stick with me, and I took her under my arm and we walked out in the middle of the street. The ground was still shaking, and the flagpole was moving.

When we were standing out there I saw the scaffolding cause they were just not quite finished (with the Westward Hotel) and all that scaffolding was bouncing back and forth off the tall building.

By the time the earthquake stopped I had three girls under one arm, two girls under the other arm and in the meantime the people are running, it was just like somebody had just stepped on an ant hill.

People were just running helter skelter. I yelled at them, "Don't run, because if a fissure opens up it'll suck you in and man you don't have a chance". People are still running like crazy. The earthquake finally finished itself.

Bob Terrin and Jack Higgins were standing in the door at the 515. We stood there in the street for a few minutes or so, and they yelled out, "Hey what are you doing with all those good-looking girls."

I says, "Hey none of that Robert Hall jazz, if I'm going, I'm going first class."

I asked the girls, Hey, I'd buy you a drink if we can get to the bottles." So we proceeded to go into the 515. One of the ladies came in, and we set up candles on the bar, never realizing how much had broken in there. We walked to the back to get more candles, and all of a sudden I realized the cases of beer are tumbled over. When we got behind the bar walking through all that broken glass and stuff, Carl is still sitting at the bar, and he says, "Now son-of-a-bitch am I going to get a drink in this joint, or do I have to go to some other joint?"

I says, "You just sit still, Carl, as soon as I can find you a pinch bottle I'll set it up on the bar for you." Which of course I did and I got him a nice glass that wasn't broken. I put some ice in there, and I says, "Drink to your heart's content."

I got the young lady a drink. She says "You know, I live out in Turnagain, I'm a little concerned about my family there." Me not realizing said, "Oh its probably fine out there. Don't worry about it." I never did hear from the lady again.

After we started cleaning up the place Truman Chance said to me, "Why don't you go over to my place and if you can't get into the door there's a place where you can crawl in. I've got two portable radios over there. They're all in good shape bring them over to the "Five".

So I went over to get them. When I got back we were getting things organized. The first report we get on the newscast, "Anchorage is totally submerged." I said, well if that's the case, I'm going to have me a martini, and I got the biggest snifter glass we had in the joint, filled it with ice, took me some Samovar vodka, and made me a beautiful big martini. I proceeded to knock that off.

Old Smitty, who was the tennis pro here, also tended bar in the wintertime, came walking in. I said, "What the hell you doing down here?" " I was in bed with my wife and all of a sudden I fell out of bed, and I said, "Honey are you that horny?" We were all making jokes about what was taking place.

Then about a half hour later, the radio announced, "We have to correct ourselves on another report, Anchorage is totally engulfed in flames."

Well, then, I decided I needed another martini. I made me another big martini. By the time I finished that second one, I was swacked. In the meantime the military guys were coming through the place, making sure that people weren't stealing things off the street.

I decided to make a run over to the Club Paris, only to see that their windows were all knocked out in the front, and Bobby was sitting there with three top coats, one on top of the other, on top of the other trying to keep warm, freezing his little butt off. Everybody was fine, and they already had somebody boarding up the windows. So I went back to the 515.

By this time I was swacked out of my mind because I hadn't eaten all day. I went out the back figuring I was going to go home, but I couldn't get in my car to move it, so I thought, "What the heck, I saw a bed over to Truman's", so I just walked back over there, kicked through the plaster and stuff, got in through that little door. There was plaster all over the bed. I just knocked it off and I just lay down on the bed and pulled the cover over my head.

I don't know how long I lay there. All of a sudden somebody hits me with a billy club. He says, "Are you okay?"

And I said, "Yes."

He says, "Get out of here, this building is condemned."

I said, "What do you mean, I'm sleeping."

So we had a little bit of a skirmish, but I finally got my butt out of there. I'm about half drunked up, and I walked over to the 515. And then I says, well I got to get home.

I lived out in the Spenard area. I was living with Dennis Davidson, and his wife Denise, who was pregnant. When I got home, thank God, they were all okay, so I went to bed.

Before I went home I also ran around to the Westward Hotel to check to make sure that everybody was okay down there. They were. Duane Bernardy was up on the top floor when the quake hit, so he got a pretty good ride.

The following day when I woke, Denny came into my room and said, do me a favor, Denise needs to get some food in her. So will you take her over to the post, Post #1. It was only four blocks from where we lived, so I walked her over thinking we were getting into this long line for food. When we got to the building, we stood there for about 20 minutes trying to get in. We walked around the corner, and I thought I was in the service again, because unfortunately Denise was ahead of me, and before you knew it she had a tetanus shot.

When we finally did get served it was set it up so nicely, you would think we were out on a date or something.

They had two nice plates of food for us, and I can't remember if we had a little wine. I walked Denise back home. I started walking downtown and as I was coming around the curve on the hill from Spenard and what do I spot, a pheasant. I found out later that somebody had it for a pet. I says, "What, am I dreaming?"

I got downtown and got myself involved with the Civil Air Patrol. We flew down to Kodiak, Soldotna, and Seldovia , trying to check these various places.

We went down to check on the people in Alyeska. We couldn't get through for a while because of three slides. We eventually did get over the slides, and then ate some rations that they gave us. Apparently when the quake hit they had just quit clearing the mountain or there would have been a lot of bodies lying around. Everybody was cleared off the mountain. All the snow slides stopped just prior to coming into the chalet.

We got into Kodiak, and I couldn't believe that all those ships that I had seen just four months ago were piled into downtown. One of the gals working in one of the bars was really lucky. Everybody was told to clear out of the bars right on the main street. She went running back like she was going to get a bottle or something, A guy says, "Don't go in there!" and he grabbed her and pulled her back. Just about that time the waves were coming in, and I guess part of the building got washed away, so she was just lucky the guy got her and pulled her back out.

We were pretty much getting back to normal.

I finally got in touch with the gal I had the date with before the quake, and I said," You know what, one date I'm sick, second date, you're sick, the next date nature saying we have the biggest earthquake we've ever had, three strikes, you're out."

Debby Best

Forty-Sixth Street

I was at 1202 Forty-Sixth Street. We owned a small house on a large lot catty cornered from Willow Crest School. Then in '64, it was at the end of a dead end street. Now it's on Cambridge Street across from Windemere Subdivision. I still own it.

I had been in the kitchen getting ready to fry fish for supper. There was a large bottle of oil on the stove—open. We had five kids, one foster child, and I was about three months pregnant so I had flopped down on the couch for a couple of minutes.

The house gave a large jolt and the lights went out. All the kids and Sam, my husband, were in the living room except for Diana, the baby, who was sleeping in her crib in the bedroom. The house was sort of swaying back and forth and every swing or two something would crash somewhere. All the nails were squeaking. I hoped they'd hold. I asked the kids where my shoes were, thinking we might need to go out, but nobody knew, least of all me. There was a huge crash from the baby's bedroom. Sam went to get her. A dresser had picked itself up off the floor and landed on top of her six-month crib. Thank God she was lying down. Sam came back and handed her to me.

He told Lisa, eight years old, to go hold the TV so it wouldn't fall on the floor so she staggered over to it and held on. More crashes from the kitchen and the other bedroom. After ages and ages (it was really only five minutes) the shaking stopped and I peeked into the kitchen.

There was a small hutch against one wall where I had sugar eggs drying. Also there had been milk cartons of dirt where I had started pansies and petunias. Above the sink there had been four place settings of china on a shelf and on the top shelf of one cupboard there were six jars of pickled beets. Add the oil from the stove and mix all these ingredients. I went back to the couch and sat down wondering how, without water, was I going to get that mess up. I do not know, to this day how the mess got cleaned up. Maybe Sam did it. Obviously I blacked that out.

Pretty soon the house began to shake again. We didn't know anything about "after shocks" so we wondered if we were having another quake. This one was bad, but shorter than the first one. Sam decided he should go downtown to see if he could help and I told him he had his hands full right where he was. All evening people kept stopping by to make sure we were okay and all night every once in a while the house shook some more. The next day about 3 PM we got our electricity back, and water. We were lucky about the water. Lots of people lost their wells.

The municipality provided shots for everyone. The Salvation Army shipped up boxes of disposable diapers. These were the first disposables I had seen. They were made by Sears to fit into a special pair of rubber pants they manufactured. I immediately became addicted.

The mess got cleaned up. The house is still standing and has been expanded. For years afterward whenever the lights went out I'd feel a wave of panic, but that has worn of after all these years— I think.

Leonard C. Bibler

Did the Banking

I was downtown in the old Federal Building, where the post office was, checking my mail. The earthquake started and it seemed

The Elmer and Mary Louise Rasmuson home at 2701 Marston Drive, Turnagain after the earthquake subsided.

like immediately the lights went out. There were five or six of us in the building and we all ran out into the street, across from

Woolworth's. Everything started falling out of the windows that were breaking; there were dresses on the sidewalk, which was rolling like waves on water. I looked up at the Anchorage Westward Hotel where they were just finishing the thirteenth floor. The building was moving back and forth at the top and it was going so far that I was sure it was coming down. The earthquake kept going, it seemed like forever, I could hardly stand up on the sidewalk.

I had been going to the bank, because I was flying on a business trip to Seattle that night, so I headed for the Matanuska Valley Bank, about a block away. There was an after-hours window in the outer lobby entrance. One of the tellers was across the street. I asked her to help me, "I need to go to Seattle." We were crossing the street when we got the second jolt, but she helped me with my banking, and I got to my car and I headed for my business down on Post Road.

I still had no idea what had really happened. I found D Street closed by a mound of dirt with a car was sitting on top. I went to C Street and turned up. I couldn't get any further than the alley to Fourth Avenue where all the buildings were sunk. I turned around and started realizing that things were pretty bad. I tried G and H Streets. No luck. I ended up going down Whitney Road to Post Road and back to the business. I had a trucking firm, D and M Transport Service. All but one of the trucks were out on the road. That one truck had gone through the garage door and into the yard. That, and eight or ten feet of concrete blocks lost from the warehouse wall, was all the damage.

Of course, the airport was closed. I didn't get out on the airplane that night.

The Knik River Bridge was the only way out of town to the north and it was damaged so badly trucks couldn't cross it, so when the drivers came back from up north they had to park their trucks. We had to bring them to Anchorage in cars.

Mary Valero Bloes

On Elmendorf

I had taken off to go to church at two o'clock and had to come back to the office at four because my boss hadn't allowed me the whole afternoon off. At four we had a meeting, which lasted until five. At five I was exhausted and just couldn't dash right home. I was a civilian working at Elmendorf AFB. We were allowed to live in civilian "barracks" on what was called "Murphy's Corner."

I sat at my desk to read a letter from Dixie, my little cousin. Pat, the secretary, came over to talk to me about her roommate and so we sat and chatted away. When the tremor started it didn't alarm me because I have felt two such tremors before and they always stopped before too long. Pat and I stopped talking and waited for it to stop. It didn't. It was a frightening sensation to feel it getting stronger and stronger and stronger. It made a terrible noise. It made me think of being up a tree with a bear angrily shaking the trunk. Pat's eyes opened wide and we both fell to our knees when the furniture started moving. The windows flew open and the doors slammed shut. Luckily in our office nothing overturned. I grabbed for the typewriter close to Pat's head and knocked her glasses off. I said, "Let's get under this desk, Pat."

My whole concern was getting away from the swinging fluorescent lights. There were six of those four footers and they were swinging from one side of the ceiling to the other. If it shook one second more we could have had them all over the room.

When it stopped, Pat says, "I don't know about you but I'm getting out of here." My reply was, "Wait for me."

We checked the neighboring offices for people and found that everything was scattered hither and yon. Coffee pots, partitions, glass, lights, books, records, etc., all over the floor. We went downstairs and the guard asked us if we were all right.

One of the officers asked us why we didn't get out of the building. Well, it just didn't occur to me, that's why! I was so busy thinking that it would stop any minute that by the time it was shaking so hard we couldn't have traveled.

I took off in my car and Pat in hers. I stopped by Chapel Number Two to see if the Blessed Sacrament was all right. The Chapel was dark and I discovered I was wading in the overturned Holy Water. The altar boys and priests had just gotten there and were putting things in shape. No real damage there so I went home. The base had virtually no damage except a few overturned chimneys.

Now for the cute part. I wish you could see the many different kinds of seismographs that have developed. All homemade, but they work! When that little spring hanging in the middle of the room with a rubber band dangling a small nut starts shaking, IT'S TIME TO MOVE! We had a "good one" exactly a week later and you should have seen us evacuate. I was the only woman running down the stairs with a bunch of GI's and my high heels just couldn't go fast enough. We were running shoulder-to-shoulder so as I stumbled this 6'3" caught me by the arm and away we went! Now I knew what an earthquake could do and I didn't trust it to stop in two seconds.

Roland L Bloes

Helpless on a Hospital Bed

In 1964 I worked for the Truck and Trailer Company on Post Road building trailers for the North Slope. I injured my back on the job.

As a result, I wound up in traction on the fourth floor of Providence Hospital. Traction did not do the job so Dr. Perry Mead operated on my back on March 26.

When the quake hit the following day, I was helpless on a hospital bed. All I could do was watch as things started falling all around us. The building shifted from side to side and as it did, our beds rolled from where we lay to the other side of the building, striking metal lockers and rolling back again, hitting the wall. Fortunately, the sides of the beds were rolled up, preventing us from falling. There was heavy metal traction equipment hanging on the beds, and they made a lot of noise when they hit. The young, frightened nurses aides also made a lot of noise with their screaming.

Sister Phyllis, who worked at Providence Hospital, had also undergone a back operation a few days before and was recovering in a private room on the fifth floor. She later said that the window beside her bed had been the only one to fall out.

When the first tremor finally settled down, the troops from the Fort Richardson Army Post were immediately at the hospital getting the emergency power going. The patients from Elmendorf AFB Hospital also started arriving. The Air Force hospital had been damaged and its patients and doctors were transferred to Providence Hospital.

Doctors who had not been at the hospital started arriving from all over town. Dr. Mead was at the hospital throughout the crisis. He was later to learn that the land under his Turnagain home had shifted breaking his house in two, causing it to drift into the inlet. Two of his boys were lost.

My friend's wife had just delivered a baby the day before. She later said that all the mothers were herded out of their beds and rushed to the nursery where they were told not to look for their

Deep fissures line this street in Turnagain By the Sea. Some fissures were only a few feet deep. Others grew into bottomless crevasses. Men in this photo are geologists inspecting the area. It was feared that aftershocks could send more homes tumbling into Cook Inlet.

own child but to pick up a baby, any baby, and to hurry outside. Once outside, she said all the mothers started looking for their own child and with great relief, exchanged babies.

Several days after the quake, another doctor said I could go home if I had a place to go. I really didn't know if my place was still there so he allowed me to stay a few more days. My friend, Hal Smith and I were sharing a house. After a few days he came to the hospital to see me. Hal had a job at the old Safeway at Ninth Avenue and Gambell. He said everyone at the store was working day and night to clean up the damage and to restock the shelves.

Once home we found we had a few broken dishes but that our biggest problem was what had happened to our cars. Our driveway was wide enough for two cars, so that's where we had parked them. The force of the upheaval had brought the two cars so close together that we could not back out one without scraping the other. Both were brand new, one was a black Buick and the other a beige Chevrolet. It took Hal a while to hoist one car on a jack and then carefully, without exchanging paint, tow it away from the other.

During the many weeks I had been in traction and later recovering from the operation, a couple of ladies from the St. Anthony Church Legion of Mary would pay us a weekly visit. I became especially acquainted with one of those ladies. Seven months later I made her my wife. That was 39 years ago. We're still in Alaska and still happily married.

Marianne E. Schultz Boyer

Sixth and H Streets

I moved to Anchorage in the fall of 1963 to teach first grade at Sand Lake Elementary. Marian Sykora and I subleased an apartment on the second floor of the Dodd Apartments located at Sixth and H (currently the downtown bus station).

Because it was Good Friday, I had a vacation day from school, had spent the day cleaning and had just started to bake a cake. Two young men from Elmendorf Air Force Base had stopped by for coffee. Through a singles group at the Methodist Church — Methkeys — Marian and I had met several fellows in the military. The USO was across the street from our apartment, so they would ride the bus into town and stop by to talk or play cards or watch television. It was "our family" away from home. The cake mix, eggs and oil were in a bowl on the counter and I sat down for coffee. All of a sudden, the room began to move. We quickly stood up to hold the Goodall and Henne paintings and a mirror on the walls and to hold the television set in its rack. The floor movements went on and on. When they seemed to end, we walked outside and the earth started to move again. This time the parking meters were moving back and forth, so we headed back for the apartment.

We decided to look for Marian. She had a weekly Friday hair appointment at Don's Stairway to Beauty. One of the fellows had a car and as we drove down Sixth Avenue, we spotted her walking across the parking lot, looking somewhat confused—the way we felt! We continued down Sixth because we were told to head for the hills to avoid a possible tsunami. We stopped at D Street so Marian could check her job site—the Loussac-Sogn Building. I remember standing at the corner of Fifth and D. The stone panels from the outside of the Penney's Building had fallen on several cars, and we watched as they tried to lift the panels from the cars.

When we heard that a tsunami was no longer expected, we

checked on some friends and then returned to our apartment. It had a small walk-through kitchen with cabinets on the north and south walls. During the quake the cabinet doors had swung open and shut several times, spilling their contents. Cake batter was on the floor mixed with broken dishes, pots and pans. We scraped the mess together into a bag, but the floor remained very sticky!

Two German girls stopped by, looking for the fellows in an upstairs apartment. The girls had been living in a Third Avenue apartment that was badly damaged. They stayed the night with us. We opened canned food (tuna, sardines, etc.) and enjoyed our meal by candlelight—the only light available. I remember taking a walk in the snow that night. There was a very eerie feeling. You did not know if the worst had happened, or if there was more to come. We laid down on the couches and floor, but slept very little. One of the German girls had lived in Germany during the "blitzkrieg" when she was young, and every time there was an aftershock, she would scream.

On Saturday morning, we were told to leave the apartment because they needed to check all utility lines before heat and water would be available. One of our friends rented an apartment from the Gene Silberer family and they invited us to stay with them; they had a huge fireplace to keep the house warm. We walked to Inlet View School to pick up fresh water, courtesy of the military.

I remember going to Anchorage Lutheran Church on Easter Sunday morning. There was a very hushed, quiet feeling, and the sermon was one of thankfulness. I mailed a letter to my parents in Iowa telling them that I was alive and well, but I did not know how long the mail would take. My family was very relieved to receive a phone message from a ham radio operator who had connected with someone here.

Marian volunteered at the Red Cross , and I helped later in the week. Relatives and friends in the Lower Forty-Eight were trying to contact their relatives in Anchorage. I remember working with many scraps of paper with messages and phone numbers. I also remember going to Turnagain to look for an individual the following week. The National Guard allowed us through their checkpoint. We drove down the road, and the road suddenly just fell away, as had the homes on the north side of the road. Someone remarked, "I always wanted a view, but I didn't want to go through this to get it."

I had moved to Alaska, planning to stay for one year. After the earthquake, there was a wonderful attitude toward rebuilding and renewal that kept me here.

Robert H. Boyer

Kulis Air Guard

On Friday afternoon, I went to the Ninth Avenue Laundry (an old Quonset Hut), planning to go out to dinner with Harold Batchelor. He was talking on the phone and suddenly said, "Let's get the H… out of here!" We went outside and around to the back of the building. Its top was moving back and forth. We looked up and the power lines were whipping up and down ten feet. Women were standing in the alley, screaming. I could hardly stand up. I kept falling down. At the time, I thought that the Russians had dropped a bomb and that we were getting aftershocks. I had lived in Anchorage for six years and had experienced earthquakes before, but never for this long! I could not stand up or look at the ground! When I looked down later, I saw some cracks next to where I had been standing. The cracks were six inches wide.

Harold and I went to check on our friends, and all were okay so we got dinner. On the radio, we heard that the National Guard was activated so I reported to Kulis Air Guard. We had a ham radio station at the Guard. They contacted someone in Hawaii, Hawaii called Seattle and Seattle diverted Anchorage-bound airplanes to Fairbanks. We set up emergency cots and bedding at Base Supply. Many individuals and families stayed there until other arrangements could be made.

My friend Charlie Christy drove the Guard wrecker to the airport and found Olin, the chef for the Upper One airport restaurant, pinned under the control tower. Charlie was able to lift the tower with the wrecker and free Olin. Fortunately, he was not injured. The Guard was called to patrol Fourth Avenue and the Turnagain areas and to help business and homeowners remove their own items. The Guard also flew supplies to other affected communities.

I was assigned to photograph damaged areas including Turnagain and downtown. I flew to Seward where the train locomotive had been moved 100 feet from its tracks. My friend Jim Campbell (a fisherman) lived there and lost his house trailer and boat. In Kodiak, the downtown area was flooded and washed out. Boats were scattered everywhere. I also photographed the destruction in Valdez caused by the tsunami there. Even four or five days after the quake, fires from the oil tanks were still burning.

Portion of a Chilligan Drive home shows on the right perched on a bluff where no bluff had existed before, Cook Inlet and the tidelands in the background.

Charlotte Bradley

Romig Hill

I was coming up Romig Hill from work. I thought at first there was something really really wrong with my car. Then I saw the ground crack. I thought it was kryptonite, like the story of Superman. It was the end. I was passing Ed Wolden, advertising manager at Carr's, who was coming down the hill. He and I just looked at each other.

I was sure it was the end of the world. There was no other explanation. I went all the way to my house on Iowa Drive in Spenard. My husband, Joe was in his pickup listening to the radio. I ran up to him saying, "What happened?" He said, "Shut up and go look at the house." He had watched everything come out of the cupboards. One of the top shelves had garlic powder, which was all over everything, and we had a large aquarium, which had spilled so everything was covered in garlic and fish water. The cat stayed under the bed for several days.

There was only minor damage to the house but one we were building at the time had really strong rebar, but the walls that had already been put up were destroyed.

Erv Brooks

18 People, 1 Bath, No Water

I remember March 27, 1964. I was feeling a bit under the weather, and did not go to work that day. But I was well enough to pick up my wife and newborn son from Presbyterian Hospital. Some friends had stopped by after work to see the new baby. We were sitting in the living room when we felt a gentle rocking, "Another earthquake, we've had lots of those, no big deal." Then the first BIG jolt hit.

We immediately decided the house was not a good place to be and rushed out to the yard. As we looked back, my nearly two-year-old daughter was looking out the window. My friend and I collided in the doorway as we both went to get her. One of us did, and we were all in the yard beside the driveway. We decided to get in the car for two reasons, it was bouncing so much we were afraid one of the kids might fall under it, and in case the power lines came down. As I sat in the car, I could actually see waves in the roof of the house. I remember waiting for it to fall down, but it didn't.

The violent shaking continued for what seemed like an eternity, but I believe it was only about three minutes. When it stopped, we looked around and saw little visible damage in our area. The house came through exceptionally well; the only obvious damage was the broken bottles and contents of the cupboards that were spread all over the floor. We didn't think it was too bad until some neighbors, who had been downtown, came home and told about the devastation there.

There was no electricity but we had battery-powered radios and a station was able to get on the air with an emergency generator and start disseminating information. We heard about the slide in Turnagain and how widespread the damage was. A warning was issued for a Tsunami in low-lying areas in Anchorage (There was no tsunami in Anchorage) so I drove across town to warn some friends who lived at

Eighteenth and Arctic. No traffic signals were working so intersections became four way stops. Traffic moved well, perhaps better than when the lights were working.

The husband, an Air Force pilot, was not home so I took the wife

A huge fissure in front of the house at 821 Eighth Avenue.

and kids to our house. In the meantime, our friends who had been visiting went home but returned along with neighbors because of a strong natural gas odor in their area. Later some friends who lived in Turnagain arrived. They lived a few blocks from the bluff but were afraid of aftershocks. The pilot also arrived so we had eighteen people, ten adults and eight children, making for wall-to-wall people in our small house.

Eighteen people and one bathroom---with no water. But the sewer was still intact and we could flush by pouring water into the bowl. The problem was getting water. We melted snow on a Coleman stove (carefully avoiding the yellow stuff) for water and boiled what we needed for drinking. No electricity also meant no heat, so after inspecting the fireplace and chimney, we kept a fire going all night. The fire was inadequate to heat the house with the fifteen degree outside temperature, but with blankets and sleeping bags no one froze. What with all the aftershocks some of the people never slept all night.

Saturday the electricity came on for about an hour enabling us to run the furnace and take the chill off. It came on more or less permanently the next day. Also two of the families returned to their homes freeing up the living room floor. We got water back on Sunday although we still had to boil the drinking water. The last family moved out on Tuesday and things returned to near normal.

Helen Butcher

Flat Tire

About 5:30 PM I was halted on Spenard Road, after crossing the railroad track. I felt I had a soft tire, then a flat tire, but when I finally braked at the traffic light, I knew that it was an earthquake. People ran from the grocery store at the corner of Minnesota Drive and Spenard , getting away from the falling supplies from the shelves. No one could move over the undulating roadway. As soon as the rocking quit, drivers put their cars in gear and raced to their homes. I headed for 2400 Douglas Drive in Turnagain.

While residents were evacuated from the Turnagain area, and no one permitted to enter, National Guard personnel maintained their small campfire and visited with boys and their dog as they guarded the area.

My kids, Mike and Ann, had held onto the large mirror that was above the piano in my living room, and then they went across the street, and rescued two children until their parents arrived. I couldn't see much damage other than the ground outside. There were broken Clorox bottles from the utility room, smelling up the house.

Soon my bosses and a couple of others came by and persuaded me to join them, as they had heard that houses on the bluff had gone over the cliff. We watched Bob Atwood walk up on the stretched out street, still holding the trumpet he had been playing when the quake struck. (The manufacturer replaced the horn later on.) His first concern as he came up level with the street, was his wife Evangeline, but someone knew she was safe at a friend's house. Their house was broken up, but was still seemed to be intact. Next-door though, Dr. Hines house was gone; it was a pile of lumber, debris, sticks, and rubble that remained on the inlet level.

As our utilities were broken, or just plain gone, we were invited to join our nephew who had a light plant to give us light, with water, heat and hot water. Aunt Imy moved over, to join the crowd. Everyone was tired, so we stretched out on the living room floor for a nap. When Bud and Marian came from the east end of town, their first impression was that we all had been gassed. Gramps tended his tomatoes, which were outside in a greenhouse. Rosene had plenty of food for all participants being a Mormon supplier.

By the time we got back to our house, the place was guarded and only those people who could prove they lived there were allowed in. We moved over to Ed and Flossie's house for a few days. I wandered down to the end of Turnagain Street, had soup from a military makeshift kitchen, which had been setup as soon as possible. The mailman tried to deliver the mail to as many as he could find. All who had houses over the bluff found something to take up. One man had a vacuum cleaner over his shoulder.

Others flew outside and some even refused to come back for the longest time. Husbands had to go out and persuade them to come back.

Gwen Christianson

ACS Building

I was the supervisor in charge of operator services at the Alaska Communications (ACS) building on Government Hill at the time of the earthquake. My husband was with the Anchorage Police Department. In 1964 US Air Force 1929 Communications Group handled long distance communications. I received a letter of commendation for my service following the earthquake.

Anchorage skyline and C Street from Government Hill. Anchorage Cold Storage ended up as a pile of debris and other buildings slid down C Street and demolished the cold storage plant.

The following letter was written to my husband's parents.

April 4, 1964.

We have been working so many hours since the quake that I haven't had time to write previously. I alone managed to put in forty hours of overtime those first few days and Ralph is still at twelve hours a day seven days a week. We're both exhausted but we keep going. We had another quake exactly one week from "the day" but it only lasted thirty seconds. Believe me it was a good one. We evacuated the building temporarily and ten operators refused to go back in afterward. I can hardly blame them. My nerves are just about shot too. We have had tremors almost daily since Good Friday and you really feel them on the third floor of the ACS building. The building was cracked on the side but they say it is safe.

We were home at the time of the big quake, we got outside immediately and we kneeled down in a snow bank. It was impossible to stand. Black Jack, our French Poodle, was right with us and Runt, our Siberian Husky, was chained to her house. We were plenty scared as we knelt there and watched everything rocking and bouncing. The Rambler bounced up next to our house but it wasn't damaged. When we could go back into the house it looked like a cyclone had hit inside. Plants all turned over and a lot of glass breakage, otherwise there is no visible damage to the house. Our well is dry again but we've got electricity and heat back. The section that was hurt the worse of course was downtown and the exclusive Turnagain area. We're very thankful that more people weren't injured or killed.

I'm going to send you some newspapers covering the disaster soon. I'll close now. Write soon.

Love,
Gwen and Ralph

John Clare

Alaska State Police

I remember dressing and heading into the office and seeing a VW bug hit a raised broken section of pavement, flattening all four tires. The driver may have been in a hurry to get home.

At the office the men arrived in various stages of dress, full uniform, partial uniform, whatever they could grab. The office was in disarray. No computers at the time, so all records were on four by five cards. The cards were scattered across the floor, thousands of them.

The phone system was out and the only communication was through the police/fire radios. A patrol car was sent to Providence Hospital to stay there and supply communications to the hospital.

I was sent to Portage Flat to watch for a possible incoming tidal wave. All the roads were split and cracked and heaved.

I moved to higher ground after watching a bit. I remember thinking; this isn't very smart of me sitting down here. After the danger from a tidal wave passed, I was dispatched to the Turnagain area to work.

Since there were no gas pumps working, we had to cut the chain on the gate at International Building Supply and use the gas stored in their above ground gasoline drum. The next day the owners, Bill Plett and Ted Ziemlak were informed and graciously donated the gas.

So there you have it, not very dramatic, but I am thankful our story is not dramatic.

Marium Clare

O'Malley Road

We moved to our five acres in 1963, the same year my husband joined the Alaska State Police, later to become the Alaska State Troopers. We lived in a little prove up cabin on the property to which we had added one more room. We couldn't afford a well or septic tank, so hauled water in five-gallon army cans from a neighbor. We used a home made port-a-potty for the family, so when the earthquake hit we were pretty well set with water on hand and a self-contained toilet.

John was on nights with the troopers so was sleeping. I had made a batch of chili on our little apartment size stove. I heard a rumble like the familiar sound of a truck coming down the road. O'Malley was still a gravel road, so it wasn't uncommon to hear a truck on the road.

When the first jolt hit, the chili tumbled on the floor and into my silver chest.

We had no storage, so it was on the floor in the kitchen. The TV and fish bowl suffered the same fate.

Our children were six, seven, and nine. As the shaking continued I yelled at John several times. He finally jumped out of bed and ran outside with us in his underwear. We stood outside in the snow hanging onto the car for what seemed a long time. We could see the trees swaying side to side as waves rolled down O'Malley Road in swells.

My husband dressed and reported for duty. He was gone until the next day when he checked in on us and was gone again. We had about fourteen friends and their families from Turnagain who came out and stayed with us for a while. We had people sleeping on the floor, but we had a wood stove to provide heat. Everyone was warm.

Dorothy Cobb

Bank on Northern Lights

While my husband was at home I was at work. We heard a loud roaring noise and then the bank building began to shake and roll. I was employed at the First National Bank of Anchorage, Northern Lights Branch, and the building is nearly all glass on three sides. We had a few customers in the bank and they all left in a hurry. We were told to get under our teller counters, but as it got more, then more intense, and the ceiling tiles began falling, filing cabinets turning over and with the possibility of the windows breaking, we were ordered out of the building.

I tried to walk, but finally many of us decided it was easier to crawl out on all fours. I lost a shoe on the way, and when we finally got outside the parking lot was a sight to see. The parked cars were moving up and down in perfect rows, one up and one down. The people in their cars out in the streets were rolling around and bumping into one another. People from the Caribou Department Store were trying to get out of the store. Of course there was no electricity and many of them were still upstairs in the dark. It was a very eerie feeling, like time had stopped for a few minutes. Then the sirens began.

We went back into the bank and tried to gather up the money to lock up. Then we went home. We did not realize the intensity of the quake until later.

It was very hard for us to go to sleep that night and for several days after with so many aftershocks. We almost thought about moving back to California, but Hey!! California has earthquakes too, so we stayed and made Alaska our home and have never regretted it.

Tilford Cobb

Artesian Well

The day of the earthquake we were living on Arctic Blvd at the Spenard Acres Trailer Court, which my mother and stepfather owned. Arctic Boulevard was just a two-lane gravel road with very little traffic. My wife was at work and I was home with our three children, fourteen, eleven and three. As soon as my wife got home from work, we had planned to go to the movie at the Fourth Avenue Theater.

All at once we heard this low rumbling, which increased until it sounded like a bunch of tanks coming down the road. It began to shake real bad, and I realized we were having an earthquake. I gathered the kids, and we stood in the doorframe of our lean-to, where we could look up Arctic Boulevard. Some dogs were barking and running like crazy, the street looked like it was flowing up and down like the water in small ocean surf. The power poles were swaying back and forth like tall willows in the wind, but as bad as they swayed, none of them broke. In the ground, a crack opened up and closed several times puffing out reddish dust.

The well in the court was very deep and had had a twelve-pound artesian head pressure. This stopped after the quake. We were able to pump out the muddy water, and once it cleared we then supplied water for anyone that needed it for a few days.

The court did not have too much damage; we were without electricity for a while but we were very fortunate.

Arlene Cross

At the Movies

Something strange came from the heavens piercing a stone in the town square, in the movie, *The Sword in the Stone*, which was showing at the Fourth Avenue Theater on March 27th 1964. The stage curtains were vibrating, the sword was shaking, and the chandeliers were bouncing back and forth across the ceiling. The screen went dark and the lights stayed out. A loud voice rang out, "Sit down, this is an earthquake." Everybody sat back down and we all rode out the 1964 earthquake in one of the few buildings in Anchorage built to earthquake specifications.

After getting a rain check for a movie, we left the theater. The windows were broken in the Five & Ten cent store next door, but we didn't notice that parts of Fourth Avenue had sunk. Our car was in the Loussac Library parking lot. It had bounced a car's length from where we parked it. We drove by J C Penney. The siding was all over the street. We crossed several small fissures on Seward Highway; came to one so wide we had to go back to Dowling Road and over to Lake Otis Parkway. The same fissure extended there, but someone had already put planks across and we were able to continue on home. There we found a mess. Noodles, rice, dried beans, etc. all covered with jam and jellies plus lots of broken dishes.

My children were ten, thirteen, and fifteen at the time of the quake. To this day when we have a quake they tense, until they are sure it isn't a big one. My daughter illustrates the '64 quake with a chair. A tiny shake of the chair is a light quake, but the chair swinging from side to side is the Good Friday Earthquake of 1964.

Fourth Avenue and A Street. Denali Theater marquee sits at sidewalk level. The Anchorage-Westward Hotel is the tall building in the background.

Jean Paul Cechowski

I Said the Dumbest Thing

The day was cloudy, cool, and snow was on the ground. It was Good Friday and I had the day off from Creekside Park School. I had a touch of flu and was in bed when the state of Alaska rocked and so did my bed. My husband threw open the front door, I staggered to an arch, the cat went under the bed, and our brave shepherd went under the table. We watched helplessly, hanging on, as the refrigerator went over and then back to upright. The tops of the trees whipped to the ground and then back up. Our car rolled back and forth helplessly. But it was the noise, like an approaching train, which overwhelmed me. My, it was NOISY!! After we regained our footing, I said the dumbest thing, "Well, that wasn't so bad!"

We had no great damage because the house sits on a gravel hill, but we did lose our well—no running water for about five months! Try that for a while!

Tom Dale

Elmendorf Warehouse Leveled

We were getting ready to go to church when it started. All the cupboards opened up and all the dishes started coming out. I was in the second story of the apartment, which was in one of a number of wooden buildings. We went to get in the doorway of the building.

I was working on Elmendorf, in a concrete warehouse, which was leveled. The next Friday a bunch of us went to the PX for lunch when it started again. We got up and ran out. We kept falling down.

Beverly Dalzell

No Bowling That Night

While standing in the "connect and disconnect" office at Chugach Electric, talking to Carl Jenkins, the earthquake started. The ten-foot window of the building was waving; the folks and cash register out front were going from one side of their space to the other, back and forth. Then the General Manager and the Comptroller each left their offices and headed for opposite exits, hell bent for election. Carl and I just stood there and watched the light poles along Gambell Street swaying and the folks at the Safeway and Pay and Save Stores running to their cars. Some stayed to pick up a few things they might need. It's called "looting." Some people really think fast even in a time of disaster.

Obviously there was no bowling that night so I picked up son Bobby and Bob's eighty-year-old mother and took them out to the house on Birch Road as the oil floor furnace was still lit and the house was kind of warm. We were greeted with cupboards that had emptied into the sink, etc., mixing black tea and ketchup and a little spice. I put Grandma to bed with lots of blankets. Bobby was in his sleeping bag and I was on the couch. We slept well. It was a few days before power was restored, but we made it through the experience of a lifetime.

Bob Dalzell

Chugach Electric

I left Chugach Electric for home to prepare for an evening of dinner and taking my mother to mass at Holy Family Church. While waiting for her to get dressed the earthquake started. I heard her say something about not being able to stand up. I went to her room and she was laughing while trying to get her dress off the hanger. I told her she better sit down as we were having an earthquake. I got her to the sofa, which kept going back and forth until the quake stopped. The things on the table were just as they were before it started. The TV fell over on the footstool, but the kitchen was a mess.

Bev came and got mother. I went to Chugach where we worked getting the power back on. Hunk Petronavich and I went to Alaska Native Hospital on Third Avenue where we surveyed the damage. City power was trying to get their diesel oil for the generators. They got one diesel going, but it died when the hose collapsed from the diesel tank. They were then out of compressed air to start the diesels, so Andy Johnson, operation supervisor, had us go to the Anchorage Oxygen Plant on Gambell and Seventeenth (where the Sullivan Arena now stands) and picked up three loads of bottled nitrogen for the city power plant to be used for starting the diesel instead of compressed air. After city workmen got a metal fuel line installer from the army tankers to the diesel plant they were able to start the first diesel for standby power.

After this, we spent 72 hours isolating power lines, mostly in the Turnagain area before getting relieved and going home.

Greg Dixon

I Was Very Impressed

I was raised Catholic and our family had moved into a new church at about 22nd and Arctic. The dirt road stopped right there. They had picked up an old military surplus building and made it into a church. It was Good Friday, and I was an altar boy. I was at church doing something connected to that.

A friend had a new mo-ped motor scooter, and he was going to let me drive it. I had just got started going around a block or two. I took off and went down the road. Of course I wasn't going very fast, and all of a sudden it felt like I was getting a flat tire. I started to get off, and it knocked me down.

One woman was trying to get out of the house with her son, and every time she would try to take a step she would get thrown back, back and forth and back and forth.

There was a Buick inside an open carport. It was slowly shaking down the post that held up the carport.

It just kept getting bigger and bigger. It kept growing and growing. I was impressed with that. Cracks opening and closing. Let's see, "atomic bomb". Lots of things ran through my head. To me it was just another earthquake, a real good one. I was in the tenth grade, fifteen years old, and I was very impressed.

Then I went back to the church to take the bike back. When I got there the priest said I should probably go back home, I agreed so I walked down to about Nineteenth Avenue. At the time Spenard Road was the busy street, and I got down to where Chester Creek went over a culvert. Of course the cars were held up. Like a teenager, I just thought that was cool. I walked down I street, and met up with Russ Meekins. We were both teenagers then. He was coming from town, and I was going into town. He was across the street, "The whole town is down."" Okay Russ, Okay.

I got up I street about Tenth or Eleventh and saw some broken chimneys, but nothing that looked like much damage to me. I kept walking and saw my house. It looked like somebody had just taken it and shaken it. Most of the family was there, and my father started talking to us about the survivalist kind of things. My job was to go to the gas station on Ninth Avenue and C Street and get kerosene. I still didn't see too much. I was curious to know what Russ was talking about, the whole town being sunk, so I wanted to walk

A GI a field kitchen was set up on the Ninth Avenue Park Strip. Food, coffee and water were made available.

downtown. Even in that short a time the streets were blocked off. I walked down to see what I could see, and I could hear from the police station, so I was impressed with that.

I went on home, and of course we didn't have any power, no water, so the next thing was to get something for water, and start picking up things. From that point we were just trying to figure what to do next.

I was still trying to figure out how to get to town and see, but I couldn't get within a block or two. The radio station came on and the first thing I heard was that all of Turnagain was wrecked. I heard about downtown being sunk, Turnagain being wrecked. Okay, but I still hadn't seen anything. I was curious.

West High School originally was a two-story building, and it was now a one-story building. After about two weeks we had to go to school at East High. The road going to it was just a dirt road, and it was pretty much by itself. Northern Lights Boulevard did not exist.

The Hillside Manor Apartments were just off Fifteenth. During the earthquake they just kind of slid down the hill. All this was going on just two blocks away, and I didn't even see it.

As a teenager you only key in on certain things. It was just excitement. The military was giving out C Rations, and they contained cigarettes, and we knew we weren't supposed to be smoking.

When the aftershocks came I had figured out what was going on. My father was remodeling the house, and I was sitting on some planking that was laid across some beams. I had just gotten up when they fell to the basement. By then I had figured out what was happening. It was more real to me.

Mary Anne Donlan

Oh No, What If?

We were living in a small frame house in south Mountain View. It being Good Friday we had boiled Easter eggs. I started ironing and the kids were playing on the couch. My husband decided to take a shower. A gentle swaying began and I yelled to the kids, "Stop jumping on the couch!"

Then the movement became really violent, making it hard to walk. I looked out the bedroom window and saw the utility lines going round and round like a jump rope. I dropped the iron on the floor but was afraid to unplug it, so it burned quite a hole in the tile.

When the shower spigot began moving back and forth and spewing water out into the bathroom, Ed decided it was time to get out, even though he was still soapy. He wrapped himself in a towel and gathered us all together at the end of the hall. As we crouched there I thought it must be some kind of invasion because it was so noisy. Ed said later, the first thing that popped into his mind was the Bible verse, "Naked I came forth and naked I shall return!"

We spent the night with a neighbor who had a fireplace and ate hard-boiled eggs for dinner. Life began to return to normal the next day but we all felt a little off tilt and a curious lassitude seemed to possess us.

The scariest moment for some came the exactly a week later when most people were doing their grocery shopping. There was a heavy aftershock. People pushed through the lines and bolted into the street and clerks left their stations. Groceries were left behind in the general pandemonium as everyone wondered, "Oh, no! What if!"

Irene Dow

Children Lined Up on the Lawn

I didn't feel anything until that first big tremor; it just shook the whole building. I was at 746 F Street right across from the Episcopalian Church, working for Bright Mortgage Investment Company. The boss had gone home, and it was such a beautiful day. The sun was out and I was watching all these little cute kids going into the church, all the little girls all dressed up in their Easter outfits. Then as I got ready to leave, one big shake knocked me across the room, and then it just started really rocking and rolling. When people talk about solid earth, it wasn't solid; it was like waves on the ocean.

They took the kids out of the church onto the lawn, and had them lie down on the lawn on their stomachs, and the quake kind of threw them up in the air as the ground rolled. It was the weirdest thing.

I got behind my desk, and then two desks came together, because everything was moving, and I thought, "I've got to get over my desk," and the light fixture came down and took a chunk out of my desk. Took a little chunk out of my hair; good thing it didn't take a chunk out of my head, or I wouldn't be here talking to you.

Then I ran out to where my car was parked, right outside of the building. Several people were hanging onto it and it was just moving from side to side. I opened the door and was hanging onto the door as the others yelled, "Don't stand there! The balcony's going to come down on your head." I had to crawl to get away. Some people who had been upstairs told me afterward, that if you wanted to put a foot on the step, it would be up here, and then it would be down there.

We were managing that building, so when it calmed down (it seemed like five hours) I got a man to go with me into the room where the heating system was to see if anything had become detached, and took the keys and we went into all the offices to see if there was anybody dead, but there wasn't anybody there. A friend of mine came down to see how I was, and he drove me home. I had just moved to the brand new Sleeping Lady Apartments, off of Third and Barrow.

My apartment looked fine when I walked in, but the kitchen!!! Everything had fallen out of the cupboards, and the refrigerator

While many streets were totally destroyed, or greatly damaged, this one in the Turnagain area only suffered a small pressure ridge.

door had evidently opened, maybe several times, because, even though the door was closed, there wasn't a thing left in it. Molasses, milk, sugar, liquor, everything but one bottle of Vodka had a little left so my friend and I had a drink. There weren't any glasses; they were all broken, so I think we drank it right out of the bottle.

Then the pounding on the door. The National Guard came down, with bayonets. They were just young kids, and they were just as frightened as we were. They said, "Out of here, everybody out, there is going to be a tsunami." I said, "Get that thing out of my face." He had that bayonet right in my face, and my friend said, "Have you ever used that?" And the kid said, "No". She says, "Well, she's right." "People are frightened enough, without you going around with that bayonet, flashing it around." And he said, "We have to go to higher ground." I said, "Where is higher ground?" He didn't know.

Since the phones were out, I decided I'd better go to my employer's house on Lake Otis Parkway near Fifteenth to report on the office. They were cooking in their fireplace; the kids were thinking this was a lot of fun. I had picked up a radio at my apartment that had batteries, and we found out what was going on in the rest of town, so my friend and Carl immediately went out to Turnagain to see if they could help. We ended up with a house full of people that lost their homes. They were sleeping on the floors, and Kay and I were up all night keeping the fireplace going and tearing up sheets for diapers. And it just kept shaking and shaking. People didn't sleep very much. They just went to bed with their clothes on and slept for a couple of hours.

On F Street we never did lose water. It had once been an apartment building, so there was a little kitchen, and there was a full bath with tub and shower, so we, at least, could get clean. I checked on my friends and invited them down for showers.

I volunteered with the city and the Red Cross. People from Outside were getting in by ham radio and trying to find their relatives. We would go out and try to find people, maybe some elderly lady who lived by herself, so I was running all over town.

A week later we had another big one, about noon. They had just been telling us, "It won't happen again for 100 years." Boy everybody was—I was—ready to leave. Get out of Alaska.

Art Elliott

East High

I. The Earthquake

My wife Jane and I came to Alaska in August of 1963. Our son Tom was going to be in the Sixth grade and our daughter Nancy was in the third grade, and I was contracted to teach at East High School. My wife, Jane, taught at Scenic Park for the first year, and later taught many years at Airport Heights. I might just go back a bit and say that one of the reasons we came to Alaska is that my wife is an identical twin and her twin, Mollie Jean, along with her husband Fred, and daughters Linda and Rita and son Kevin had come up in 1958.

Down to March 27, 1964.

The kids and I went to Alyeska to go skiing. There was a bit of a white out at times, and so we got home a little early. We live, then as now, on the South end of Alder Drive, a block away from my sister-in-law and her family. Since it was Good Friday my wife said, "Better take Tom and get his hair cut." I heard there was a new barbershop opened over on the corner of Lake Otis Parkway and Northern Lights, so we went there. Johnnie was the barber and he had a Japanese assistant. We got there around 5 PM and waited. There were two chairs. About 5:30 things began to shake and shake very hard. The Japanese barber took off his smock and got out of there, and Johnnie never heard from him again.

We decided, Tom and I, to get outside because things were falling off the shelves. Our car, a 52 Chevrolet, was sitting outside. The car was rocking back and forth and jumping up and down, and the telephone poles were swaying back and forth like a row of fly rods. I was thinking it would be safer in the car. I said to Tom, "Get in the car." There was a little girl there, four or five years old. I said,

"You better get in the car with us." She said, "No, I'm not supposed to get in the car with strangers." I said, "It'll be okay, today." So, I scooped her up and we sat in the car rocking back and forth and up and down. When you looked down Northern Lights it looked like the street was a roller coaster. We sat there. I knew it was a good earthquake. I don't remember us saying anything to one another. We were just sitting there rocking back and forth. Five minutes doesn't sound like a very long time, but in earthquake of that intensity, five minutes seemed very long.

Well, eventually it stopped. We opened the door, and that little girl made a beeline for home. To this day I don't know who she was. We went back in the barbershop and Johnnie trimmed Tom's hair up a little bit and said, "Come back on Monday." It was better than a week before we made it back.

When we started up the car, I turned on the radio and there was nothing. There was no broadcasting. All the stations were down because the power was off. I found out later that if there were an earthquake the power would be shut off. Eventually, the power came on and we were listening to KFQD.

When we got home we found my wife and Nancy kind of shook up, but we didn't have any damage. The area we live in, right across from the Airport Heights School, is pretty much on a gravel foundation, so, while we shook as hard as anyplace, there wasn't much structural damage. We had a few little things tip over, but not much damage to speak of. After a while, my sister-in-law and the kids came. Fortunately, the earthquake struck at such a time that most people were off work or casualties would have been much higher. Anyhow, that evening they were all at our house because we had an oil fired furnace, which, if and when power came on, would provide some heat. Up the block at Jean's place they had natural gas. They were with us a couple of days.

While Jean and the kids were at Penney's, my brother-in-law, Fred, had been up the street. He came back to their car and it was smashed flat. He didn't know where the family was at first. The following day he and I went downtown and looked at Penney's and, of course, his car was still under the rubble. Over on Fourth Avenue, the north side for two blocks was all down. That side of the street dropped about twelve to fourteen feet. The theater was down there—the Denali Theatre—the marquee was just about touching the sidewalk, but the lights on it were not broken.

When the station wagon was uncovered and Fred and I were over there getting things from it, I found one of my sister-in-law's shoes. I said, "We've got to find the other one." He said, "Aw, never mind." I said, "Well, if I don't find the other one, Jean will have to buy a new pair and then, since the twins always dress alike, my wife would have to buy a pair too."

II. The Schools

There was no school. West High School was shook apart. Government Hill was shook severely, and all the schools were closed for about two weeks. When they reopened, West High was moved to East, and the two schools put on shifts. East (where I was teaching) would have the first shift with the students getting there at 7 and teachers at 6:30. That was fine for me since I had worked at jobs where I had to get up early in the morning. The first day was rather interesting. At that time Northern Lights did not extend to East High School from Lake Otis Parkway, and so the traffic all had to come down Bragaw. Joe Montgomery was the principal of East. He had arranged for the police to be down on the corner directing traffic when the buses came, but wires were crossed and they weren't there. Joe was pretty upset. Once we got it working right, the buses with the West High students would go around the back of the school, let them off and then drive to the front to pick up the East High students. One batch of kids came in the back as the other was going out the front. It worked pretty well. The students were a little in shock. I want to say this about our kids — many of them worked at helping get things out of houses and other places around town. At Airport Heights School, we had people from Old Harbor staying there. The Red Cross had arranged that.

We had many, many pleasant years in Alaska. After that earthquake I was sure I wasn't going to go back to Minnesota because I wanted to find out what was going to happen next.

Dr. Maynard Falconer, Jr

Shaken In Bethel

After loading up the new red and black Nash Rambler station wagon with all that I owned, I drove it to the Seattle Docks for delivery in Anchorage, Alaska. (In 1964 you were allowed to put everything you could in your car and ship it north.) I then went to the airport and flew to Anchorage, arriving the first week of March 1964. The Optometric practice I had purchased was located on the corner of Ninth Avenue and K Streets.

Dr. L. W. Hines had scheduled me to see patients in Dillingham and Bethel. I packed three trunks of optical instruments and equipment and headed for the Wien Airlines flight to Dillingham. I spent several days in Dillingham during the Beaver Roundup. Being from out of town, they asked me to judge the Miss Dillingham contest. It was held in the high school gym. It was during this contest that I had my first beaver tail hamburger.

The trip to Bethel was very much appreciated by the town people. They met me at the airport, served me a "Harvey Wallbanger," and drove me to my lodging above the Swanson Brothers General Store.

On Good Friday, I went over to a lodge for a family style dinner. Ten people were just about ready to sit down for dinner when the room began to rock. It continued to sway for what seemed like minutes. I sat down in one of the over stuffed chairs and turned on the radio. The Armed Forces Radio broadcast, from Fairbanks, had gone on emergency status. For fifteen minutes it reported on disasters. The tower at the Anchorage International Airport was down, Seward was on fire, all power was out in Anchorage, J C Penney store had collapsed, hundreds of people had been killed due to slides in the Turnagain and Downtown areas of Anchorage, airports were closed, Kodiak was awash with high tides and no power.

Tsunami warnings were in effect for Valdez and the rest of the West Coast of the United States.

Suddenly the fifteen minutes of negative reporting was halted. Immediately a positive air was projected. Information was now given on what to do without water, power, and food. Bulletins on how to cope with debris on roads. Air traffic and emergency locations situated through Southcentral Alaska were located.

Some of the men at the lodge worked for Wien Airlines. Wien had just landed a plane at Bethel. The men immediately went to the airport, boarded a plane and flew toward Anchorage, landing at the military bases.

Very little damage occurred in Bethel.

Those of us not affiliated with an airline had to wait several days before we could fly into Anchorage.

When I arrived in Anchorage I stayed at the Roosevelt Hotel (now Inlet Hotel) in downtown. The house at which I was a guest before I left was totally destroyed as it slid into Cook Inlet. Luckily the day before, my car, packed with all my worldly possessions, had been moved from Turnagain Arm to the downtown parking lot at Ninth Avenue and K Streets.

I opened the office as soon as possible and took care of the optical needs of many. The Red Cross sent numerous people over to the clinic for vision services.

My wife was still in Seattle finishing her job with the Seattle School System. She called the Red Cross in Seattle trying to get more information about my whereabouts. When she mentioned my location in Bethel to the operator, the reply was, "My dear, we won't hear from those remote locations for months."

My father, Maynard Falconer, Sr., the director of design for the 13th Naval District, was called from his office in Seattle to fly immediately to Kodiak. Kodiak was one of the three military installations directly under control of the navy. (Adak and Barrow were the other two.) Although my father was a civilian he was given the rank of commander when flying to Kodiak. His job was to get Kodiak on its feet. The plane was filled with tools, electrical equipment and loads of baby diapers. When he arrived at Kodiak he immediately placed as many of the military personnel as he could under his command. He started getting the electricity into the city so hospitals and stores could operate. It was cold and damp so fires were built on the harbor shore to keep workers warm. Access to the local liquor stores was good payment for the civilian and military workers.

Cheri L. Hansen Funk

In Fairbanks

We were living in Fairbanks at the time but I remember exactly what I was doing when we felt the quake. I was nine years old. I was lying on our bear rug watching this show called *Fireball XL5*; it was a marionette puppet show. My Mom was making macaroni and cheese and fish sticks for dinner, my brother Bill was sitting in our rocking chair also watching TV. I felt the floor kinda move and I yelled at my brother to quit rocking so hard cause he was hitting the floor and making it shake. He stopped rocking and said he wasn't doing anything and at that moment, the quake hit and the whole house jerked. We all jumped up and ran to the outside door and stood in the doorjamb and watched things go nuts outside. The car was bouncing from side to side, telephone poles were swaying so much, and it looked like they were almost laying down on the ground, tiny pebbles were being pitched into the air. It was the scariest thing I had ever experienced. After things calmed down, we watched the devastation in Anchorage on the television, and our hearts went out to everyone there.

Patricia Swafford Garrett

London Bridge Is Falling

When I remember the earthquake I have to start with the winter before that Good Friday of 1964. For me it all started in November 1963, when we drove to Anchorage from New Mexico.

My new husband was nineteen. I was seventeen and expecting our son in the spring. During our long and winding drive through Canada and the Yukon, there were many days that the AM radio of our 1956 Mercury did not come in.

I felt obliged to fill the silence. I told my husband about something my best friend told me, that an earthquake fault ran along California all the way to Alaska. She said it was predicted that we would have a huge earthquake, the lost city of Atlantis would rise from the sea and California would fall into the Pacific Ocean for good. He told me I scared him when I talked like that.

Like many newcomers to Alaska in the early 1960s we had very little money, no Arctic clothing and not a clear understanding of what life in this far north state would require. My husband and I laughed at the large brown round toed boots with felt liners and golden yellow shoestrings his mom had waiting for us in Spenard.

We lived at the Wonder Park Apartments on the west end of Northern Lights Boulevard Our apartment sat close enough to the railroad track that I could hear the train blow its whistle at night.

One day a tremendous shaking began and the thick milky white icicles that hung over our only window snapped, broke off, and crashed into the wooden walkway under the window. Our TV abruptly went off the air. It unplugged itself from the wall and rolled across the floor. A small lamp fell over and broke. Our dog started to whine and cower. Snow whooshed off the roof. I thought the manager was clearing the dangerous icicles from the roof.

Once the ice fell and the snow slid off, a loud roar started. The sound came from all around me and I could not pinpoint where it started nor ended. I became frightened.

I knew a little about the Cold War, understood Alaska's strategic location and the threat from Russia. I remember thinking then that it must be a war. I decided that airplanes were roaring overhead and bombs were causing the ice and snow to fall. Then I saw the scrawny spruce tree outside our door whipping back and forth like a jerky windshield wiper.

I supplemented my husband's minimum wage by babysitting two children under the age of three. I remember cuddling the two on a full sized bed, while I knelt beside them on the floor. My knee ground against glass from a broken baby bottle. The three year old began to cry. I patted his back and started to sing, "London Bridge is falling down, falling down, falling down."

When the frenzy of motion stopped I could hear people running along the wooden walkway, calling back and forth, checking on neighbors. I remember trying to stand and my knees wouldn't allow it. I wobbled and plopped back down on the bed and cried right along with the two little kids.

Our power was off. I wanted the fatherly voice of our local news TV announcer, Alvin O. Bramstead to tell me what to do, but the TV was quiet and the screen was black. I could not pick up KHAR with my small transistor radio. We couldn't afford a phone and I don't suppose they worked anyway.

I thought of my husband across town and hoped he was okay. I wanted to be with him. My mother in law told me to dress warm and to wear the big ugly boots, and for once, I listened. She also told me to pack a few things to bring with me, "in case of emergency." Very pregnant, I followed her outside.

I may have been slightly hysterical by then. If chunks of falling ice, snapping and zapping power lines, spilled coffee on my newly waxed linoleum, and wildly flinging trees were not emergencies, what would rattle this woman?

A friend of my mother in law had a Rambler station wagon. We loaded into it to go check on my husband. There were lines of bumper-to-bumper traffic going in both directions on Northern Lights Boulevard and Spenard Road. Everyone drove slowly, calling out and asking about others. People stopped on the road, hugged each other and wiped tears as they found each other. I finally saw our Mercury coming toward us. We honked the horn, flashed the lights, rolled down our windows, and yelled loud my husband's name. He saw us and waved back. We were in a narrow place on the road and couldn't pull over, but I knew he was okay so I felt better. His mom started to cry when she saw him.

When he saw us headed for Anchorage, he assumed we were headed to the Community Hospital down on the Park Strip to have our baby. He tried to turn around to follow us, but the traffic wouldn't permit it. Since we knew he was okay, we just drove around looking at all the topsy-turvy sights, while he drove back downtown and sat at the hospital parking lot waiting for us. The hospital was being evacuated and they ran him off. He imagined us beside the roadside delivering his first child in a snow bank. We were invited to stay at a place out at Mile Seven on the Seward Highway. I thought, "how will I ever live way out there in the sticks" "what if I go into labor?" At seventeen, everything was all about me.

At this place "way out in the boon docks," south of Dowling Road, we had a gravity drip oil heater that kept us warm. We boiled well water and added Clorox and Kool Aid before drinking it. We had propane stove for cooking. The freezer was packed full of salmon, moose and caribou for hearty meals. We had a wringer washer to keep our clothes clean and I used a honey bucket for the first time.

Most of all, we had the example and generosity of someone that knew how to live in Alaska without city utilities. I don't know what we would have done without him.

We learned later that across from our low rent apartment, some nice houses slid into the Inlet, and that gas lines were leaking. Worrying about explosions, trying to stop sightseers and hoping to prevent looting the National Guardsmen blocked our way back home for a while. They thoughtfully let my husband walk into the blocked-off area to our home to look for our dog and gather up my brush hair rollers, blankets, food and clothing. I don't remember looting being a problem. I do remember Foodland offering canned milk, corn syrup and diapers, which we went to pick up just in case our baby decided to come during this time. They also gave us canned goods, wilting vegetables, fruits and thawing meats.

None of my memories are unique. They are rather dull compared to some stories. However, when looking back I appreciate the kindness, compassion and generosity of the people in Anchorage towards each other during that time. Anchorage came together in a tremendous community effort to dig out and move forward.

Kathy Gates

Good Friday Earthquake

Magnitude 9.2 Largest in North America in the 20th Century March 27, 1964

2774 Marston Drive
Anchorage, Alaska
The Gates

8 AM—Today is Good Friday, a beautiful sunny, crisp day and I have the day off work.

10 AM—I am giving my mother a permanent and my neighbor, Jean, is visiting with us.

2:30 PM—Jean has gone home, and I have Mother home.

4 PM—The handwork on my Easter outfit is finished.

4:30 PM—I would like to sit down and rest but I need to vacuum my floors before tomorrow, for tonight we are going to church, and tomorrow we are going skiing. These sunny March days are good for skiing and tanning.

5:30 PM—Herb isn't home yet. The steak is frying, the potatoes are cooked, and I have just finished my cleaning in time for supper. There are Linda's wet boots. "Linda, come here and put those boots down on the furnace. "Sorry, Mother, I forgot."

5:36 PM—Suzie is shaking her dust rag and has just shut the door. What is that noise? It is the roar of an earthquake. "Linda!" I scream. Luckily she doesn't even finish her trip to the furnace. She manages to get up the basement stairs through the garage and into my arms just as the shaking is getting too violent to stand up, and the basement is crumbling. We stand in the doorway between the garage and dining area while Suzie hangs onto the front door. Hanging on is the only way we can manage to stand up and not be thrown around. Our house is jerking cracking sheet rock, and snapping tubing and pipes. What a horrible sound!

We are rocking way up on the side then back the other way. There go the dishes off the table. Suzie cries, "When is it going to stop?" "I don't know, but hang on, stay by the door." Our new car is slamming back and forth in the garage. Why worry about that? The fireplace chimney just fell on it. I believe the quake is slowing down, "Come on kids, we can't get out the front door. It is wedged. We will have to climb over the car." Oh no, the quake isn't slowing. It is starting up again more violently. We go out the back garage door and see a wall of dirt rising up behind our house. No, it isn't rising, we are sinking. "Oh God, I think it is going to fall on us. We had better go up to the front of the garage. There goes Holmberg's house down in a chasm, collapsing with two by fours flying out through the roof. My other neighbor's house is breaking apart. I scream, "Jean, Jean!" Edna, my neighbor across the street on a huge wall of dirt that is tilting toward the inlet. She yells, "Jean is out front!"

We pray, "Please, may my Herb be okay, and please, please stop this. Please, God." We don't have many big trees, but the neighbors across the street have a lot, and they are crashing, lashing, and writhing. Then a crevasse opens in front of us as mountains of blue clay spurt up in the front yard. If it would only stop.

5:40 PM—After about 5 minutes of Hell, the earth quits wrenching. Frantically I climb over the car to get our coats, my purse, and boots. I grab my billfold and checkbook out of my purse and put them in my pocket. My hands are free to climb over the crevices and up the wall of dirt. I don't see my neighbors, the Holmbergs. Then they answer my call. They are standing on the only piece of ground by their car that didn't go down.

Our dog cries when she can't get up. We turn around to help her, but she finally makes it up. We run like crazy, yelling, "You better get out of here. It might happen again." We get to my parents' house about five blocks away. Mother is in the house picking up glass and dirt from her upset plants. Here comes Herb. He is okay!!! I run to catch him so he won't go home and think we have been buried alive. The girls and I kiss Herb and hug him!!! I sadly tell him, "Our house is wrecked lying down in a big hole."

Herb has come from Hewitt's Drug Store on Fourth Avenue where the stores have dropped down so that only half the storefronts are visible at street level. In the drug store all the drugs are spilled everywhere, a smelly mess.

We think we should go get some clothes. I am shaking scared to go down there for fear of another earthquake or landslide. Finally we get up enough courage and rush to gather some of our clothes and insurance papers. We throw a blanket off the bed and get my new thirty dollar ski pants, my best sweater and skirts. They are so heavy I drop them. Herb gets our important papers, his guns, and

The dwelling at 2751 Marston Drive, owned by Drs. Robert and Helen Whaley was completely destroyed. Nothing much could be salvaged, but the attempt was made.

suits. We have so much we can't carry it, so we leave the guns. Just as we go out the door a terrible tremor comes. We drop everything outside in the dirt hanging onto our insurance papers and scramble out. After all, is it really worth the risk?

116

7 PM—A notice comes over the radio that Valdez has been hit by a terrible tidal wave and is also on fire. We go to my parents and just stand around deciding what to do. No lights, no water, no sewer. Then a warning comes to beware of a tidal wave. We go to the next block to get gas and Smitty said most insurance doesn't cover earthquakes. I read our policy by dash light and it says earthquakes Excluded! A $30,000 house we built ourselves from payday to payday, all paid for. We go back to my folks and try to eat, and then the kids in sleeping bags with their clothes on. All night the tremors continue.

March 28 - Morning comes and the army sends out guards and patrols to prevent looting and haul water and sewage. They are really a big help. We decide to salvage what we can of our personal things since the fine lines of the insurance policy exclude these in an earthquake. We haul our things manually up over the bank. GI's who work for my husband, and my father come to help. We are frightened every time there is a tremor. When a camera fan or sightseer comes along we enlist their help in the tug of war up that embankment. Then comes the sad part, taking out our cabinets, carpet, baseboard, bathroom fixtures, fireplace, and light fixtures. After building the house yourself and living in it for eight years you become quite attached, and feel bad to have to tear it up. Our life savings are sitting here in the twisted torn hulk.

We are not alone. Seventy beautiful homes are completely destroyed in our subdivision alone. And lest we be ungrateful, some lost their precious loved ones.

We have moved to an apartment where five of our neighbors who lost their homes are living. Earthquakes are horrible. You not only lose your house, but a home, and your neighbors you have lived and visited with for years, and worse yet your loved ones or your life.

Sol L. Gerstenfeld

North Mountain View

I heard the earthquake, it was a rumble, but mostly I felt it.

I was right here at home (in N. Mountain View) when the earthquake struck. I was going out to dinner so I was all dressed up and just about out the door. At the time I had an oil range with a hot water coil in it, and an electric fan blower. First thing I checked the stove, and it was still running, which meant that the oil supply was still there. The bathtub was full because I used to run hot water into it. It kept the coil cool and free of clogging and the hot water would heat the other room. As the quake went on, I heard the water splashing over the tub, so I pulled the plug, and as it drained, I was thinking to myself, "Ooooh when is the tub ever going to be full again," because the electricity was off for the water pump.

I kind of surmised everything was under control here, and then I checked to see how the neighbors were. I was a member of the Civil Air Patrol and an auxiliary fire fighter at the time, but I had been hurt in judo so I couldn't put on my uniform because I wasn't fully capable. Nevertheless, I figured that I could make sandwiches and coffee or something and whatever I did was that much less for somebody else to do. On the way into town, I stopped off at Merrill Field, and they seemed to have things under control there, so I went on into town, and it was amazing to me. City Hall was crowded. (The fire station was right there, then) but it was a beehive. There was no commotion, just hustle, bustle, and a buzz. We ran out of Civil Defense armbands, so people had kerchiefs around their arm to show that they had been assigned to a job. It was amazing how they all just flooded in there and kind of took charge.

They sent me with a couple of other guys in a pickup down to the railroad yards for gasoline to run the generator. The tanks had ruptured, and dams had been thrown up to contain the oil. We were afraid of setting it off, so I stayed with the pickup on the road while they walked into to the building to get the gas. There wasn't even time to blockade the road, when here comes a guy wants to go to see how his boat was doing. I said, "Well you can't go down there. We're not even going down there" At first he wouldn't have it (a one-track mind) but he didn't go.

Only one of the four-radio stations on the air was KBYR. They had their own power plant. The phone system was busier than the dickens, so people from all over the state that needed services were calling into KBYR. KBYR would pass the needs out over the air, and people would call them.

What really impressed me was the way things came together. Things were moving creatively and constructively. After 9/11 you saw the same thing; people coming in with all their skills and pitching in.

There was a man that had a generator of his own, and had a filling station out in Muldoon, who was offering five gallons of gas at the regular rate for anybody involved in Civil Defense, so I went out there and I showed him my two cards and he filled up my tank at the regular rate.

The grocery store next to Brewster's in Mountain View was closed because stuff was scattered all over, and people didn't know when were going to be able to buy things again. However the owner would open the door for anyone, ask what he or she needed and pass stuff out the door and take the money.

When I went back to work at Elmendorf in airfreight, a forty-foot vanload of meat came in on planes for the town. So did clothes for the Salvation Army, so much so that the Salvation Army had no place to store them, so we kept them for a while. The military helped the town a lot.

Our fire department equipment and the military's fire department equipment was not compatible, but we knew that and had worked out agreements and practiced in advance so we could help each other out. Thanks to automatic shut-off valves, which cut the gas supplies and automatic sprinklers there were no fires.

Unfortunately, we don't seem to have learned much from the earthquake.

Robert Gilmore

1218 H Street

I am relaxing in the front room reading the evening paper, the *Anchorage Times*. In the kitchen my wife Helen is preparing dinner with a pot of beans simmering on the stove. Daughter Becky is upstairs watching TV with her sister Robbin and brother Ron. It is a quiet Good Friday and I have had the day off from my job as Chief Map Draftsman with Sinclair Oil and Gas Co. Suddenly the room sways and Helen says, "We're having a quake!"

In our two years in Alaska we have felt several tremors and we aren't too alarmed. However the motion continued and the frame of the house starts cracking and making a splintering sound. Helen's eyes get big as she realizes this is no ordinary tremor and she runs into the kitchen where the pot of beans and the contents of the kitchen cabinets are being thrown to the floor. Everything loose starts flying around.

Outside I see large waves rolling across the ground and our car is being rocked up and down like a boat on rough seas. Our neighbor, Gerry Witkowski, runs out her front door to get into her car, but it is pitching and bouncing and the seismic waves are getting bigger so she has to retreat back into the house. Her husband, Norm, is clinging to a tree in the back yard, which is lashing back and forth like a giant whip. Helen and I both run to the stairway and call the children to come down where there is nothing that can fall on us.

Becky yells, "The TV is trying to fall down!"

"Let it go!" I answer back, "and get down here." I hear the TV crash as she scurries down.

All three children join us as we brace ourselves at the bottom of the stairs. Out the kitchen window, I can see the "L" Street Apartments building (Inlet Towers) in a cloud of dust. The walls are fracturing and shattering like glass as the concrete walls crack into the form of "X's" all down the sides of the building.

As I hear the roaring and cracking and breaking of glass, I can barely keep my footing. Outside everything is moving and dust is flying and I can only think, "This must be the way the world ends!" Our chimney disintegrates, rumbles down the roof and crashes to the ground. The horrible waves keep rolling right through the house and I wonder when will they ever stop. Four minutes is a long time to be in terror.

After the waves die down and we can collect ourselves we look around the house and feel very lucky that only a few things are broken and scattered. The electricity and water are out so we need to find a place to stay for a few days. Luckily, we have friends on Elmendorf who invite us in. After a few days, we are able to move back home and try to clean things up.

All of downtown Anchorage is shoved several feet to the west toward the Inlet. "L" street has a jog in it from the westward movement. My office with Sinclair has been destroyed. It was on the second floor of the Daily News Building between Third and Fourth Avenue on C Street and everything has dropped several feet. There is a large hole in the ground where I would normally park my car. So the huge task of moving our office begins. We move into the vacant "original" Providence Hospital on Ninth Avenue and L Street and I continue my job there.

Elva Hahn

A Yuckie Gray Time

My son and I were at home. I was in the bathroom, indisposed. All the water in the back of the tank started to give me a shower. I came out to the kitchen and was knocked down twice. Everything on our shelves came alive but did not break. I couldn't stay up. My son said, "Mom, it's a bomb." We got under the table. Just then, a hand came in through the door and a voice said, "Give me your hand. It is not a bomb, it's an earthquake." It was my husband, Ralph. He led us out. The sound of the quake was so unusual. Trees were swaying to the ground. Many snapped off.

I had a little pocket radio. It took an hour to find a station. We soon learned why. We knew we would have to do something for survival, water, etc. There was an old two-burner wood stove under the house in the basement. Ralph got it out and we made do with what we had. The next morning I made breakfast for neighbors and ourselves. There was no water. No electricity. We could not take the car out. We were told to go back to our homes and stay there. I canvassed the neighborhood between Lake Otis Parkway and Tudor to Muldoon, getting notes from a lot of families in the neighborhood, and made contact with a ham operator in Arizona who was able to get messages through.

It was a week before I went into Anchorage, but it was so depressing I had to go home. We realized we were lucky there weren't too many people living here to be hurt or killed. There were big brown snakelike heaps all around from where the earth opened and then closed puffing up the dirt on top.

There was a lot of talking about the quake and there was lots of fear. It was easy to cry. The sun was not shining; it was a yuckie gray time. Around the twentieth of April the sun finally came out and everyone got busy. Rakes and shovels and wheelbarrows were all bought up; you couldn't find one in town.

Slowly, slowly people's spirits came back, and they can never stop talking about the earthquake and reliving it.

There had been a shortage of clay to make pottery, but after the earthquake this was no longer true. There has been an abundance of clay for pottery ever since. Other than that, I can't say anything good came of the earthquake.

A fissure buckled and split this house at Eighth and M Streets. This was along the fault line that ran from Fourth Avenue, along L Street and into the Turnagain area.

Norma Lepak Hannan

Shoppers' Surprise

Late on that snowy Good Friday afternoon, my former husband and I arrived at the Super S Drug Store on Fifteenth and Gamble to shop for Easter rabbits and baskets. We were both happy to have had the day off from teaching and to have recruited a new twelve-year-old baby sitter for our three children under five. The fourth was due in four months, so he went with Mom! At exactly 5:37 PM as we trundled our cart, the floor began to rumble under our feet. It sounded like a freight train! I thought, "An earthquake!? No, maybe an atomic bomb?!"

I knelt, covered my head with my coat awaiting the FLASH! Eerily calm, I thought maybe this was the way my life would end! It felt like a boat heaving and dropping on a stormy sea. During the next five minutes, I peeked out from under my coat to watch in awe as all the items fell off the shelves and the floor rolled like great giant waves. The fluorescent lights above dropped and dangled from the ceiling and the stores' front windows cracked and broke. With my fear now diminished, I concluded this was no ordinary earthquake!

There was no power and no checkout clerks in sight, so we departed without rabbits and hurriedly drove across Anchorage, which had the appearance of a WWII war-torn city. Goods overflowing from store doors simulated oversized coal deliveries. We drove around cracks in the streets and wondered how extensive the damage was.

Now time seemed to stand still. As we rushed into our Spenard home, we were relieved to find our three wide-eyed children contentedly sitting on the couch. Our new sitter had everything under control — even the spilled refrigerator contents had been cleaned. Our well water was pitch black, but we still had electricity. The radio began broadcasting messages of people trying to locate their families or to let them know they were safe.

We were happy to learn that my parents and brother's family were all okay. With no heat or water and tsunami warnings, my brother's wife and three young children soon arrived to stay with us. For the entire next year, everyone told only earthquake stories, some funny and some tragic. Alaskans helped Alaskans in every way imaginable.

A fissure caused this small house at Third and A Streets to be broken into three pieces.

Cathy Heyworth Harris

First Prayers

I was happily watching my favorite television show, *Fireball XL5*, when my very first earthquake gently rocked our neighbor's living room, and then abruptly stopped. "What was that?" I asked, having somehow missed noticing earthquakes for the first eight years of my Alaska life. My mother replied that it was an earthquake. I settled back down, satisfied.

Two seconds later, all normal life ceased to exist. Our neighbor's home became a boat trying to stay upright in a sea of crashing earth waves. All I can remember is snippets ...

• Being on the second level of a raised home, and watching the cars in the driveway float up out of sight above the roof, then head back down and disappear again as the house went back up.

• Our neighbor holding onto the television on the mantel so it wouldn't fall over. She watched in horror as her china hutch fell over onto her living room table, and shards of glass flew everywhere as we tried to maintain balance and deflect projectiles. I think she always regretted choosing the television over the china hutch.

• Her daughter on her knees on the floor (in shorts, no less, during the March Alaska winter) bloodied from rug burn.

• Holding onto the davenport on rollers with my mother, watching the power lines break apart with blue arcs and the earth roll whole forests down and then whip them back to the other side with a violent snap. Between the roll of the earth and the roll of the sofa, it was hard going.

My whispered questions to my mother began: "What is Judy doing on her knees?" "Praying", my mother whispered. "Praying?" I queried, "What is that?" "She is praying to God". "Who is God"? "She is praying to God to make it stop." This was all way too much for an 8-year old raised with no concept or knowledge of God, church, praying, or a power greater than yourself. My parents had obviously succeeded in their plan to move to Alaska after World War II, to bear and raise children to be free thinkers, away from the influence of other's beliefs.

The praying didn't seem to have much effect at first. My mother finally burst out in hysteria that the nuclear bomb had gone off, and we were all going to die. A defining moment, when you realize your parent is scared and vulnerable.

Finally, finally, finally, the violent shaking began to subside into utter silence. It has been almost five minutes from beginning to end.

And what did this free thinker conclude? That when God decides to come visit you for the first time, you begin to pray for a second visit.

A log home on "O" Street tilted upward by a pressure ridge.

Lorene Harrison

The Hat Box

The painters had finished with the bathroom, and I was putting up the curtain when it started. Of course, I had no idea it would go on and on, so I just continued the job, and then hung on for dear life. Finally, I managed to get down and out of the house. My front yard faced the Park Strip; across it I could see the nearly finished apartment just gone — right into the ground. My neighbor lady stood in the street, trembling, very frightened. The ground was still shaking. I told her "We're okay. Let's just keep hanging on."

About that time, a friend, an Alaska Airlines Pilot, came by and offered to help. I just said "Take me to the Hat Box!" (That was my store.) Before we could go one block we were stopped by a crevasse, but by a roundabout way we reached the store in the old Anchorage Hotel near Fourth and E. One of my clerks, a new hire, was still in the store, running back and forth through the mess from the front door to the side door. She had been waiting on a customer who was trying on a hat when it happened. The woman ran out and the clerk, more concerned with her new job than the quake, chased her to retrieve the hat. The customer handed it over, saying, "Here, take it. I'll be back later."

The military guards wouldn't let us stay, so my clerk, with a stop at my house to rescue my little dog, took me to my daughter's house. There I found a note on the door "We are in Bob's car. Will be at..." We chased them down and found them sitting in the car with the three kids and some crackers, wondering "What next?" I joined them, and after forty-five minutes, we relaxed some and went to a friends house for the night. Next morning I went home and began the clean up.

The new Four Seasons Apartments at Ninth Avenue and M Streets were almost ready for occupancy. They were completely destroyed.

Beth Henderson

A Giant Stomping

On the day before the earth shook so violently, our well that had supplied us with pure, clear, sparkling water for ten years suddenly went dry — no water. Also, our German shepherd, Sage, started acting strange.

On the afternoon of the day of the earthquake I went next door to my neighbors with two buckets to be filled with water. While I was there the kitchen started shaking. I finished filling my buckets and went out to their back door porch. I had to hang on to the railing to remain standing. I could not get off that porch. My neighbor, still in her kitchen, was screaming hysterically. The trees in front of me were snapping back and forth. I finally decided to start crawling home because the shaking seemed endless, but it did stop and I got home. My mom, who was staying with us, said the piano had been dancing in the middle of the room. She was able to hold the china cupboard closed, after one cup had flown out. My daughter, Claudia, five, was watching David and Goliath on TV, and my son, Grant, six, was outdoors building a snow fort. As he came home he said he had been sure there was a giant stomping around out there somewhere.

The downstairs shop room was in total shambles, tools everywhere. I grabbed a compressed gas torch that was spewing explosive sounds outdoors and threw it in the snow. Except for some askew stones in the fireplace, we were essentially unscathed.

My husband, Bob, had flown to Seattle on a business trip two days before and was still there on the day of the quake. In his hotel room, he turned on the TV and heard the news that because of an Alaska earthquake Anchorage was leveled, on fire and that there were 5000 people dead. He went to the airport made reservations on Alaska Airlines and Pacific Northern Airlines. However, they could not fly because there was no clearance to land in Anchorage. Finally, the President of Pacific Northern said, "We will board and fly up there. If we can't land we will have to return." On that flight up he could see that the snow had avalanched off the cornices of the mountains and Valdez was on fire. Bob, ever the optimist, assured himself that he had a good strong home and that his family would be fine. I later had reports from some of the other passengers who praised Bob for reassuring others and helping keep spirits hopeful.

When they arrived in Anchorage they learned that the airport tower had collapsed with one fatality, but finally home, he was relieved to find his house intact and his family safe.

As for our water-well going dry the day before the earthquake, there is some scientific explanation that there could be a connection. And how about the unusual behavior of our beloved German shepherd? Was he aware of the earth trembling before it all happened???

Dan Heynen

It's An Ill Wind That Blows No Good

I was a high school student in 1964, and I had a headache on the day of the great Alaska earthquake, enough of a headache to take two aspirin and a nap in the middle of the afternoon. The bed shaking and the noise of all the paint cans and hardware falling off of the shelves in the garage, which adjoined my bedroom, rudely ended my nap. I stumbled into the dining room where my mother was trying, without much success, to hold her glassware on the shelves of a tall cabinet. She would grab for the crystal on the right side of the cabinet and watch the items from the left crash to the floor. Then she would move to try to catch the objects on the left, and the items on the right would end up on the floor.

In the midst of this, our dog, a collie named Bonnie, came running through all the broken dishes and headed out the door into the back yard. She had been lying at my brother's feet while he watched TV and practiced his trumpet (during the commercials.) Once the earthquake got rocking and rolling, the dog jumped over the music stand, scratched my brother's chest, peed all over him, and then came running our way.

I remember asking my mother two questions: Is it ever going to stop? Do you think this is the end of the world? I'm sure those thoughts were going through the minds of a lot of other people at that time. We were lucky. We lived in a wood frame house in City View, and we had no damage. In fact, for a while we were unaware of the disastrous effects of the quake. My dad had been out grocery shopping and he came home telling us of the pandemonium at the Piggly Wiggly store. Everything falling off of the shelves onto the floor, the electric doors not working. Then another friend stopped by who had been down town on Third

Avenue in his Volkswagen bug. He watched the road in front of him drop away several feet, so he asked the driver of the car behind him to please back up. When he had room, he backed up a bit, and just as he did, the roadway upon which his car had just been sitting dropped away.

Several days later we joined many other volunteers to help people remove their belongings from what was left of their homes. We were at the Turnagain slide area, and had to climb down a cliff with ladders, walk a twisting trail to homes that were tossed and broken on the frozen ground above us. Then we would climb into the damaged houses, and carry belongings back the way we had come to put into trucks for the homeowners.

I attended East High, which was undamaged. West High lost most of their second floor and was closed, so we went on double shift with the East High students on the early morning shift. One of the positive results of the quake for me was a part time job. I had worked the preceding summer at Pictures Inc. on Eighth Avenue. The day after the quake, their shipping clerk quit and was on a plane to any place but Alaska. During April and May I was finished with school by noon and could then do the shipping at Pictures Inc. to save money for college.

I still have a very healthy respect for earthquakes, and when they get to a certain severity, I am automatically on my feet and heading for the door. Some things you just don't forget.

Peggy Hicklin

Immunization Clinic

I was home with my five-year-old son and a friend of his, sitting at the supper table. Being used to earth shakes from time to time it took us over a minute to realize that what we suddenly felt was something more than usual. We all went to the living room and sat on the floor. We didn't think to look outside. The house swayed from north to south. I thought to save a table lamp from falling, but a lurch as I made my move, made me knock it to the floor, ending its use.

Not much else suffered within or without in our immediate surroundings. The east side of town was found to be on the most stable ground. Greg's parents came, his mother in tears. They had come from a service at St. Anthony Church where the shake was very noticeable. Apparently a stop at their house on the way over revealed kitchen cupboards open and contents scattered on the floor.

Our shaken neighbors gathered in the street to trade experiences and wonder if the event would continue. The heat was off, but the weather mild. (I've since bought a wood stove in case.)

The next morning I got a call to set up a typhoid immunization clinic at Airport Heights School. Further, there would be families whose homes were demolished by a tidal wave at Old Harbor coming to the school for shelter. The Red Cross was to take care of their basic needs. I was to see to their immediate medical needs and get all pregnant women to the Native Service Hospital for check ups.

Hoards of people showed up for the immunization clinic we held. The Sunday following, our church was jammed with attendees we had not seen in ages, if ever. I can't remember more enthusiastic singing. Everyone needed something to do to relieve his or her anxiety.

A group of nurses flew down from Fairbanks to help, but by that time we had things pretty well under control. We had to find places to bed them down for the night.

It was a long time before I got down town to see the tremendous havoc on Fourth Avenue and to J C Penney store … and still much later the Turnagain area, which received the brunt of the shake.

A curious couple looks over the Ninth Avenue slide area.

Phyllis Holliday

Providence Hospital

I. The Earthquake

In 1964 I had a family of four — my two sons, my husband, and myself. We came from southern California so we were not too dismayed when the quake started, but when it didn't stop, that was another story. I was coming home from the new hospital on Providence Avenue where I worked. I shopped at Safeway and, as I stood by the car, I said to the young boy who brought the groceries out, "I think I'm going to faint." The ground was moving and rolling under my feet, and it made me lightheaded. And he said, "My feet are trembling and my legs are trembling." And then we heard this loud noise that sounded like a train under our feet and the ground was moving. I had pulled up in the parking lot on ice that had water on it, and so the car was sliding back and forth. I fell and slid under it. He was able to get a hold of my leg and I pushed myself out with the help of another man. I saw the trees touching the ground, I saw the power poles with the lights coming off and hanging down on the cords and swinging and the poles dipping another way. It was a very traumatic look. The air was absolutely still as it started to snow.

I jumped into the car and got out of there. I drove down what is now Minnesota Drive to West High School, where the second story had fallen into the first story. It was a two-story high school that was now a one-story high school. There was a big crevasse between the high school and where I wanted to go — Forest Park Trailer Court where I lived. So I took a chance and drove into the crevasse and bounced out the other side. I got home to find my husband and my youngest boy in the trailer just frantic because they didn't know where I was or where my other son Terry, who was a teen at the time, was. My husband worked on Elmendorf and had just seen movies of the atomic explosion and what to expect. He thought that was what had happened, so he dived under the table with our son Bill, only to have the china cabinet fall over and everything in it broke all around them. The refrigerator came across the floor. Mattresses came off the bed. All the clothes were off the hangers and when we opened the closet door the contents spilled out. We had a big crevasse along side the trailer. We were in an area where that crevasse came up through the golf course, and through Chester Creek, and on into town.

Our teenage son, Terry, was driving near the corner of Ninth Avenue and L and he turned the corner and almost went over the new hill that was there. At the Four Seasons Apartments he went in and helped get people out. When he got home he had a child with him, about a twelve-year old. I said, "You'd better get that child home. That mother is going to be frantic." He said, "Well he lives in Turnagain and it's bad out there," but he took the child home and got caught when a road gave away on him. He helped people get out of houses there.

We went out to the car to listen on the car radio to what had happened. The announcer was giving information on all the devastation and what was going on. We were not able to stay in our trailer. We had some friends who lived on the East side of town who had no damage, so we went over to live with them for about a week.

II. At the Hospital

I went to the hospital to work and stayed there for several days, as I was head nurse on maternity and gynecology. (I took my young son, Bill, with me.) The earthquake upset a lot of pregnancies. Many patients came in in false labor. We were very busy. Elmendorf sent over their caesarians. We had several of those going on for the next two days. We were so swamped they brought their own help, their own anesthesia, their own nurses and so on, and then left the patients there until they were stable to be transported back to their own hospital. Their hospital was very damaged.

We also received all the patients from the hospital downtown on L Street, across from the old Providence Hospital, which was badly damaged. We had patients on the floor on mattresses; we had just a dynamic situation going the whole time. Some of the help came in and some of them had to stay home to take care of their own problems. Staffing the hospital was quite a problem. It was organized chaos.

The Elmendorf military people came over and set up a big power plant so we could have lights and they also drew water out of the creek into the main pipes. There were no lights in the patient rooms, only in the hallways. They were dim with electric cords everywhere. As I remember, the elevators were not working either. The basement of the hospital was crowded with people who had nowhere else to go. They had to be fed and cared for. I think the hospital had the only lights in the area. Families of patients stayed full time in case of repeated quakes and because the patients were afraid to be left alone.

Back corner of St. Mary's Residence parking lot, a nursing home at Eighth and L Streets under the direction of Sisters of Charity of Providence. A corner of the old Providence Hospital shows at far right. Following the earthquake the parking lot had two levels.

My son Terry helped in the emergency room for days and days. He just stayed at the hospital and helped people get out of the car when they came to the emergency room and helped patients out of the emergency room to the floors. He also carried food to patients and family visitors. He was a real trooper, as all of the teenagers were. They were wonderful. They hopped-to, there was no silliness, no giddiness, no running around, no wanting to do this and that. They really took a hold and did whatever was asked of them.

III. Aftermath

We had a major aftershock the following Friday after the big one and that shook a lot of people and a lot of people left after that. By then, they had the bridge on the highway to Palmer repaired so you could get out of Anchorage. For the first few days, there was no way to leave. The bridge was out and the airport runways were closed. The Airport tower had collapsed and a tower operator was killed. Even though I didn't feel trapped like some did, it was a very traumatic experience. I did learn it was not possible to die of fright. If that was possible I would have been gone, I was that scared.

We just continued to do anything we could to help reestablish our friends and ourselves and to get back to normal. My husband was in the Civil Air Patrol and flew groceries and immediate emergency equipment down to Kenai and Soldotna because there were no roads that were open to those people. He was at that for weeks.

Darlene Holt

Disaster Headquarters

The earthquake made me realize how helpless people can be. This Friday started like most had for many years, when I went to work as Assistant Billing Supervisor at City Hall from eight to five PM; however, that's where the similarity ends. Arriving home that evening, I started to prepare dinner, when we felt an earth tremor. Having experienced these occasionally since 1951, my husband came to the kitchen doorway to ask if I had noticed it, when all of a sudden everything lurched, including us!

I soon found myself on the floor with the food, which had fallen off the counter tops. For a split second, I was undecided about what was happening. I managed to crawl into the hallway where all but one door had closed from the motion. With the next jolt, a twin bed slammed into the last open door, which shut with a bang! From an open archway to the front room, we saw things flying through the air or falling over. However, after what seemed an eternity everything was still and quiet.

Cautiously we started to look around to assess the damage. The first thing we realized was there was no electricity. That meant no heat, stove, refrigerator or radio that would work in the house. We would have to eat a cold meal, put on extra clothing for warmth, and find a candle for light. My husband remembered a battery-operated radio in the car and went to get it. All of a sudden I felt myself swaying again! How bad would it be? Where should I go? Where would it be safe? Again I experienced that helpless feeling until the earth was still again.

Using the pocket radio we were able to listen to the news, although at this point they were unable to tell anyone how extensive the damages were. Furthermore, they were issuing tidal wave warnings as an aftermath of the earthquake.

After sweeping up the debris from the kitchen floor, we went to check on some friends in the next block. On the way over there, a fissure across the road was just about too wide to drive over, indicating extensive damage. Indeed these fears were confirmed after seeing the second story of West High School had collapsed! We were relieved to see our friends were fine, although they shared the same anxiety.

Everyone I talked to shared the same feeling of not knowing what to do. Many were trying to locate friends and relatives, and this tense situation was aggravated by the aftershocks, or tremors, which continued for a couple of days.

The next morning I received a request from the City Manager's office for my help at the disaster headquarters. Upon arriving I noticed, amid the confusion and chaos, the strained and tired faces around me, and became aware that some of these people were frantically trying to locate relatives or friends. The main business district had been closed to the public, for both safety and looting reasons, so I was directed to get permission to go through this area to City Hall, check the utility records of the hardest hit area, and account for all people living there.

With a pass to enter the area, I gingerly picked my way along the littered, cracked sidewalks until I came to a huge pile of bricks and mortar. Looking up, I was horrified to see the whole corner on the top of the J C Penney building had collapsed! Immediately I realized the danger of walking so close to the buildings and hastened to the middle of the road. Although the City Hall building appeared to be safe, looking across the street on the next block I could hardly believe my eyes! The whole block of business buildings had sunk, with only the signs and roofs above the ground. After seeing this, I had to muster my courage the enter City Hall, and it was with great relief I greeted another person who was waiting to assist me.

We immediately started checking the books, and as my cold, stiff fingers thumbed through the faceless pages of the utility records, I couldn't help but wonder if all that remained of their life might be their names. They had been as helpless as I to control their destiny, for that period of time the earth's crust was moving so violently.

It was during this time a group of friends gathered at my home and the topic of conversation was naturally on earthquakes, which was uppermost in everyone's thoughts. We all agreed there was nothing any of us could do should it happen again and the only safe place would be on an airplane or helicopter if a person were fortunate enough to be in one. We understood when natural disasters happen such as earthquakes, which are beyond anyone's control, how helpless we can be.

Peter Jenkins

API

On the evening of the Good Friday earthquake I was at work at the Alaska Psychiatric Institute. I was the charge nurse of the recently opened third floor unit holding fifty patients all of whom had been transferred up from Morningside Hospital in Portland, Oregon. I had gone down to the nursing office on the first floor. The evening supervisor was not in the office. All of a sudden the floor started to move. The office was quite small; it contained a desk, a chair, and three four-drawer filing cabinets. All were moving to and fro across the office and I was trying to avoid being struck. As the motion became more and more violent, I was scared, to put it mildly. I was reminded of the V1's that came over London in '44 and '45 where I was then living. These were un-piloted planes carrying a ton of explosives, which flew around and finally dived into the houses and exploded.

As staying in the office seemed dangerous, I made my way outside and edged up clinging to the flagpole. All the cars in the parking lot were bouncing up and down as if going over a very bumpy road. When the motion finally ceased, I went back into the building and climbed the stairs to the third floor. An LPN by the name of Dorothy Jones had gathered all the patients into the elevator lobby and had them sitting on the floor singing hymns. Everybody was calm and in control. Dorothy did a wonderful job in handling this very difficult situation.

The evening supervisor (Dodo Matsko) and I conferred as to what to do. As we explored the damage we found there was little electricity, no phone service, and no water. However the building seemed safe and in no danger of collapse. The radio talked about the massive earthquake but there were contradictory reports of what was going on. We decided that we would have to take our own measures. As the elevators were out of service (and were to remain so for several months) we moved the patients from the third floor down to some empty units on the first floor.

The biggest initial problem was the lack of water; the patients were using the toilets without any means of flushing them. Luckily there was a lot of snow outside so we organized parties to go out and fill every garbage can we could find with snow to melt and pour down the toilets. Of course a garbage can filled with snow is less than a quarter of a can with water, so many trips were needed. We raided the kitchen supplies for juices of various kinds so that the patients could take their medications. Of course we also had to move the mattresses and other bedding down the stairs and get the beds made up again. Many staff members were anxious about their families; my wife was eight months pregnant with twins and there was no way to contact her or any other family member. We finally got everybody settled down and somewhat organized.

While all this was going on an elderly gentleman was wandering about the building asking questions. We pretty much ignored him and found later he was the new medical superintendent, Dr. Bowman, who had just been hired to run the Institute.

Needless to say many of the night shift were either late or did not show at all. I finally left about 3 AM. We lived in a small trailer and lean-to in a trailer court on Muldoon Road. At home I found the trailer empty and my wife next door. She had ridden out the quake sitting in a chair with our year old son on her lap while holding up a bookcase and TV so they would not fall on her. For some reason I opened the refrigerator door and a container of sour milk fell out and spilled everywhere. My wife had soured it on purpose to use in a recipe. She was not happy about the mess but I finally got it cleaned up.

The next evening I was the evening supervisor. Shortly after I took over I was informed that the patients from Harborview in Valdez were being transferred to API as the building in Valdez was too damaged for them to return to. They had spent the night in the cars of the staff and some commandeered school buses, which had moved them up the road to safety. These patients (about fifty or sixty, all of whom suffered from various degrees of developmental disability) and four exhausted staff who had been with them for over twenty-four hours, arrived about 6 PM. These four staff members had done a magnificent job of caring for their patients in extremely difficult circumstances. I later found out that the husband of one of them had been swept away from the dock at Valdez when the tidal wave hit.

Many of these Valdez patients had difficulty communicating so one of the first things I did was send someone over to Providence Hospital to get wristbands (we did not normally use them.) We needed to be certain we administered the correct medications to the right patient. This was very important as a number of them had seizure disorders and had already missed several doses of their meds.

As we were somewhat short of staff and I now had all these extra patients to look after I asked the Hospital administrator to see if the emergency service center downtown could get us any help. About two hours later six National Guardsmen showed up, complete with their rifles and ammunition. I decided to lock their weapons up in the pharmacy, the most restricted room in the place. When I opened the door I found a small disaster. A gallon bottle of gentian violet and another of acriflavine had been knocked off the shelves and broken. We cleaned up as best we could, stashed the weapons and got the drugs that were needed for our new arrivals. From then on it was just a matter of getting everything organized and settled.

One of the concerns was that the water supply might be contaminated and I, with many others gave several thousand typhoid vaccinations.

The following Friday, as my wife and I were driving down Fourth Avenue, suddenly the bars emptied all their patrons into the street. In the car, we hadn't felt the strong aftershock. To us, the scene was comical, like something out of a silent movie.

Pearl Jensen

Ninth Avenue and L

On the way home from work, I stopped at Dr. Hines office near Ninth Avenue and L to pick up some new glasses that had been ready for me. I just sat down to wait in the armchair by the window

Total destruction in parts of Turnagain, and somehow this greenhouse managed to stay atop the jumbled earth to move some distance from its original location.

when it started to shake. I thought, "Well, it's going to stop," because usually they did. But then, it was shaking so hard for so long, I couldn't get up. I looked up above me and there was a light fixture on a long pole with a globe on it, and that thing was swaying back and forth. I thought, "I gotta get out of here, that thing is going to fall on my head." But I could not get out of that chair until it stopped shaking! I watched a double metal filing cabinet tip over on its side. That was something to see, that filing cabinet falling.

Right across the street on Ninth Avenue I saw the Four Seasons collapse. That big apartment building that was going up. It was just the steel frame, the steel beams up there. When I was finally able to get out of the chair I told the woman that was behind the desk, "I'll be back later," and I took off. I ran across the Park Strip because I lived on Eleventh and my kids were home. My youngest girl was in the first or second grade. I ran there as fast as I could and found that the young man who lived on the other side with his parents had gotten the kids out and put them in the car. They thought that if it really got bad, they would take them somewhere.

I went in and all the things had fallen out of the cupboards. The top half of the secretary desk had broken off with all my china cups, all broken. There was food on the floor, syrup, and of course it was getting dark. There was no water. We got a garbage can, got some snow to clean up the mess.

My fourteen-year-old son hadn't been feeling well and had been in bed upstairs. There was a bookcase near the head of the stairs. The books chased him down the steps. He was scared. I was scared too.

We didn't have any electricity or heat or water. The military set up tents on the Park Strip and people could go and get food and water.

Whenever there is a little tremor now, I just get goose bumps all over. My earthquake indicator here is that chandelier. When that starts swinging...

Frank Jones

Craig, Alaska

I was the skipper of a fishing boat out of Craig, Alaska. They reported that a big wave was coming. The water was like a pot of water on the stove just before it boils. All the boats were waiting for the big wave and it didn't come, so we went home. The wave went down to Crescent City, California and damaged and killed people there. They told us it was eighty feet tall and we wouldn't have survived in our boats.

There was a bar in Craig on the waterfront and the bartender said, "Well, boys, this is it. Help yourself to all the booze you can carry." There was no wave, after all, but by then he had no stock left.

Norval Kane

Sixth and Karluk

At the time of the quake I was visiting my friend Herb Gerals and his family in their house near Sixth on Karluk. They had two children, one a baby and the other about two. We were in the kitchen when it happened. I was sitting in a chair with the older child on my lap. Johnny was on the other side of the table holding the baby. When the shake began to get very strong I could only stay in the chair and hold the boy. Johnny went under the table with the baby beneath him. His wife was near the door leading to the entrance. She sat down in the doorway. We could see the trees in the yard being violently shaken. Of course the cupboard opened and everything imaginable came out and crashed. They had a black iron ring with a three-piece chain attached to the ceiling. This held a potted plant. When the shaking stopped that plant and pot were smashed on the table but the ring was still intact. We never could figure out how the pot got out of the ring.

After we found that no one was injured, Johnny's wife looked at the devastation and said. I think this calls for a drink. She located an unbroken bottle and made us a drink.

Afterward, while evaluation was going on a call went out on the radio looking for a geological survey report that dealt with underground conditions in the Anchorage area. (The survey office was pretty much damaged at the time.) I just happened to have a copy so I got to take it downtown to them.

I was fortunate in not being hurt and losing nothing of value. It was an interesting experience but once is enough.

Les and Berneice Kelm

Geysers on Campbell Lake

In 1964 we were living on our homestead, off of Dimond Blvd. and Victor Road, in the basement we had built. We had the upstairs finished only enough to use the bedrooms. We had three daughters and two sons. Our son was out delivering the *Anchorage Times*, our evening paper at the time. The other children were all at home and Les was home from work. We were boiling eggs for Easter when we felt the first small shakes. I remember saying "Oh, just an earthquake."

Then, I grabbed my youngest daughter who was three and stood in the doorway between the kitchen and dining room. Suddenly things were falling off the shelves I used for cabinets and my eggs fell off the stove. It was very frightening for the children. As it intensified, I began to think it was the "end of the world!"

We had a room divider that was a free standing bookcase with lots of books, a large television, and an aquarium on the top shelf. The aquarium was filled with five gallons of water and numerous goldfish. With a loud crash the divider tipped over and there was water and fish everywhere. I was really frightened that someone might get electrocuted, but then Les discovered the power was off. The quake lasted almost five minutes and by then we were all in a state of shock, but very thankful we were all right and still had our home, with only minor damage.

Suddenly we realized our son usually crossed Campbell Lake on the way back from his paper route. We were frantic until he returned, all excited. He and two friends had jumped up on the bed of an old truck and watched the ice on the lake break and crack, the water shooting up like a fountain. Our own "Old Faithful" geyser.

We had a battery radio, which we turned on as soon as everything settled down and were just horrified at what we heard. By 7 PM they announced that we would probably have a tidal wave and I could visualize it coming right up Campbell Lake and to our house. I felt I couldn't handle a flood at this state, so we went up to a friend's home on O'Malley Road where we stayed until 1 AM when the alert was called off

A welcome message for those looking for survivors in the Turnagain area. The family that lived here escaped, but the house was demolished.

We went to our home and bed. Off and on all night there were little aftershocks so our sleep was anything but peaceful. To this day one of our now-grown daughters calls us every time there is a little quake. The phone rings and I know who it is and her comment is always the same. "Did you feel that?" So I know she is still somewhat affected by those awful memories.

Easter was not quite the same that year. We attended church. People came in whatever clothing that would be comfortable and warm and expressed their thankfulness that we survived and we did what we could to help those less fortunate. My personal feelings were that material things aren't very important in the long haul.

Lois Kenny

Aurora Village Area

On my way home from work I had stopped at the grocery store where REI is now. I got in my car and I thought somebody was pushing it to make it jiggle. I saw the ceiling of the bank come down. I started to leave, and the man at the car next to me said, "Maam it's not over yet," and I said (I can remember this as plain as day) "Well, I'm sorry, I have to leave." And I left.

When I got home my teenaged girls were all right but shaken up, and so were the animals. I realized that I had forgotten to get bread, and our battery radio was dead, so I said, "Let's go back and see if we can get anything," Well you couldn't get in the grocery, but at the nearby drug store they were standing at the door and if they had what you needed, they got it for you. I didn't have exactly the right change, but they said, "That's all right" and gave me the radio batteries for whatever change I had.

The girls had gotten dinner ready, and it stayed warm enough that we could eat. My husband had been to the commissary the night before and the groceries were sitting on the floor in sacks, so we didn't lose many stores. We got our first water from the Air Guard and after that we went out to Raspberry Road where we had friends with a well.

My husband was in the National Guard and they had been out for a two-week encampment. It was just ending and they were out on the parade ground for their final inspection. When the quake hit, the band hit the ground just like they'd been knocked down. The officers all took hold of hands and stood in a circle. He and the other local officers were kept there that night, except for a quick trip to check on their homes and families. Then we didn't see him again for a week.

I can remember about a week after the quake we had quite an aftershock. My youngest daughter and I were out of there like we'd been shot, but our oldest daughter was walking up to a friend's house a block away and didn't feel it at all.

Onie King

Unbroken Easter Eggs

The day was a busy one at the King household. In the forenoon we had boiled eggs, lots of them. While my children, LuAnn, Mark, and Craig colored and decorated them, I baked a special cake, shaping and decorating it to look like a rabbit, with long paper ears and coconut in the fluffy white frosting. It was carefully placed in a bed of green Easter grass on the dining room table. It made a nice centerpiece and the children proudly placed their eggs in the grass.

The children came inside as I started the evening meal. I was later very thankful for that. I had something on each of the four burners of my small cook stove. My husband, Don had just arrived home from his shift at the airport and lay down on the sofa while he waited for me to call him to dinner. When I felt the first tremor, I commented to my husband, "I think it is an earthquake." He started to smile and said, "No way." but that smile was replaced very quickly. My children ran to the kitchen to cling to my legs. Don told us to get in a doorway and the children and I managed to get in an archway, but he was out the front door and in the front yard before I had a chance to say a word. The fastest I ever saw him move. The children were crying, clinging to each other and me. They were praying, saying, "God please don't let us die." I was scared myself trying to calm the children and keep my balance. Our poor house sounded like it was going to fall in around us. There so much noise. I could hear things falling, glass breaking, the tremors seemed to last forever. Out the window I could see Don trying to stay on his feet. He yelled for me to stay in the house. I could see the electric wire swinging back and forth in longer and longer arcs. It was then that I started to get frightened for my husband. He was trying to get back into the house but couldn't. The ground itself was sort of rolling in waves. Our brand new Corvair was moving all by itself, about twenty feet back and forth. I could hardly believe what I was seeing.

We had a light fixture that could be pulled down from the ceiling to hang close above the dining room table. As the house shook it came down full length and was swinging like a pendulum. It was swinging so hard that it looked at times like it might hit one of the windows.

We had a small kerosene generator and some kerosene lanterns so we dug them out and got the generator going so that we could have electricity and heat. We would run it for a while, turn it off for a while, and then turn it on again for heat or cooking purposes for ourselves and some of our neighbors who weren't so lucky and had no electric, no money and nowhere to go. They would come during the day, cook, get warm, and visit, then return to their own homes to sleep in cold houses.

We felt like we were lucky to have not had more damage. But the quake had shaken us up so that when the aftershocks hit we'd head for a safe place expecting more. We were afraid to let our small children out to play because the ground had big cracks in it. Some were fifteen or twenty feet deep, and several inches wide. The thought of the children falling in them was always on my mind. In fact at the middle of the intersection of Dimond Boulevard and Old Seward Highway the dirt had been pushed up in a pile about five or six feet high by the quake. It was cracked and tossed up in a small mound.

A good end to this story is the fact that the dinner I was cooking that day, rode the stove without falling off. Even the bunny cake and eggs stayed on the table. So later on after things settled down, we were able to have our meal (albeit cooled off) as a family.

Armond Kirschbaum

Fifth and B

Originally from San Francisco, I grew up with occasional earthquakes there. When my wife and I moved to Anchorage in 1948, it actually felt like home when we experienced mild tremors. That all changed in March of 1964.

I had a store at Fifth and B where we sold art supplies and Sherwin Williams Paints. When the motion started I assured my employees and a lone customer, Mr. Al Bennett, that it was only an earthquake … not to worry …! The motion became more intense and continued to build. I looked out my store windows and saw Mr. Bennett trying to hold his bouncing car down in the parking area of the store. By then, quarts of Kem-Tone paint were bouncing off the top display shelves. I caught one or two, but four or five more hit the floor popping their lids and spilling the contents of paint. I gave up the effort of can catching and moved outside of the store. From my parking lot I could clearly see the Westward Hotel (now the Westward Hilton) rocking side to side like a tree in a blow. A temporary elevator scaffolding on the east face of the hotel was rocking with the building. While I watched, the platform on the top floor broke loose and dropped about three floors to catch in the scaffolding. Directly in my line of vision was the Savings and Loan Bank at the corner of Fifth and C. (The building today houses Baker Interiors.) The C Street side entrance had just emptied a batch of employees when about fourteen feet of red bricks above the door let go, as if someone had thrown an eject switch. All the bricks piled in a mound where people had been leaving seconds before.

I turned to the center of the street and looked west toward C and D Streets. The large slabs of pebbles and concrete that were attached by cleats to the front of the J C Penney store were swinging back and forth like pendulums on grandfather clocks. This action suddenly pulled the entire front of the store off as I watched in disbelief. The store floors were now open to the street.

They say the big quake lasted about three minutes but to me it seemed much longer. My store suffered no damage other than clean up — fortunately!

Following the earthquake ground surface was lowered an average of thirty-five feet in the Turnagain area. Displacements broke the ground into blocks, which were tilted, into various jumbled angles.

Joe Kish

All His Fault

I was in the back bedroom reading. My wife, Gloria, was cooking French fries, while the crab cakes kept warm in the oven. Our six year old daughter, Ida, looked into the oven and excitedly exclaimed, "Mommy, they're jumping around." A few seconds later everything was jumping. At first I thought the washer-drier was unbalanced so I rushed to change the load, but by the time I reached it I knew better. Bouncing off both walls, I made my way to the kitchen to see if my wife turned off the gas. She had and had moved away from the stove, but a pan of fries had been rocked off the stove and fell upside down onto the floor. With all that fat on the floor, I slid past the stove, checking it on the way, and almost slid through the picture window. I stood there and watched the lamp poles dance. The cat went halfway up the wall before he lost his grip, and then ran under the bed. The dog went under the coffee table. Ida was crying because she didn't understand what was happening. Our fourteen year-old boy Joe figured it out and just hung on.

When the ground stopped shaking I got a flashlight and went under the trailer to see if everything was okay. It was. All the blocking was still in place; water and sewer lines were all in place. So were the propane tanks (no natural gas at that time). Back inside Gloria told me we didn't even have any broken dishes. We were so lucky

Neighbors soon started to come out to check on each other and for mutual reassurance. We were the only house in the neighborhood with a stovetop coffee pot, a twelve-cupper. All others had electric pots and no electricity, so they came to our place for comfort and coffee. It's surprising how caffeine can help people at times. The dog let all children pet and hug him, but the cat stayed under the bed.

My next-door neighbors at the time blamed the quake on each other and me. He and his wife had been married for some years without children. About 4:30 that afternoon he came home and yelled, "Hey, Joe, guess what! We're going to have a baby!" I said, "That's an earthshaking bit of news."

Monday morning when I went into work the boss sent me to Fairbanks to work at Eielson AFB for six weeks, which was okay with me. Got me out of the clean up.

Geologist Dr. Ruth Schmidt measures the width of a fissure in the Turnagain residential area while houses in the background tilt after being thrust upward. Boxes on the ground behind Dr. Schmidt are for the purpose of salvage. Many residents lost everything. Some residents reclaimed some of their belongings.

Lester A. and Dora A. Klatt

Big Ditch

Our family was all at home. In the living room our son and daughter kept the radio from falling. In the kitchen some shelves emptied out on the floor, including a can of bacon grease that made the worst mess for cleaning up. As we looked out our front windows we could see our pickup moving back and forth in front of the birch trees, sliding sideways and digging ruts in the snow. New growth birch trees swayed constantly. We thought the movement would never stop. When it did, of course, it took quite a while for our nerves to settle down before we decided to venture outside.

In our walk around the homestead we noticed one very big change: where the upper ground (which is mainly sand) meets the lower area (all peat) there was a ditch formed about a foot wide and a foot deep, with a distance of at least one half mile.

All of these thoughts remained with us these forty years, even though we experienced no real damage. This area continues to be our home, and our family and we find it a good place to live.

Robert and Ruth Knutson

A Small Boat on a Rough Sea

Our two young daughters were watching a children's TV show. The freshly baked pumpkin pie was cooling on the counter. Spaghetti and sauce were boiling in two separate saucepans on the stove when it started. Off went the power. A violent shaking began.

Oh, my, there must have been an atomic bomb, I thought. We three plus my husband Bob immediately ran to the hall leading to the bedrooms where nothing could fall on us. We sat on the floor close to one another. The shaking continued for a very long time. It did stop, eventually. As Bob describes it," we felt as if we were in a very small boat on a very rough sea."

We took inventory. Water had sloshed out of the toilets. Some lamps had fallen over. A couple of vases were broken. The top section of our china cupboard had bounced forward but had not tipped off. The glassware in the top section leaned against the glass front but was not broken. A bowl had fallen into the pumpkin pie. The spaghetti was ready, so we had dinner.

Two sets of neighbors appeared to check on our losses, which were minimal. Our former landlord and family appeared, wanting a place to stay for the night. They lived at the bottom of the hill we lived at the top. As there was the possibility of a tsunami they felt safer up here. We built a fire in the fireplace and hauled out the sleeping bags. During the night our "guests" went home as they felt the danger was past.

We were very lucky. On Saturday afternoon the power came on in our neighborhood. We had lost our water supply, however. The water table our well was on had disappeared. Our neighbors to the east allowed us to hook a hose to their outside faucet. Water flowed through that hose with no problem until May 17 when we had a very cold night and the water froze in the hose four times. Bob had a busy night thawing out that hose! City water had become available during our well years so we hooked on after the thaw.

Within a week our girls had invented a new game shaking the dining room chairs and shouting: "The Great Alaska Earthquake."

Pat Korsmo

Having Fun

I was nineteen, had my first apartment, and had just come home from the Hill Building. I was lying down on the bed, about to fall asleep and it started this horrible rocking. I don't remember the noise, I just remember the shaking. It just kept getting worse and worse. I started thinking, maybe I'm going to have to get up, but by that time we were in the real midst of it, and I couldn't stand up. I was all dressed except I had nylons on and no shoes. I was crawling off the bed, just falling off, crawling on all fours through the bedroom out the bedroom, out the living room to the steps of the porch on the first level of the apartment building. It was a long barracks type building at Thirteenth and I, where Sagaya's is now.

Dad and Mom and the rest of the family lived in one of the other buildings, the reverse of mine. I remember crawling out the door and crawling into the snow because it was real crusty and dirty. I ran over to my mom and dad on what is now Twelfth across the courtyard. Halfway I met a couple with a child and the woman was just hysterical. We hugged each other holding on until it got over with.

I left them and started running to Mom and Dad and they were all sitting in the car, and I said "Why are you in the car?" They were getting ready to go find my brother who was sixteen and on a paper route on Fifteenth in that area near the bluff where there was a spa at that time and the Hillside Manor Apartments that went over the cliff. When they found him, he wanted to know, "Why are you here?" He was walking and didn't even feel it. To this day he still swears he didn't feel it.

I didn't lose a thing, but I had little to lose. Mom lost every piece she had except one bust of Madonna and Child that just flew in the air. My sister yelled to my brother "Catch it Richard, catch it" and he did. Recently when I moved my Father to the Pioneer Home we packed that statue carefully, because it always meant so much to them. It was just about the only thing that they could salvage.

I couldn't go back to work in the Hill Building right away because of the damage, so I was detailed to the Native Service Hospital. The next Friday, when the second earthquake hit, we were inventorying these tall metal shelves. They started shaking and a guy yelled, "I think we better get out of here." What was funny about it was, the hospital was on a cliff, and people in wheelchairs beat us out. They were yelling, "Get out of my way," We all ran toward the cliff, and then decided, "This is the wrong way," We wanted the street side. I don't know what we were thinking. I was following the wheel chair people.

After the quake, my weekend was ruined, all the bars were closed, and for the next month all the guys I knew were out guarding the city. I was really bummed about that, but next I was assigned to a barracks on Elmendorf, near the men's dorm. I was so young, and I was in my glory. All those GI's. I really had fun. That was a real blast.

Hilda Lacey

Needle Circle

We lived on Needle Circle, off Tudor Road. It's now between the Old and New Seward Highways, but then the New Seward Highway had not been built and Tudor Road was a two lane, forgotten, out of town, trail.

There were eighteen houses in a circle. I was home cooking supper with my oldest daughter, age fifteen. Things started shaking. I didn't think about a big earthquake, and then my cupboard door in the kitchen flew open and all the dishes came crashing down. I had the table set for five with everyday dishes. It was not disturbed, but the fine German china in the cabinet was broken. I caught the Grandfather Clock and laid it down on a chair.

I came around to the kitchen. I was serving chicken and french fries for supper. There was ketchup on the ceiling. I bent over the stove and the refrigerator fell on my back and I was trapped. My husband had come home from work and taken a nap in the bedroom when the bed began moving around the room and the noise awakened him. The bed lodged in front of the door so he couldn't get out. He saw the swaying trees out the window. When he was able to get out of the room he rescued me from being caught between the refrigerator and the stove.

My son on his paper route was knocked to the ground. My youngest daughter, second grader, was across the street visiting with a man who was working in his garage. To protect her from his swinging tools he threw her into the snow bank. She wrote a story for school about that event.

We didn't have too much damage. One pipe broke on the heater in the garage. There was a crack in the garage floor and the porch separated five inches from the house.

We all slept on the living room floor that night. The TV tipped over but was not broken. We were very happy to be together. Not a window was broken, either. Amazing. It was a new home in 1960. We had our own well. But we weren't to drink the water until it was tested. Someone came around with honey buckets and water supply. We were pretty upset waiting for the aftershocks. We were lucky there was no big damage and nobody was hurt.

Total destruction in parts of Turnagain, and somehow this greenhouse managed to stay atop the jumbled earth to move some distance from its original location.

Marlene Leslie

Clay Products Drive

My husband, Bill Leslie, and I and our three children had just eaten dinner. Bill and I were still sitting at the table at our home on Clay Products Drive. The three kids had gone off to their room somewhere.

When we heard the sound of the earthquake, which was like a roar, and began feeling the trembling, we yelled at the kids, and said come here we're having an earthquake. We had had experiences with small tremors before and they were always kind of interesting.

This one however kept going and going until it got frightening. My husband and I both went into the living room to see if we could find the kids. At that point the house was shaking so badly we could not stand up. Bill was trying to go down the hall to find our daughter, Gail, who had not come out to the living room to join us. He kept being knocked against the walls of the hall. When he found Gail crawling on her hands and knees out of the bathroom, he did the same. He got down on his hands and knees and crawled out to the living room, where all five of us just laid there on the floor until it was safe to stand up.

The kids were crying, "Make it stop, daddy." And that was kind of feeling I had too. Kind of a helpless feeling of not being able to do anything.

We did not actually observe what was going on outside because we were laying flat on the floor (not the recommended way to go through an earthquake).

When we did feel we could get up and walk without being knocked over and began to look around we found the refrigerator door had been thrown open. Eggs, mayonnaise everything you can think of had been thrown out of the refrigerator onto the floor. We had hot dogs for dinner. A bottle of catsup was still sitting upright on the table, yet everything had spilled out of the refrigerator. The cupboard doors were open. Things had fallen out of those. But that catsup bottle remained upright on the table.

We went into the bedroom. The house had swayed so much that the closet doors had been taken off their tracks and were lying down in the room. The chest of drawers in two of the bedrooms had been knocked over. So the shaking had been real violent, but yet it looked like there wasn't any harm other than a few hairline cracks above the window. There were many broken knickknacks. A vase full of daffodils that were on the coffee table in honor of the coming Easter Sunday was broken all over the floor.

The Turnagain landslide was the most complex in the Anchorage area. Almost 130 acres were completely devastated by displacements.

We had a full basement; so Bill went down to see what it looked like down there. I heard him yell at me and not knowing what in the world was wrong I tried to go down there with him. The whole one corner of the basement had just kind of disintegrated. There were still the reinforcing rods, the steel was still there, but all of the cement blocks had just crumbled around it and fallen away. That was just one corner of the basement. One girder that ties the basement to the house had split along its entire length. It's a 2x12. And that one wall was just leaning in. It did not fall over, thank goodness, but the top of it leaned in about three feet. It would have fallen over if the earthquake hadn't stopped when it did.

We didn't at that time have any tile or anything over the cement floor. The floor was in big chunks and it looked kind of like if you've ever seen a flood and when it dries out, the flood has caused the ground to be so wet and then when it is dry it breaks up into chunks. Some of the corners and edges are sticking up. There was nothing smooth about it. It was just chunks and corners of this one and that one. I wanted to cry. We had no electricity, no water, no telephone, no anything. We were not sure what to do at all. My husband was a plumber. We could smell gas, so he turned off all the appliances that were gas and we went outside. At the time I was a smoker but the gas was so strong that I was afraid to light a cigarette. But yet, at that time I needed a cigarette.

Everybody seemed to be going outside, all the neighbors, so we did too. Not sure what to do. Everybody was scared. Our neighbor and good friend, Austin Joy , who lived on Chilligan, about three blocks down Clay Products Street from us, came walking up. He said he knew his kids were at Alyeska, his wife was not home, he did not know where she was, he couldn't get his car out of the driveway because half of his driveway was gone. He said all the houses on the west side of Chilligan Street were gone. They disappeared. They fell over the cliff along with half of his road and half of his driveway, so he was walking up to see what happened to us. We told him to come on in. We didn't know what we were going to do either, but we knew we just couldn't stay in our house.

We all kind of gathered there, and then a car came driving by on the street with a megaphone saying, "Evacuate, leave the area, there is a tidal wave coming, everybody evacuate." It went down the street and then came back up, "Everyone evacuate."

Austin didn't want to go with us because he didn't know where his wife was and he was worried about her. He asked us for a battery-operated radio so he could listen for news of his family. They were making announcements to separated families as to where their loved ones were, whether they were okay or not, which roads were passable, and which ones you could not get through. We hadn't even listened before that.

We decided we could get the car out of the garage, even though our garage floor was cracked and broken, but we could still get our car out and go. We didn't know where we were going to go, but since they said to leave we didn't want to be hit with a tidal wave as well. We are about two or three blocks off the inlet. We piled in the car with our family, plus Austin Joy who agreed to come with us because we had the radio. As we backed out we could see that all the trees were leaning to the side and at all different angles. We could also see it looked like there was a vacant area down there, but we didn't realize the destruction that had happened. Frank Feeman Junior who lived down the street in front of us, closer to the inlet, came to us as we were leaving and said, "Mr. Leslie, we have some people who are down over the bluff and can't get out. Do you have a rope that we could have?"

Bill gave him the rope, not realizing how badly the land had broken off. He just gave him the rope, said, "Go ahead, you can use this," and we left. I'm not even sure where we went. It was some-place on Arctic Boulevard where it was higher ground. But some of the roads you couldn't get through very well. But we did, we went out towards the woods and sat in the car all night. During the night when we were sitting all cramped in our little Ford Falcon, we did hear the announcement that Betty Joy was at Thelma's and she was okay. That made Austin feel better. One radio station spent their airtime trying to connect families.

There were frequent tremors, but that's how we spent the first night. When we did come home it was maybe five or six in the morning, cramped, tired, we decided we would go ahead and try to get some blankets and things. We had some friends that lived in mid town, and we would go ahead and see what happened to them, and maybe stay over there because we thought it seemed like midtown did better than the Turnagain area, where there appeared to be a lot of destruction.

We took Austin home, because he saw Betty's car sitting as close as she could drive to her house and knew she had come home. So my family went over to our friend's house and stayed there for one night. We came back home because our friend's two-bedroom house was crowded with all of us, plus their three children.

When we got back home, we did have electricity. Bill converted our furnace back to oil so we could get some heat. Before we got heat, we took an army blanket and tried to block off all the doors and tried to heat just the living room area with the fireplace. Our fireplace isn't a heat--a–lator but that was how we kept warm. We kept our coats, everything right by the front door. We slept in sleeping bags on the floor in the living room. Tremors were continuing to occur. At this time we knew of all of the destruction and we panicked every time there was a little tremor. Everybody was ready to run out, outside, out where we didn't know. We were prepared to go at all times, day and night. We still didn't have any water. The National Guard was bringing the water. We would have to go up to the corner to get a barrel of water, and that was what we used. All the water lines were broken.

There were guards all around. You had to show your identity in order to get into this area. There was a lot of looting. All the houses were badly damaged and people were stealing things right and left. You did have to prove where you lived and where you were going. There were guards up there that checked ID.

Bill came home, and said, "Those poor guards up there, couldn't you bake them a cake or something to take up to them." Since those were such trying times, and sometimes I can be a little bitchy, I just really pitched a fit, "I have no water to cook with, and I have all this mess here trying to clean up eggs and all this off the floor with no water." I really didn't want to bake a cake. But since he asked me and I was a good wife, I baked a cake so he could take up to the guards. But it was pretty irritating that he was out trying to help all the other people convert so they could get heat, and here I was feeling sorry for me. All the inconvenience and he wants me to bake a cake. In his own way he was getting me to focus on doing something positive rather feel like there was nothing I could do. I can see that now, but it was just a real hard time then. He was trying to help me.

Eventually somebody came by and began to lay four-inch irrigation pipe on top of the ground. Pipe all along the street to get water to houses. Each house was given a hose that hooked onto this pipe and then put onto our outside faucet. That way we could get water into our house. That's the way we got water through the summer.

Electricity, sewer, water, and all the gas lines were all in preparation to be redone, and slowly but surely we got all of those back. The telephone seemed to be the first appliance we had that actually worked again after the earthquake. It was probably just a few days when the telephone rang, and that was kind of a good sign. Hey, things are going to work out to normal.

We lived upstairs. We just didn't go downstairs. We had to get it repaired before winter. They decided it was safe for us to live here.

It wasn't going to fall over any more, and the house was not going to collapse. So we could live here, but it was hard to get contractors. Of course we weren't the only home that had a lot of damage. We were able to get the house lifted. They put in a complete total wall. They reinforced the corners on the front wall so they were able to save that one. Everything else was repaired. Of course nobody had earthquake insurance back in those days. The Small Business Administration came in and gave us loans to repair homes at 3% interest. Which is what we did. We borrowed the money to repair the damage and things eventually got back to normal.

I never want to experience another earthquake of that magnitude. However, it was a humbling experience to go through that one. People would ask why we stayed here. There were all kinds of reporters from papers and magazines that came around for interviews and they said, "Why don't you leave instead of repairing it, why don't you just go?"

But it's our home. In fact, the friends that we stayed with in midtown that didn't have any damage left because they didn't want to experience another earthquake. They moved out that summer. But we didn't even consider that, we love Alaska, we love our home, and I will probably live here the rest of my remaining life.

Barbara L. Lilly-Brown

Camping Inside

It was afternoon, I was eight years old, and my brothers and I were watching our favorite TV shows *Fireball XL5* and David and Goliath, when things began to shake around the trailer house living room. The TV went black but the shows were not really over. The power had gone out. I got up from the living room floor to get my mother, who was outside shoveling snow. It was hard to walk as the floor was rolling like the ocean. After making it to the door, I opened it and tried to see my mom, but it was not easy as the ground outside was rolling across the yard. I saw our neighbor trying to run across the waves from next door and wanted to laugh because he looked like a drunken sailor. I looked toward the driveway and our car was bouncing back and forth over the rolling waves. This was all happening pretty fast but at the time it seemed to be in slow motion.

I remember that when the shaking and rolling finally stopped, Mom and the neighbor made it to the trailer at about the same time. Looking around inside of the trailer, I saw my youngest brother happily splashing and playing in water that had sloshed from the bathroom.

Our dinner, a big pot of spaghetti sauce, was very close to sliding from the stove to the floor. One more shake and it would have.

We all wanted to know when our TV show and the lights were coming back on. Mom said we had to wait until Dad got home. So we waited for Dad to come from work with news of what had happened. He finally got home and told us there had been an earthquake and things were a mess everywhere. The next day we went driving around and could not believe our eyes at some of the things we saw.

My brothers and I thought the next week or so without power and running water was like camping, only it was camping inside.

Cara L. Lilly

Mile 7-Seward Highway

The Bob Lilly family of five lived at mile 7-Seward Highway, in a trailer. Bob worked swing shift for Northern Consolidated Airlines and was on the job. I was shoveling snow, the children watching TV and keeping an eye on their eleven month old brother playing on the floor.

I didn't know what was happening. I couldn't get the shovel of snow up and over, so I put the shovel in the snow bank and rolled with the quake and tried to stay upright. The ground rolled like the sea. Trees, power poles and lines were swaying back and forth and bending to the ground. The family car and trailer were moving like toys. My thoughts turned to the children and their well-being. Soon the trailer door opened. Our daughter, Barbara swinging back and forth called, "Mama, mama." Our neighbor, Jerry Widener, was returning from J C Penney. He stopped quickly, jumped out of his car and ran over, taking her inside and staying with the children until I made my way to join them.

While I was rolling with the shovel and wanting to get to the children I looked to the Klatt Cemetery to make sure the dead weren't rising.

At last the quake stopped and I made it inside. All was okay. The eleven month old was having a ball playing in water from the bathroom and kitchen sink. He looked like a duck paddling in a pond. The others wanted the TV back on so they could finish watching David and Goliath. The power was off and stayed off for several days.

Bob made his way home to see about the family. There were crevasses along the route, some a foot wide. We had heat to stay comfortable, got the Coleman lanterns going for light. Another neighbor, Don Shower , had a Laundromat close by. He invited everyone to get water there. People helped each other with what ever they could.

Downtown Anchorage, Spenard , Turnagain as well as many places over the state were hit hard, losing everything, even lives. I am thankful for our blessings yet mindful of the ones that lost their all.

Robert E. Lilly

Anchorage International Airport

I had gone in early on the swing shift at Northern Consolidated Airlines at the Anchorage International Airport to build up an engine for a quick-change unit. We had just hoisted the engine from the cart and moved it aside when I heard a huge rumble coming. I made the remark that I was "Getting out of there!" One fellow, grinning like a mule, was still standing there was I went out the vehicle door when the shock came.

I thought, "Is it ever going to stop?"

Looking out over the airfield the ground seemed to roll like the swells of a bay. Autos were hopping around and things were falling in the hangar.

The engine we were working on was swinging on the chain hoist. Fortunately, we had removed it from the shipping cart and away from the crate or it would have been destroyed.

When it settled down, there was a haze in the air, cutting zone distance vision considerable.

A Reeve C46 buzzed low the length of the runway. The pilots were surveying the safety of the runway. One of their mechanics contacted them on the ground control frequency from a radio on one of their tow vehicles and they landed safely.

A cargo handler drove down from the terminal and told that the control tower had collapsed, killing a controller. The tower came down on Northwest Airlines' kitchen.

We went back into the hangar to access the damage. Things had fallen over and down without much damage.

The rest of the swing shift started trickling in so the four of us headed for our homes to check on them and our families.

On the way home on the Seward Highway south I came across a

small traffic jam. I thought that they could converse later, but that wasn't it at all. It was a crevasse about a foot wide and as I crossed, I could see no bottom. A large spruce tree was split in half. One side on each side of the breach!

At home, I found everything was in good shape. We were then living in a 36'x8' trailer home. The power was off, but we had enough heat to be comfortable and with my Coleman lantern we had light!

Mattress, cushions, chest, lamp and miscellaneous items salvaged from a home in Turnagain.

Our neighbor owned a Laundromat close by that had a huge water tank inside. Fortunately, it was full when the power went off. He invited the neighbors to obtain their water there.

With water, heat, light, and propane cooking stove, other things were a minor inconvenience.

The good Lord was watching over us.

Vivian MacInnes

Sixth and E

We lived at mile 2.1 O'Malley Road in a new house we had built and moved into only three months earlier. Don, my husband, and I drove together to our respective jobs in downtown Anchorage, leaving our two children, Debbie age six and Scott age four, with our baby sitter Alma Merrigan, affectionately known as Muggins.

For the most part, our working day was over, though Don, an engineer for Paul B. Crews, was at a client's office at the Loussac-Sogn Building on D St. between Fourth and Fifth Avenue, and I was at my office at Sixth and E Street. I felt the tremor and recognized it was an earthquake, but didn't realize just how bad things were going to be until the building started really shaking and file drawers were being thrown out of their cabinets and across the room. One of the insurance adjusters and I managed to get down the stairs and out into the street. The ground was heaving and rolling so badly we could not stand up. So much was happening around us that I did not even think about being frightened. The street was rolling as if it was a ribbon, the plate glass windows of the grocery store on the corner were being bulged and stressed until they shattered. The cars in the parking lot next to the building were dancing all over the lot and into one another. I could see the back corner of the Penney's building and it appeared to shift at the second floor. I remember the noise of someone screaming, of breaking glass and a rumble I was never sure about. I still had no idea how terrible it was.

Don arrived soon after the shaking subsided. He had witnessed the concrete panels on the front of the Penney's building fall and land on cars below. We heard later that two people had died there. By this time we were both pretty worried about our children and we started home. The going was very slow. We could see large cracks in the earth, some crossing the road making detours necessary. We saw where trees were split down the center and separated by these cracks. We had people stopping along the way telling us of the devastation in the Turnagain area and other parts of downtown. With each passing minute and the bits of news picked up, we became more and more frightened for the welfare of our children and Muggins.

We arrived home to find everyone shaken, but unhurt. We had damage to our house but considered it minor in the face of what

Geologist Dr. Ruth Schmidt looks at the results of the vibration, sliding and settling of loose glacial-alluvial deposits together with the shaking of water logged clays and silts that was responsible for portions of this area sliding into the sea.

could have been. Jack and Nova Simpson and their two sons, Mark and Erik, spent a few weeks with us, as their home was too badly damaged to be occupied. We had no electricity for most of the first week after the quake, but managed fine with a tank of well water, and two working fireplaces for heat and cooking. We celebrated Easter with our next-door neighbors, Gene and Dolores Roguszka, who cooked and served a wonderful dinner for all of us. It was amazing how people banded together and showed a real concern for each other during the trying times of no utilities, no communication and in some cases no homes. I think we were all shaken down to earth, literally and attitude wise.

Along with many other ordinary citizens, Don spent the week after the quake going through the damaged areas helping evaluate the downtown buildings' conditions as well as to make sure no one was trapped in the damage. Most of the buildings had not been built with earthquakes in mind. His office lost the entire concrete block wall of the second floor. As it crumbled and fell, it struck their secretary as she was attempting to leave the building. She was seriously injured. Not only were buildings shaken apart, but also the ground literally dropped from under many of them.

I worked for Northern Insurance Adjusters, and even though there was almost no insurance coverage for the damage, we were interested in checking out just how bad it was. The damage was wide spread in most of the bluff areas, and the areas closer to the tidelands of Turnagain Arm. Many of the homes were completely destroyed. It looked as though some giant plow had gone through turning the earth and plowing under streets, houses, automobiles and anything else in its wake. It was truly unbelievable.

The days after the quake we kept hearing of the damage in the other areas of Alaska. It was so overwhelming that it was very hard to take in. With each new piece of information, we again felt so thankful to have our family and friends intact that we wanted to reach out to everyone less fortunate.

For weeks after the quake everyone was very jumpy. I felt as if the ground was unstable and soft under my feet. Every time there was the slightest aftershock or tremor we were all ready to fly out of any building we occupied. To this day our daughter, who is now in her forties, still turns pale and flees at the slightest tremor. Our son, on the other hand, told his sister at the time that it was just an old "earth quick," and he apparently still feels the same, for his memory is that of a four year old.

Future Malvo

"My Kids, My Kids"

I was walking near the parking area at J C Penney—getting ready to do my last minute Easter shopping. I was still outside when things began to move. There was no help available. Everybody was running for his or her life. My kids were at home with a four-teen-year-old babysitter, so when I saw the buildings were falling, I became hysterical. I started running and screaming: "My kids, my kids, my kids." I ran—jumping over the crevasses in the earth. It was about 45 minutes walking distance to home. The cabs were generously packing as many people as they could in their cabs. About three-quarters of the way home I got a ride in a packed cab. I was still hysterical repeating, "My kids, my kids." The cab driver tried to calm me, telling me my kids were okay. The kids were on the second floor, and they had tried to go downstairs, but the stair-way swayed, so they got under a table upstairs. That's where they were when I got there. We spent the night next door with our neighbor, who had heat. We burned candles.

Another thing I experienced was how people came together. The merchants were very generous about giving us food. The military distributed water in tanks for us to drink, telling us not to drink the city or well water. The large grocery stores just opened their inventory up. Most of it was on the floor. They gave us the opportunity to come in and get food by the basketful.

The kids and I left because of the earthquake. In May we went home to St. Louis, Missouri. After a couple of months I decided Alaska was the best place for me, so by August we were back. While we were there, the kids shared their earthquake horror stories with their cousins. They would sit for hours at a time, holding their cousins spellbound. Some of it wasn't quite true and sometimes I tried to correct them.

They had never experienced thunder and lightening. After three or four weeks there was a terrible storm. The kids held onto me, crying "earthquake, earthquake." I tried to console them and said it was not an earthquake, it was a storm. No matter what I said, it was an earthquake.

One of the homes completely destroyed by pressure ridges, upright blocks and tilted collapsed blocks. Three people lost their lives in the Turnagain area.

Lou Marsch

Oh, the Aftershocks

I was preparing dinner. My husband Burt had arrived home from work, hungry and was changing clothes as the quake began. He was standing in his shorts and had to pause to maintain his balance, but he lost it as the shaking intensified. Our frame house swayed, house and floor lamps and other furnishings crashed to the floor, aquarium water sloshed out, the doors of the cupboard over the refrigerator flew open and jams and jellies cascaded out and shattered. Our two-year-old son's face turned white. Burt (still in shorts) took his hand and I picked up our three-month-old baby from the couch. We unsteadily wove our way to the outside door. The trip was dangerous. Canned goods were pouring off the shelves. When we got to the outside door, we saw the telephone poles and wires swaying, and blocks from our neighbor's chimney falling. We then decided it was safer to stay inside near the doorway and wait for further developments.

Finally the shaking stopped and an eerie dead silence hung over the city as snow was softly falling. Of course, we had no electricity, no lights, no heat, and no water to clean up the mess in the kitchen. Fortunately, we had a fireplace. With blankets we sealed off the kitchen, bathroom and bedrooms to conserve the heat from the fireplace, which we burned continuously until our utilities were restored, four or five days later. We cooked on the fireplace, including heating baby food and bottles. We obtained water from a central distribution points in the city.

The first night after the quake was one of the most nerve-wracking experiences I've ever had. I slept on the living room couch to keep the fire going and would nod off, only to be awakened with a terrifying start by aftershocks, which continued all night long. I think the aftershocks were worse than the major quake.

Tom Marshall

Third Avenue

I was alone in the office of the Petroleum Branch of the Alaska State Division of Mines and Minerals Building on Third Avenue waiting for a phone call from the operator of an offshore drilling rig in Cook Inlet. I was reading a book by a Dutch geologist, Peter Umgrove, who was disagreeing with the then new concept of earth crustal movement called "continental drift." Umgrove believed that crustal changes occurred in a catastrophic manner, which he called "pulses." One of those pulses was about to happen.

I was only mildly startled at the initial swaying of the building, but when the top section of a steel filing cabinet fell on the desk and put a permanent crease in the book I was reading, exiting the building became the top priority. I was closest to the rear basement entrance of the building, but had convinced myself that this was no earthquake; it was a Cold War atomic bomb attack. Consequently, I ran for the front door facing the Fourth Avenue business district. In retrospect, it was foolish to think that the choice of escape routes would make any difference to an atomic bomb, but it almost certainly saved my life because the first floor collapsed over the basement entrance.

Running at full tilt down the hallway to the front entrance was not possible because of the violent shaking. At the place where the new cement block annex joined the old cast concrete building, a four-foot gap had already developed and the old buildings were sliding down the hill toward Ship Creek. I jumped that gap with only inches to spare and thought perhaps the worst was over. It wasn't. The roof of the old building mysteriously started to rise, exposing the gray sky, and then fell on the walls, crunching the clothes closet door and the front door so that they couldn't be opened. I decided to break a window and get out while the getting was good. I grabbed a heavy mailing tube and headed for one of the large plate glass windows facing the front parking lot. Suddenly, my Scottish blood told me not to break a $500 front office window when there was a $20 window in the library that would serve just as well. I broke that window and had one leg outside when I heard a loud screeching and rumbling sound as the Warren Painting Company Building tore off the vertical steel siding of our building as it moved by at a brisk rate. I withdrew my leg and then broke the $500 plate glass window. I high-jumped a mineral display case and surprised a group of would-be rescuers who were unsuccessfully trying to pry open the jammed front door. They figured someone was in the building, because my car was parked in front.

I couldn't drive home because the car keys were in my coat in the clothes closet and the door was jammed shut, so I started running. On Gamble Street a lady offered me a ride to Fifteenth Avenue. There a minister picked me up and drove me to my front door in Airport Heights. Two thoughts dominated my mind. How did my family and my house survive and did the oil and gas-drilling rigs withstand the shake?

A joyful reunion occurred at my front door. My wife, Donna, and five- year-old son had weathered the quake mainly in the front doorway safe from a falling television set and gun cabinet. They were uninjured and I had only a small cut on my little finger from climbing through the broken window frame.

My neighbor, Everett Skinner came to our house within minutes of the quake and offered to check out our basement hot water heater and turn off the master water valve. Sure enough, our 50-gallon heater had "walked" about ten feet to the middle of the basement floor, trailing the 220-volt electric lines and the broken water pipes while still remaining upright. Otherwise, our house was largely undamaged.

The next hour was eerily quiet. We enjoyed a candlelight beef pot roast dinner. The quiet was ended by a knock on the front door. It was Karl and Phoebe Vonder Ahe. They had been at a birthday party on the top floor of the fourteen-story L Street Apartments where they lived. The quake slid Phoebe from one side of the large party room to the other, giving her some bruises and a black eye. Karl managed to hold onto a radiator pipe while trying to grab Phoebe as she slid by. Karl asked us if they could occupy the spare bedroom in our basement. We put an ice bag on Phoebe's eye and everybody had settled down for a welcomed night's sleep by ten PM.

At midnight there was a pounding at the front door. It was Irwin Mitchell, the state's mineral assayer. Mitch was white as a sheet and was obviously startled to see me. "I came to your house to tell your wife she was a widow," he blurted, "and instead you answered the door. Are you a ghost?" Mitch had made his way to the Mines and Minerals Building and found my car in front and the rear entryway nearest my office totally collapsed. He had called my name and looked around for me until his flashlight failed. I fixed Mitch a cup of coffee on the camp stove to calm him down and thanked him for his concern. He left for his home near Bootlegger's Cove but was back within the hour with his wife, Marion, and three small children. Marion was crying and would not stay in their house because she smelled natural gas and a neighbor's house had been set afire when they lit a candle. They were pleased to spend the night on camp cots and backpack mattresses in our living room, the last unoccupied room in the house. The next morning the ten of us consumed two dozen scrambled eggs.

The ruins of our office building was declared a hazard, bulldozed flat and hauled away. In a cold Olympian view of the world, earthquakes have a function. Without them our planet could be a dismal swamp or perhaps a shallow sea, but would certainly lack the majesty of our mountains.

Forty years have passed. My only souvenir is that geology book with its broken back and deep crease where the filing cabinet fell on it and pleasant memories of the kindness of strangers and neighbors.

Patricia McClure

Valdez

I began preparing dinner for my nine-year-old son, Mark, and my one-year-old daughter, Melanie. Our kitchen stove, which also heated our water, was set on low. When I turned it up, I heard a strange rumbling sound that led me to think it had broken down. Melanie started screaming. The house began to shake and I realized it was an earthquake. I yelled to Mark, who was in his bedroom upstairs, picked up Melanie, and hurried to our back door. Mark joined us in the porch a minute later with our little dog.

From our position at our back door, we saw a fissure running to the front of the house. As the ground continued to shake, the fissure would squirt brown water about six feet high. This fissure connected with another, which ran directly under the porch where we were standing, creating a strong rocking motion. I then saw an enormous wave of water raise and fall over the tops of the buildings, which blocked my view of the Valdez dock area four blocks away. This was when the dock collapsed and thirty-two lives were lost.

Then the noise stopped and it became eerily quiet. As we gathered in front of our house with the St. Amands, my sister's family, and the Lawrence family across the street, Halle Ruhl came running down the street, calling for her sons, Richard and John, telling us that a tidal wave was expected. The three families, totaling fifteen people and three dogs, got into my sister's pickup camper and left Valdez. We joined the majority of the town's residents on higher ground at about mile six on the Richardson Highway. Around ten PM many of us cautiously returned to town and our homes. The front door of the house, which had separated into three sections, would not open. (Since then, I always open a door, during even a minor quake).

Less than a half hour later, however, we lost our electricity. Suddenly, the sky lit up with flames from a fire at one of the Union Oil Company's large storage tanks. Then another storage tank caught fire! About that time, John Kelsey, the Mayor of Valdez, drove down our street with a loudspeaker telling everyone to leave town. There was concern that more storage tanks would ignite, possibly explode or spread through town. Once again, we piled into the pickup camper and drove out of town.

We returned next morning about seven, but aftershocks forced us to go back, this time to Mile 27 (a Highway Department camp). A large Army helicopter was there, sent to transport the patients evacuated from the Valdez Harbor View Hospital to Anchorage. They also brought some emergency items. We stayed a couple of hours, and then once more went back to Valdez.

At the time of the earthquake, my husband, Earl, was unloading his tanker truck at the Standard Oil Bulk Plant at Tok Junction. When told of the intense destruction of Valdez, Earl borrowed a pickup and along with Jack Steel, another truck driver, headed home. The Richardson Highway was damaged in many places but they were able to drive straight through. What a relief it was for them on Saturday to find their families unharmed, but shaken, bewildered and in awe of the experience.

On Saturday, Valdez was still without electricity. In addition, continuing tremors left the stability of our house and the St. Amand's house in question. Therefore, we decided to drive 100 miles north to Copper Center, where we were able to locate a vacant cabin to rent for the two families to share.

On Sunday morning, Earl and Jack drove back to Tok for their trucks. They and Andy Growden put in long hours transferring fuel from Valdez to Copper Center, Big Delta, Tok Junction and Fairbanks, so that repairs could be made to the emptied tanks.

Nine months after the earthquake, when we were living in Copper Center, we experienced another event of 'Mother Nature'. During an extremely cold spell (-60°), the Klutina River flooded the area, which forced us to temporarily relocate to Glennallen. However, this story is for another time.

Dolores McCullough

Homestead-Victor Road

We lived on a homestead located where Victor Road now exists, in a frame house on a basement. It was out in the middle of a field with birch trees around the house.

When the earthquake hit, I got our two children and our neighbor girl and the dog out of the house. We stood in a circle in the yard and could barely stand up, even though we were holding hands.

My neighbor girl asked in a quavering voice, "Mrs. McCullough, do you think we are going to die?" I reassured her. "I don't think so." (But inside I thought we probably would!)

The trees bent way over and would swish back upright and bend again with each wave.

It seemed like it went on and on and was never going to end.

We only lost a few things and had some cracks in the basement walls. We felt very fortunate and that the Lord's hand was upon us.

George McCullough

Palmer Highway

I was traveling south on the Palmer Highway just past the truck weigh station when the truck began to swerve all over the road. I thought the tie rod must have come off so I didn't apply the brakes, but slowed down. Finally I realized something was very wrong because the whole earth was moving.

I stayed in the truck and held the brakes on. I guess I thought this would stop it. I watched the power lines sag almost to the ground, and then the wires get so tight that surely they would break. All the trees were whipping back and forth and the noise was very loud. I watched a car ahead of me. The driver was outside the car and couldn't stand up. He staggered around and finally got back inside. When it finally stopped I started for my home south of Campbell Lake, arriving there with no problem. Much of the roadway was buckled and broken but all was passable. The whole area had a very foul odor as all the edges of the swamps were cracked, and brown water had boiled to the surface around them.

Arriving home I found everything intact with our house, just things scattered everywhere. No one was injured. I thank the Lord for that.

Lewis J. McDonald

Government Hill Quonset

I was living on Government Hill in a Quonset hut. I was typing a letter at my kitchen table when suddenly I felt the house shake. I thought, "O well, that's nothing."

Then I saw my door bending over. I went outside and my hut was jumping up and down, so was my car. When my hut stopped jumping up and down I went back inside.

I had been heating some beans and wieners on the stove; my cupboards had opened and dumped a bag of flour in my pan. The dishes were in the sink to be washed. Otherwise they would be broken.

The next day I went to Palmer to check on my folks. They were fine. There was an aftershock a week later. I was working the in FAA commissary. We all ran out of the building in no time flat.

Bill Miller

Hope

I just came from the sawmill, logging, about 5 PM. Went down to Mrs. Ray's cabin in the center of Hope. I built a fire, put the kettle on for coffee and lay down, waiting to hear the kettle whistle. I started to doze and it seemed like someone was shaking me awake. Then I realized the cabin was moving and creaking and things really started "rockin' and rollin'" so I started through the kitchen to get out and all the cupboard doors were popping open with contents crashing down onto the floor. I got to the porch and hung onto one of the posts. The ground was rolling from east to west and the trees were whipping back and forth, some tops touching the ground. I didn't know what to do next and finally things started to slow down, so I went back in the house and checked the stovepipes. They were knocked askew so I straightened them and went back out again.

I could hear someone yelling so ran into the street and saw black smoke coming out of the upstairs living quarters of the school. When I got there I found that the stovepipe had come apart, spewing smoke and soot. I used gloves to get the pipe back together.

Then I went over to Specking's whose fireplace chimney had collapsed and helped them straighten things up. We worried about a possible tsunami as warning came over Speckings's Civil Defense radio for all coastal communities.

I caught a ride to Mile 18 (Snow River—bridge out) then hiked across the RR track and caught a ride on into Seward. All along the Lagoon there were boats across tracks and RR cars and engine tipped over. I checked on friends and helped people there. Came back to Hope several days later.

A couple of us decided to drive as far as we could (Ingram Creek) then hiked on to Portage Glacier Road. All the bridges were out, RR tracks were torn, up in the air and bent like a snake. There was gray mud and ice everywhere. Ice cakes inundated the gas station and restaurant and the RR station looked like someone tried to break it in two. Twenty Mile RR Bridge was still intact. We climbed up and across some of the bridges to get back to the car. They were about eight feet above the ground. We saw rabbits that had become caught in the willows and alder bushes. It was a desolate looking place.

Some twenty highway bridges were destroyed between Anchorage and Seward alone. This one pictured was across the end of Kenai Lake.

Jean M. Miller

ANS Hospital

Shortly after returning from work at the Alaska Native Medical Center, then on East Third Avenue, I was shocked with a jolt, which caused my dinner sandwich to stick in my throat.

As it subsided somewhat, I ran to the living room. Then things began falling off the walls. I caught the TV and put it on the floor. Things were flying out of the refrigerator, smashing on the floor. My poor dishes, glasses, and Alaska Johnston knickknack collection all fell.

I tried to get out of the small basement apartment I shared with my husband. He was in Kotzebue tagging polar bears for Alaska Department of Fish and Game. The brick fireplace in the recreation room outside my apartment was moving horrendously. It was my only escape outside but I didn't want to be killed by a falling fireplace brick. I went back inside, unable to stand up. While I was on my knees it was time for prayers.

After forever, the house stopped moving. I ran up the debris-cluttered stairwell that led to the house upstairs. After searching all the rooms, I panicked thinking I might be running over debris-cluttered bodies, but the family had run barefoot outside in the snow. They spotted me in one of their picture windows. We were all shaking and stricken. The boys told me, "You should have seen the house and your car jumping all around."

We looked toward the airport and screamed. "The tower is gone!"

We returned to the house cautiously to inspect the damage. Going back into the messy apartment was sickening. Before I could begin to clean up, the landlady told me she heard a message on her two-way radio that all doctors, nurses and hospital personnel were to return to duty. By then it was dark. My car started and the headlights provided light. Otherwise everything was dark and very eerie. Some of the roads had electric lines down plus the streets had cracks. When I got close to downtown, National Guard and police stopped me. I explained I was a nurse trying to get to the hospital where help was desperately needed. They told me which roads might be open and tried to reroute me around power lines and other obstacles.

At the hospital it was quite chaotic. I reported to the children's ward, my duty station. We were told to dress all the children in street clothes in case of evacuation. Maintenance men brought mattresses from the warehouse. We laid them in rows on the hallway floors while also taking care of any injuries.

The floors were sticky with spilled medication, cough syrup, etc. Ugh! Honey buckets were provided, as we had no running water. Do you know, when you are thirsty for water, juice and milk won't cut it! I opened sterile water, gave the kids one ounce to wet their lips (if they promised not to tell).

On the supervisor's rounds, I received a surprise message. My mother called from Cleveland, Ohio and got through to the hospital and asked if anyone had seen me alive. She was told they had seen me and that was all she wanted to know.

By midnight patients were sleeping and I was allowed to leave. Back to the obstacle drive home as I had to return at seven AM. The after quakes kept me awake. That's why I'll never again sleep on a waterbed. It's a horrible, scary feeling.

Lots of action at work the next day. Many patients were discharged to make room for casualties. On the way home I noticed Safeway on Ninth Avenue and Gambell was open. I was so thirsty; I bought a case of Squirt and a case of beer. I was also so tired I did not look forward to the mess at home. To my surprise, the lights were on and the place was spotless. There was my husband, Lee, sitting on a chair. He had flown home in the super cub that the polar bear guide and hunter owned. They must have left as soon as they heard the news on the radio.

I remember driving down the highway to Portage. There were cracks in the road, bridges out, and temporary repairs by the National Guard. We visited Mary Lou Redmond whose family owned Diamond Jim's. Gosh darn it! She looked like she just came out of a beauty shop!

Phyllis Ann Thorne Miller

Postmaster, Hope

Excerpts from a letter written just following the earthquake:

I haven't begun to relate the complete story of this terrible earthquake—there are so many heartbreaking sides to it, also the wonderful human warmth that shows through our otherwise self-centered little shells. Everyone has helped the other fellow whenever and however possible, and have felt so much better for it! I have heard many say, "wouldn't it be grand if people were like this all the time?"

We in Hope were very, very fortunate as none of our buildings were lost—at least not yet—when the ground thaws we are afraid some of the old building may fall. We all lost dishes and other breakables—some chimneys were broken, the school sustained several cracks in the walls. Our store promptly spewed every can, bottle, bag, box, etc. onto the floor and then sent the shelves down on top of the pile! I'll never be able to tell you why, but there were only two broken jars in the entire jumble—one pickles, and one dried beef.

I can't put off trying to relate how the actual feeling of the quake was to us, I guess, even though just thinking of it puts me into an apprehensive mood all over again. Burrel, B.H. and our two teacher friends from Elmendorf, who had driven down to spend the weekend, had been working on our house and had just started home after putting two twenty feet long, eight inches wide logs up as part of the gables (they weren't fastened down yet either!). The guys in the car and said it was like being on a bucking bronco!

Laura was visiting a playmate and was running in the street screaming when her Dad got to her. She and her friend had been upstairs in the other store visiting the lady owner when it struck, and how they ever got out of that building is a mystery. Burrel said he saw it swaying back and forth, four feet each way, besides hopping up and down, and that building had been leaning at a 15-degree angle anyway, for years!

I was home—had just finished cleaning house and it shown like a new penny. The people we are renting this from while building ours had come to Hope for the weekend and he had just come in to give me some eggs. We just stood there expecting it to stop any moment, but instead it became progressively worse. He is elderly and I was afraid we were going to be knocked down, so grabbed him and headed for the yard. It kept getting stronger, so we went to hands and knees. It was like bouncing marbles up and down on a cardboard lid. The rumbling sound was sickening and I could hear cracking sounds. Mr. Buttedahl and I were holding onto each other, but my sensation, as I am sure most people shared, was that I was alone with God.

We've learned all our lives that we are strictly individuals, and when a crisis like this comes, the meaning is all too clear. Now I know why we must put our own house in order and that we are "our brother's keeper." I recall in that terrible FOUR and ONE HALF minutes, thinking that God didn't make it happen, and I also re-member my prayer. It was very simple: "Please, God, make it stop. Oh Lord, stop it please." Then, "may He forgive me, I got mad and was hollering 'Stop it!" as two children in an argument. Thank God it did stop then—nothing could have withstood that violence any longer. I came back into our house and oh, me! Everything was smashed on the floor. I got the radio and went back outside to wait for Burrel and the children, fearful of a tidal wave, but was spared from that.

The tides, however, are our big problem as they figure the land has been tipped or the ocean level has risen. We are due to have higher tides the 14th of April by the book and we are trying to determine just where they will come in addition to the higher ones we are already experiencing. They figure we are at least five feet lower. We aren't doing any more work on our house until we see where the 14th tide comes. If worse comes to worse, most of the village will have to relocate. Oh, that beautiful log house! Hope is on a good gravel bar and we think that is what saved us.

Pat Millette

Brady's Floor Covering on Fourth

We had just moved up here and rented a house by the Chugach Mountains in a subdivision called Scenic Park. We had dropped off the children to see a Walt Disney movie, at a theater on Fourth Avenue while we went to Brady's Floor Covering. All of a sudden the building started to jiggle, jiggle, jiggle. Ted and I had lived in the Bellview area and we were used to earthquakes, but this was something. I grabbed the counter. The carpet rolls were beginning to fall, the linoleum rolls were moving. The big windows suddenly shattered. There were long spikes of glass coming down, which was scary. I just hung on. The building jerked very hard. Everything was every which way. The rumble was so loud you could not hear anyone speaking. The loud roar just kept coming. I wonder what caused that roar. It was an old sturdy building and it rocked from side to side, but it held up.

Ted said, "Let's get into the car and pick up the kids." I had to hang on to him to walk. We went out the back door and the car was bouncing. It calmed and we were able to run to the car and get in. As we came up to J.C. Penney's a corner of the building crashed on to the street. We watched it fall on a car that was just smashed. We couldn't drive further, so we left the car and ran down Fourth Avenue to find the kids. Ted ran ahead. As I trotted down the street, all of a sudden there was no street beside me. It had dropped down ten to twelve feet. The bars across the street had dropped down. There were people in there. A drunk said, "That was sure a good drink I had." I said, "I hope you can get out." He said, "I'm not worried." The theater had not fallen down. My daughter was twelve and sons were ten and nine. The boys were standing with their Dad. Patty was back getting our money back. They gave her money for three children's tickets. The clerk said we could go to another movie. We said, "Not today." The kids said the grown ups yelled and screamed and ran out, leaving the children there. They just bounced around in their seats.

A man on the radio said, "be prepared for aftershocks."

We started home. There was food at home in the refrigerator and freezer, but Ted stopped to get milk and a bottle of bourbon. In the little store everything was in a jumble off the shelves. He found what he wanted but said, "Boy, what a mess."

At home we had a Great Dane puppy named Tiger Lily because she was a brindle, gold and black stripe. She was shaking and glad to see us. That night we had some earthquakes and things came out of cupboards. The Grandfather clock went bong, bong, bong. Ted and I slept on the floor in the living room, near the kid's bedroom. The Great Dane slept with us, still a little frightened. It was an interesting experience. We were very glad when it was all quiet.

One of the military bases delivered water in big water tanks. They let us know when they were coming and we could fill our jugs with water every day. The hospital sent notice they would give shots. Don't remember what for. The kids got them at the school's suggestion.

We had about two or three earthquakes a day, then it was down to one a day, then one or two a week and then no more. I was playing baseball in the streets with the kids when there was an aftershock. Everybody stopped and said, "This is fun." I didn't think so.

Betty Smith Motes

The Onion God

I lived off of Tudor Road at the tail end of the dog musher's lot. We had an acre and a quarter up on the hill. My house set up close to the road.

We had a guy who boarded with us. He was just a couple of years older than my son. We had a little house in the back yard that was a cabin we had made, and he slept in there and he had dinner at the house.

My youngest daughter was around sixteen or seventeen and she was doing the cooking. Bob didn't like onions and he didn't like them chopped up so he was giving Le Vita a bad time about chopping up the onions on the chili.

We had a big pressure cooker of beans on the stove, and it was a big one. Anyhow, she was making chili in a cast iron skillet on another burner and had the hamburger and stuff in it. She was chopping up onions to put in the hamburger and Bob was giving her a bad time because he didn't like onions in anything. He kept telling her she shouldn't put the onions in anything. He told her she shouldn't put the onions in the chili. He told her again and again. She didn't pay any attention to him at all and went right on cutting. He said, "You just wait, one of these days the great onion god'll get mad at you." And about that time the earthquake hit.

When we were done shaking the big pressure cooker with the beans stayed on the stove. Then Bob looked at Le Vita and said, "I told you the great onion god was going to get mad at you."

I had an ironing board set up as I had been doing ironing. La Vita's husband came in with a bouquet of daffodils. One of us put them in a vase, and it was sitting on the ironing board. But when the earthquake hit, La Vita ran over to hang onto the vase of flowers. She was concerned with the glassware and rushed over to rescue the flowers. That was when the chili hit the floor.

C. Dale Murphy

J C Penney

On the day of the earthquake, I was the Shoe Department Manager at the J C Penney store that had been open for one year. At the time of the quake the store was open and doing a thriving business on that Good Friday.

When the earthquake hit, everyone except four employees, C. Dale Murphy, two lady associates and Charles R. "Bud" Harris evacuated the store. These four rode out the quake in the office on the fifth floor. When all the lights went out three of us positioned ourselves on the floor by a pillar. When the floor started moving up and down the pillar I knew we were in deep trouble. Finally after about six minutes of pitch dark, the front wall peeled away from the building and we saw the light. There was the inlet in full view.

When the quake subsided, we left the office. The door was at an angle and we had to lift it up to get out. We ran to the stairwell stepping over hunks of concrete, made it down the stairs and to the back door. As we emerged from the building all the people across the street were yelling "run." They though the back wall of the five story building might fall at any time.

When the dust settled, we could hear voices coming from the building. There were three boys trapped in the elevator. They were brought out through the trap door from the second floor. Later, a hard cover book was found on the floor of the elevator with the middle of the pages all cut out. This had probably been made for shoplifting.

When the front wall of the five-story building fell, it smashed a car with a lady inside. A young man walking the picket line (Penney's was being picketed at the time) was hit by falling concrete so there were two casualties.

J C Penney store on Fifth Avenue and D Streets. Two people were killed when walls collapsed and smashed automobiles parked in front of the store.

Mikell Lilliebjerg Murphy

I Wonder If They Felt It Downtown?

We were living in a very little house in the woods near where Service High School stands today when the Great Alaska Earthquake struck. My husband had returned from taking our rowdy foster child to his mother's home to celebrate his twelfth birthday, and we had just sat down to enjoy a glass of wine and a rare quiet evening together.

Then the shaking started, but we weren't at all disturbed. After all, these little tremors happened now and then—they lasted a few seconds and were nothing to worry about. But something went wrong this time. The shaking didn't stop.

Indeed, it went on and on getting stronger and louder until the wine had sloshed completely out of our glasses, and books and dishes were tumbling off their shelves all round us.

By that time we had struggled to our feet, and my husband was shouting over the rumbles and crashes to stand in the doorframe. But our two beagles were hysterically dashing around the room and no doorframe on the planet would have seemed safe to me by then. I wanted out of there!

The dogs lurched outside to the open air and away from the creaks and groans the swaying walls were adding to the uproar. The house was obviously being torn apart, and there was no way I wanted to be inside and under it when it came down!

But once outside and into the cold March evening, the noise and danger were still there. The ground was rippling and heaving so much that we couldn't stay on our feet. I was thrashing around on hands and knees in the mud and snow of spring breakup alternately crawling and staggering down the driveway as fast as I could go to get away from the screaming of old planks and nails as they were pulled apart at the corners of the walls and then slammed back together in our little shack of a home.

The chimney was alternately leaning away from the house and then smacking back into it. The tall birches in the yard were being lashed back and forth so violently they were almost slapping the ground on either side.

From my knees I stared around me seeing nothing but certain ruin and unable to hear anything but the loudest possible roar of some huge and invisible locomotive that wouldn't leave the station—it just kept staying there all around us.

Once or twice the tumult would subside enough for me to scramble to my feet only to start up again, stronger than ever, knocking me once more to the ground. "Well," I thought, strangely calm inside, "so this is the end of the world. This is what it feels like to die."

I wasn't even afraid, just totally amazed and unprepared for what was happening all around me.

The dogs had long since disappeared into the woods by the time the noise and the shaking began to gradually calm down. And then it was over.

It had been going on for over 4 minutes! Try standing in front of your clock sometime for that long and imagine yourself in the middle of the road and shaking of the strongest earthquake ever recorded in North America, and you might get some idea of how I could have truly believed that the world was ending.

Now everything just stopped, and it was quiet again. But it was a quiet that I had never felt so strongly before. The earth and all that was in it was silent. Nothing moved. All was still.

The house was amazingly still intact. The chimney had righted itself with only the top two layers of blocks now sitting askew. We gingerly reentered and found a complete and total mess inside. Everything was thrown to the floor, and our tiny kitchen was awash in the contents of the refrigerator and cabinets. Most disturbing though was the sound of running water coming from the basement. Obviously the pipes had broken down there, and we needed a plumber fast.

My husband retrieved the phone from wherever it had been thrown and dialed the number for our plumber friend who had just recently installed new water pipes for us. Amazingly he answered his phone and said he'd be right over.

We were all acting absurdly normal—we just didn't yet know how else to respond to what had happened. To tell the truth, none of us really KNEW what had happened. And that phone call was the only one we made because our phone didn't work again for weeks.

Rather than fact the mess inside I went out to look for our dogs. Up and down the unnaturally quiet road I walked calling their names. "Adelaaaaaide! Ambroose! It's all right now. You can come home."

No response, and I silently swore never again to name pets such silly names. The dogs came slinking back home much later that night and were jumpy for weeks.

For now I was all by myself in a world that a little while before I had believed was ending forever. Yes, indeed! I had survived the end of the world! That awareness, combined with the current creepy stillness around me made me feel like a ghost.

Then I was suddenly face to face with a very large moose, just standing in the trees directly in front of me. He looked as confused as I felt. He shook his big woolly head and gave me a look that asked plainly, "Hey, lady, what the heck just happened here?!"

"I don't know," I replied.

"But I've gotta go now.

"Bye."

And I hurried away leaving him staring forlornly after me.

We were busy with the cleanup process when the plumber finally arrived much later. "Sorry to take so long," he said, "but the roads are a mess and I had to take a few detours to get here."

That was when it hit us that the earthquake was not just a neighborhood event. "My goodness!" I exclaimed. "I wonder if they felt it downtown?"

Almeda Murray

It Took a Week to Clean Up the Mess

I have been here since 1957. I worked at the old Native Service Hospital and was on duty on the afternoon shift when the earthquake hit. I was at the switchboard, which was surrounded by a wall. I was thrown up against the steel filing cabinet, and the blow left a straight red line down my back. Some floors were cracked. The elevators worked. Cars parked in the hospital parking lot went down. We were in shock.

Nurses ran out the front door and hung on to a flagpole. Three months later all the nurses got a letter of commendation from the President. It didn't seem proper to me since they all had left their patients.

At home there was a big gallon can of honey on top of the refrigerator. It fell onto the floor and all the honey went under the refrigerator and the washing machine. It took a week to clean up the mess.

Jackie Musgrave

Hold on and Pray

If you were in Anchorage, Alaska, on Good Friday of 1964, you got an eloquent reminder of the first Good Friday.

When the initial tremors came, you stood for a minute waiting for the earth to stop moving, and, when it became apparent that the movements were increasing in violence rather than stopping, you made a dive for the nearest doorway and hung on. Later, you heard from friends — or strangers who rapidly became friends — that they had squirmed under coffee tables, or picked up the baby and headed outdoors, or simply flung themselves on the floor.

But during the long five minutes the earthquake lasted, you couldn't do much but hold on and pray. You clung to the side of the doorway and got bumped back and forth and banged by the door as it swung wildly, and you watched helplessly as the lights went out with a sharp crackle and pictures bounced off the walls.

You heard a noise behind you and knew that the bookcase had fallen, and when you twisted awkwardly to look you saw your dresser sliding across the floor. You heard the cupboard doors open, and cans and boxes falling noisily to the floor.

And while you were being banged about like a little boat on a stormy sea, the hall cupboard in front of you flew open and the shelves disgorged an assortment of bottles and jars that crashed at your feel and skidded in broken chunks across the linoleum.

You saw the heavy mirror in the living room rocking and scraping the wall, but miraculously not falling. You saw the plants in the window tipping over and spilling dirt on the rug, and part of your mind sighed because the room had just been cleaned.

And finally, after a lifetime, the tremors subsided.

You ran clumsily to call up the stairs to see if the girls in the apartment there were all right, and when you saw their open refrigerator door and the food all over the floor, you were suddenly laughing uncontrollably.

Then you saw your sister running home from the office, and the upstairs sister running even faster because she had been in Penney's when the walls crumbled into the street, and the four of you were all hysterically talking at once.

A small "Vacancy" sign is attached to the front entry of this apartment house at Eighth and M Streets.

You didn't know anything until the radio stations came back on the air later that night, and then you learned that part of Anchorage was sunken, that the two 14-story apartment buildings were full of cracks and holes, that the lovely homes along Marston Drive had fallen into Cook Inlet.

And because you knew people on the bluff, and in the buildings, you worried.

Providence Hospital sent out an emergency call for volunteers, and when you drove out you bumped over huge cracks that ran across the pavement. You saw that it was still snowing, and you were aware of an eerie stillness over Anchorage. When Providence told you to come back at 7 AM, you bumped your way home and listened to your radio report news of the disaster.

You had company in your house that night — and for days afterward — people who had been evacuated from their homes.

You wore sweaters and stockings to bed because the heat, like the lights and the plumbing, wasn't working.

You spent Saturday at Providence, and when the aftershocks came you stiffened, then laughed with the patient who said, "Didn't know I was THAT heavy." You took to X-Ray a woman who had been in her room at the Westward Hotel when the corners pulled apart, and you patted her shoulder sympathetically and held her hand, receiving as much comfort as you gave, when the lights went out in the elevator.

You almost got used to the sight of armed guards at the corners, and the fact that you were in the "closed circle" at night because your house was downtown. Nearly everyone you knew sported a large red mark that meant a typhoid shot, and you were thankful when the electricity came back on so you could boil your melted snow.

You saw the wreck that used to be Penney's, and the twisted hunk of steel and broken glass that had been the Cordova Building only a block from home; the heaps of bricks where the Four Seasons had stood, the mess that had been the L Street Apartments. You saw pictures of Turnagain, and you got a good look at the sunken part of Fourth Avenue, and you thought of what cities must look like after a war.

And because you knew the earthquake registered 8.6 on the seismograph, you got a bad case of the shakes when a strong aftershock just a week later registered 6.5, and sent you scurrying outdoors.

You shut your eyes and prayed fervently for no more quakes.

But you stayed in Alaska. You started to pick up the shaken pieces of your life, and you mourned the loss of friends. You stayed nervous — but you stayed.

Opal Myers

We'd Like Our Check Now

My first thought when the earthquake hit was "hold a door open!" I was working at the Sabre Jet at Fifth and Gamble getting ready for the usual Friday night dinner rush. The building had no windows and I immediately thought about being trapped in there and not being able to open a door. After a long, long time, the building quit shaking and I found I had grabbed the main entrance door, sturdy and heavy with a hydraulic closure. It had dragged me along with it as it swayed back and forth, but I was determined not to let go.

I had just two customers in the dining room, a nice young couple. She was at least nine months pregnant, and I was concerned about her. When I finally made my way to their table in the dark to see if they were all right, she calmly said "I think we'd like our check now."

The aftershocks were pretty unnerving, so it didn't take us long to close the place up and get out of there. I had to know if my sister and her family were safe, so I drove out to Nunaka Valley. There were aftershocks every few minutes and it was snowing lightly so it was slow going, but the few drivers were very cautious and courteous. It was frightening to pull up to an intersection and see the utility poles swaying as if they could snap off and land on the car. My sister was not only safe and sound, but had many of the neighbors at their house because they had lots of camping gear and were able to cook on a Coleman stove with light from their lanterns.

I was living in the South addition, so, along with some others, I stayed at a friend's house where they had all the necessities. I believe there were seventeen of us there, sleeping everywhere, and sometimes in shifts as people left for work and came home.

After a few days of that, I felt I had to get away for a while, so I went over to my apartment. The entire neighborhood was deserted. Not a car, an animal or a person moving about and not a sound. After I picked up some of the mess, I sat down at the kitchen table to write a letter to my mother. All of a sudden the refrigerator started up. I must have jumped a foot out of my chair, but, at least I had electricity, and in a few days the water and gas were turned on and I was back in my own home.

Geologists view jumbled destruction in the Turnagain residential area. This was in the area where ground surfaces dropped some thirty-five feet onto the tidelands of Cook Inlet.

Lois Noble

On the Home Front

Good Friday, 1964, was much like any weekday. The store where I worked in Deer River, a little town in Northern Minnesota closed for a couple of hours to let the workers go to the Good Friday church service. That evening, as usual, we turned the radio on. There had been an earthquake in Alaska. So what, yawn. A bit later the radio said the earthquake was bad; Anchorage was on fire. Now we began to pay attention. Dick, our older son and his wife, Shirleen, were living there. The next news item had ALL of Anchorage on fire. Now we really worried.

The next morning I called the Red Cross to see if they knew anything. All they could tell me was to stay by the telephone. Our cousin had asked us for Easter Dinner. We still hadn't heard anything and were still staying by the telephone, so they packed up the dinner and brought it to us. Still nothing on Monday so Harland and I both went in to work. About ten that morning, a messenger came with a telegram for us. It had the most wonderful words in the English language. "No harm. No hurt. Dick". By then I was crying so hard I had to have a friend go next door to tell Harland. A few days later we got this letter from Dick written the morning after the quake.

"Dear Folks, (excerpts)

"Earthquake!! Old news to you by the time you read this, but very much real right now. We were driving on the open road (or rather riding — a salesman was demonstrating a car for us.) The salesman thought we had a flat. Then the road was moving, a twisting motion from one side to the other. We stopped, got out, and watched the ripples in the ground. Magnificent, awe-inspiring, really something to behold!

"It's bad, but as you realize, it's not nearly as bad as what you must have heard. Ought to be a good construction season here, rebuilding. One thing you may be sure of, Anchorage will rebound and come back. No one has really stopped to evaluate yet, but when they get over the daze, they'll be so busy they won't know what to do, and before long things will be well on the road to recovery. The people who come to Alaska are not the timid type who turn and leave because of some real or imagined hardship."

Split trees, split houses, and split apartment buildings! This house was split in two and the two pieces moved apart during the big earthquake. The potted plants stayed on the windowsill. Located on Eighth Avenue between L and M Streets.

Bill Nugent

Flying into Kodiak

I had just completed a visit to the Kodiak store. The flight was going to land at Homer on the way and eventually land in Anchorage, at least that was what we expected, but then the pilot said there had been an earthquake and the Anchorage and Homer airports were closed. They had lost contact with any airports. I asked the navigator "Can we get to Fairbanks?" He said, "I think we are

Clean up started immediately in Kodiak as bulldozers piled debris into piles to be burned. The entire dock area was demolished.

going to go back to Kodiak." As we were approaching Kodiak for a landing, the captain noticed the strange appearance of the sea. He could see the surface of the sea bottom. When we arrived at the airport there was no one there, so the crew climbed down the emergency ladder and pushed the stair up to let us off.

We drove into Kodiak. On the way we saw some evidence that the water had come up and then receded along the shoreline. We searched the car radio for a station. When it came on the announcer was saying "...another funny thing has happened. The Gulf of Mexico water is going up and down three or four feet. I'll keep you posted." They didn't know what was happening to us, but we began to wonder if the earth was cracking up. We wondered if it was the end of the world. It was pretty convincing.

In the town, we looked for the mother of one of the women who were with us. She lived downtown just off the business district. We found the house empty and we could see that some, not a lot, of water had come up into her house and was flowing back out the door. Just then, the daughter said, "There is the air raid siren! That means evacuate the city!" We had the good sense to follow the advice and went up a little hill. About ten minutes later the place where we had been standing was washed out, along with the whole business district.

We finally got to sleep about four o'clock in the morning. Two days later, on Sunday, we were able to get back to Anchorage. By this time there were newspaper reporters who had flown up from Seattle. They were telling stories. I believe there were about nineteen deaths in Kodiak, most due to the tsunamis, which were devastating to the small boat harbor and anyone near the shoreline.

It was an interesting experience; I don't think I'd want to do it again.

Yvonne O'Brien

Homestead Cabin

That March of 1964, my family with seven children lived on our homestead in a one-bedroom log cabin built by my late husband, Kenneth. I was helping my oldest daughter Peggy try on her new Easter dress when the earthquake hit. The dishes started to rattle in the kitchen cupboards. Then they began to fall out onto the floor and break. The house started to sway back and forth. I yelled at the children "Let's get out of here!" My oldest son Michael made it out of the front door first. As he got out on the front porch a strong jolt hit, it threw his right arm through the plate glass window. I was so scared, but he never got a cut. When we all finally got off the porch safely our eyes were drawn to the spruce trees that were whipping back and forth to where the treetops were almost touching the ground. I never knew that spruce trees were that limber. All my children were lying on the ground just watching them. After the earthquake, I went back into the house to see the damage that it caused. To my surprise, only a few of the dishes were broken. I had to depend on a lantern for light. We had no running water, anyway. My husband hauled water in two large silver milk cans that would last us for about two days. I made our breakfasts and dinners on the old camp stove until the electricity came back on.

A few days later, my oldest daughter, oldest son and I walked up Lake Otis Parkway to 68th Avenue all the way up the hill to visit our friends Elizabeth and Mac. They showed us a crevasse so deep that you couldn't even see the bottom. They had started driving down their driveway, but the front wheels dropped into the crevasse and they couldn't go any further.

Now almost 40 years have gone by and I will never forget how scared I was. When I think back to that time in my life I thank the Lord for keeping our friends and us safe. And you know what? That old cabin is still standing.

Christine Opland

Johan Sebastion Bark

I was wearing my slip. We had gone to Good Friday services, and all four of us were changing into our pajamas, while watching our favorite TV show, *Fireball XL5*. The three older of us were dressed pretty much in our underwear. Mom had already gotten my little sister ready, and we ended up sitting out on the porch that way.

I remember sitting there when it started shaking. We were going to sit through it because it wasn't the first earthquake we had ever been through, but it just kept getting bigger and bigger.

Finally somebody yelled "Earthquake" and we ran out. Run is a relative term. Lars, my older brother was just wearing his jockey shorts. He got all the way out the door down the steps and he was clinging to the gate.

My little brother and I were sitting on the steps. Mom was standing in the door holding my little sister Tanya, and praying loud.

As I recall we were watching people out on the street and waiting it out. It was kind of a scary time. Things kind of worked in slow motion.

There was a church kind of catty cornered from where we live. There was this guy trying to get into his car. He would get his foot up and his car would move, he would move over to the car get his foot back up, and the car would move. I don't know how many times he did that. Lots of frustrated people.

By the time we went back in, we had something on.

My dog had fallen down the stairs, but he was fine, he had done that before. That was Johan Sebastian Bark.

The piano came to rest right where Tanya had been sitting, and it would have hit her if Mom hadn't moved her.

Mildred Opland

There Was A Holocaust

I was very busily making a spaghetti sauce. The four kids were busily watching *Fireball XL5*, as most children in town were. It was our youngest daughter's third birthday that day.

I kept stirring the sauce when the earthquake began, because earthquakes usually did not last long. Our oldest says, "This is a real one, Mom, put that stuff away." He must have been eight or nine years old, and at least one of us had an idea of what was going on. I hurried up and put the spaghetti mix in the oven and closed the oven door. I took the kids out to the entryway to put warm clothes on them, because I figured, "Okay, this is going to be hard enough, we're going to have broken pipes."

The youngest one sat there continuing to wait for the TV set to come back on. By then I couldn't walk in the house. I crawled to her, got her in one arm, and crawled on my one hand and two knees. We all got to the doorway, put on our ski equipment and watched people trying to walk down the sidewalk.

We were right on the corner of Eighth and F. This one person I remember tried to hang onto the parking meter, but the parking meter kept tipping back and forth so they couldn't hang on.

Bricks were flying out of the big yellow building downtown. It was the one between F and G Streets. We watched the bricks and blocks falling. Bricks didn't hold together too well, they don't give. Our house didn't have much damage. Pipes broke, cupboards dumped.

We needed to get hold of somebody, and let them know we were okay, but of course we couldn't. We couldn't call out or anything. A cousin of mine who lives in town, Ivan Goody, (an accountant) drove by and found we were okay, then got hold of a person who did radio transmissions and got a message out to someone in the

United States to let them know that everybody was okay, both families. That was the only word our relatives had of us. They needed to know we were okay, because the radio said that there was a holocaust. They imagined Anchorage had gone.

My sister lives in Wisconsin, and she later said, "The radio here said that Anchorage was nothing but a holocaust." She said she thought the whole thing had gone up in flame. Anyway my concern was Bob, he hadn't come home from work yet, so I didn't know where he was. We were okay. His parents lived two blocks from us, so the kids and I walked down to check on them, and we ended up staying at their house. They had a little paper burner in the basement, so they could have heat. We spent three days there. It was the most comfortable place we could be, and there was nothing else we could do.

There was no water, and we couldn't clean up the mess at our house. For a family of six you buy honey in big containers. Honey had dumped, peanut butter, sugar, and popcorn. It was a royal mess. The cupboards were on the side of the house that was swaying. We had a fishbowl sitting on a shelf that was also swaying, but there was a post that kept it from going off the shelf, so the fish was still okay. It bounced, but it was okay.

The kids played earthquake games forever after. And *avalanche*. We had a basement playroom, and they would go down the steps on boards and things, and yell "Earthquake", all four of them. Eric was the expert at that, he was the skier.

They were a little afraid at the time, but I think our cat was the most afraid. We had a cat and a dog. They just ran up and down the stairs frantically. They just didn't know what was going on.

Bob finally came home. He was okay. At any rate we all got together at his folks house. He was very busy the next three days. After the water came back on the oldest boy and I took pails of water and flushed the kitchen and scraped up the dried up mess with ice scrapers and collected it in buckets. It was a mess. We were picking up books afterward from the shelves. The kids had this one Sunday school book, it was called, God Speaks to Us. Bob picked it up, and said, "Yeah, and in no uncertain terms!"

We went to Easter Sunday services at church in our ski clothes, the same ones we had worn for three days. We went to Central Lutheran Church at the time, which was only half a block from Bob's folk's house. We couldn't have services upstairs as there was too much damage so we were holding them in the basement. There weren't many people there because they couldn't drive.

I got water from the National Guard. They went around town with these wagons with buckets on them and we got water from a tank.

I wanted to see the damage downtown, so I took my three year old with me, and she saw the soldier standing on the corner, and she said, "Mister, my brother has a toy one of you." I got a good laugh on a serious day.

Bob's Dad and I sat and wrote letters outside for days at a time.

We couldn't sleep. At a time like that possessions don't really mean a thing. It wouldn't have mattered if the house had gone as long as the family is okay.

It's just a weird feeling.

Salvage operations under way in the Telequana area of Turnagain.

Robert Opland

Fourth and K

I worked at the district attorneys office, which at that time was located in the State Office Building at Fourth and K. Work was over at 5. At 5:10 or so one of the assistant DAs and I went across K to a place called the Memo Pad to have an end-of-the week beer. The bar was located in the Austro-Alaska building on the North side of Fourth on the corner of K. We sat down and I remember the wait- ress came over to the table, and she said, "We don't have any Miller's, Bob." So I said, "Well, what do you have?" and she started to recite their inventory on beer, which was unnecessary. I knew what they have, I don't know why I even asked, so I ordered a Budweiser, and it will probably come as no surprise to you, that is the last time I ever ordered one. I had poured a glass full from the bottle and so had my friend, and we had each started to drink when all of a sudden the building started to shake to beat the band. After about ten, fifteen seconds I expected it to stop because that was about as long as I had felt an earthquake before, but it didn't seem to be stopping. I heard the bartender do what I think now was a very smart thing. He called at somebody who was sitting near the door to open the door and hold it open, so when the earthquake quit we had a door we could get out of. That was important because when we went out the door, here was a wall of dirt facing us. The pavement on the other side was up there about six feet and the pavement we were standing on was six feet lower. Some of this Cook Inlet clay had turned to mush as it does when it is vibrated in a certain way that earthquakes manage.

The support for the upper banks that Anchorage is built on ap- parently is underlain, to some extent, by that clay and when it started to turn into soup, why the bottom just literally dropped out.

And so there was, say, about twenty to twenty-five feet along that location that I called the drop zone. It just dropped away, from four to ten feet deep. That drop zone started out behind the Memo Pad and back toward Third Avenue. Then it continued up that alley until it got to about Seventh where it turned and headed toward what was then Providence Hospital. (According to a story I heard, which I kind of question, as it was going toward Providence Hospital two nuns stepped out of the hospital, saw what was coming, and dropped to their knees. And it turned and went over and hit the Four Seasons.)

Anyhow that was the particular drop zone that I was in. I did not feel it drop. I felt a lot of shaking. I didn't know the building had come apart until I stepped outside and looked in that direction and here was this wall of dirt. I could see where the building had broken at the same place. The whole building just broke apart. The current Austro-Alaska building is new, and not exactly in the same location. The building I was in was very thoroughly condemned.

Everything came out of the back bar at the Memo Pad. A lot of it broke. I finally decided I'd best climb out of the hole I was in and go home. We clambered out and I walked home and the other fellows came along to make sure there wasn't any serious damage. While things were a mess, later when the government offered grants and low interest rate loans, it turned out that all I had was one leaking steam joint in the heat system. Hardly worth filling out all that paperwork.

Nobody in town had water, sewage. Water was cut off for everybody because they didn't trust the mains. Even if they would hold water, they didn't trust them to not have sewage in them. So, they brought in irrigation piping by the planeload. The whole downtown area had irrigation pipe running down every block. You could hook up a garden hose to it. The military moved into the downtown area to prevent looting.

There was a building on Fifth and K that was used by the Arctic Health Research Institute. Two of their employees were the high mucky mucks in the local ski patrol system. I was in the patrol, so somehow, we all met down at this building to see what we could help with, without skis. It turned out that our main job was to rescue a bunch of germs. They were studying what was the lowest temperature life could be acclimatized to and they had some microbes in a freezer chest that they had down to something like 25-

30 below zero after about fifteen years of experimentation. They really did not want the temperature to go up because then all the bugs would get killed and they would have the fun of starting out all over. One of the people from that office had an emergency generator at their house, so we got hold of a four-wheel drive, I can't recall where, and got it back in there and put this freezer on the truck and succeeded in getting it over to the fellows house and they got it plugged in, so I helped rescue several million bugs but that's about all. I was down in the hole at Morrison subdivision but we didn't find anybody who needed rescuing.

The weirdest one to me, this fellow that I had been with in the Memo Pad and I went back there and looked in the back window, which had not been broken like the front ones had. The only thing that had apparently not been disturbed were the two bottles of beer and the two glasses of beer that were sitting on our table. They were still sitting there and the chairs were right in place. They were just sitting there.

We spent our first night at our folks place. Then a friend of ours from Dillingham stayed in our house, kind of a guardian you might say. He took care of the pets.

About fifteen years ago, I went Outside for a meeting. During a break in the meeting one of the guys that knew I was from Alaska asked me if I was in Anchorage at the time of the quake.

"So was I," he said. I made a quick estimate of his age, and I said, "Well, if you were in Anchorage when the quake happened I can tell you what you were doing when it started."

"Well how can you do that?"

"Because you were watching, *Fireball XL5.*

His eyes got big. "Well that is what I was doing."

"Every mother in Anchorage in those days used that for a babysitter while they cooked supper."

Jean Paal

The Highland Fling

I. The quake

When I commented on the small earthquake we were having, Harry glared at me for interrupting his story. Then the big one hit, slamming us sideways and he interrupted himself, yelling, "Get under the table!"

We were at the Highland Fling, a popular watering hole on Fourth Avenue, between D and E Street. It was a long, narrow establishment, with a restaurant on Fourth Avenue and a back bar opening onto the parking lot which ran the length of that block. Behind the parking lot the land sloped steeply down to Third Avenue. On Friday nights, some staff from the *Anchorage Daily News* and friends would meet at the Fling for "twofers. I sometimes joined in. That Good Friday in 1964 was to be the last such gathering because the ADN was set to change from an evening paper to a morning paper that weekend. When I got there, only Harry Groom, a free-lance photographer had arrived. I slid into his booth, the one nearest the restaurant, and faced down the long narrow bar. A mirror backed it with shelves displaying the establishment's varied stock-in-trade. We had just been served as Harry began his story.

The powerful initial slam east to west broke the power line to town and everything stopped, lights, motors, all the ambient noise except temporary screaming from the other patrons who ran into the street. Then it was strikingly quiet, except that as the swaying continued, the bottles began to slide off the shelves and break — sway west — crash, east — thud against the mirror, west — crash. (To this day, the smell of spilled whiskey evokes those minutes.) Under my ear, I could hear the screech of nails pulling out. In the restaurant, one other couple had moved under the table — old

Zack Loussac and Ada. We could hear her gently reassuring him. And there we stayed — for four minutes. Time it on your watch; it's long! There was plenty of time to consider what was happening. I took Harry's hand and told him I loved him. I didn't mean it romantically, and he understood and said "same to you." Otherwise we didn't talk much. After a while, Zack and Ada left. After more time, I observed to myself that if it didn't stop soon, I might die. I began to wonder about my kids and my house, and then, suddenly, I wanted desperately to get home. I looked down the bar and noticed it seemed to be sagging in the middle. I remarked to Harry that under the table was a good place to be if the ceiling caved in, but not so hot if the floor caved in. "What are you talking about?" he asked roughly, then turned to look. "Let's get the H... out of here!" We each ran for our cars, his on Fourth Avenue, mine in back. I had to jump over the widening sinkhole in the floor.

When I got to my car, I found it teetering, high-centered on the rim of a ten-foot crevasse. I was frantic. I had to get home. I tried to cut through the bar to catch Harry for a ride, but I couldn't make myself go back into that black, dust-filled room. I ran, as hard as I could, around the end of the block past Hewitt's Drug Store. (The window was out, and I actually had a brief impulse to loot a huge display box advertising Chanel #5.) Harry was standing in front of the Fling. He saw me and shouted "Where the Hell have you been. I was scared spitless. I thought you were trapped in there, but I couldn't make myself go in after you." "Thanks. Just get me home." I panted. He said "I'll take you to your corner, but I have to get home. I don't have a single camera with me!"

We ran to his car — a V. W. Bus — a high, high vehicle I managed to climb into, somehow. He looked over at me from behind the wheel. "How could I be without a camera? Can I have one of those?" I looked at what he was looking at — my hands. My hands that were still holding my twofer scotch-and-waters. My hands that had taken the glasses under the table, out from under the table, all around the block, into the car and now, as I watched, began shaking so hard they dropped both drinks in my lap.

II. At Home

No one was home. I was stunned, although I shouldn't have been. I knew, more or less, where they all were, but somehow, while under that table I visualized them all alone at home. My husband, Vic, was helping in his friend's shop. Charlie, age sixteen, retarded, was with the sitter; Gayle, fifteen, was at a girlfriend's; Joanie, eleven, had gone skiing with the neighbors.

The tiny puppy, (new that week) was nowhere to be found. The huge old gold fish was lying on the carpet, amidst the shards of his bowl. The only apparent damage to the house was some spilled

At Eighth and L Streets fissures running across the street trapped autos. Note difference in elevation of the front and back ends of the station wagon.

ketchup in the kitchen, some canned goods strewn around and a broken mirror. I wandered around aimlessly picking things up until the rest of the family began to assemble. First the sitter and Charlie returned from picking up her husband. They had been in the car on Ninth Avenue when the apartment building at M Street collapsed before their eyes. To my immense relief, I saw Gayle walking up the alley, frightened and amazed after watching, from a across the street, the apartment building on Sixteenth collapse. The outer walls peeled away and they saw into the apartments, including a man naked in the shower. Next came Vic. He had run into the street and watched some linemen on a cherry picker have the ride of their lives. On the drive home, from Spenard , he had gunned his old Buick like a stunt rider over the tilted bridge across Chester Creek. Finally, the puppy crept out from between the two layers of a trundle bed, but for the next twenty-four hours we had no word about Joannie until someone walked out of Alyeska and reported no injuries down there.

Vic made a fire in the fireplace, and rigged up a tripod with a kettle over it. I took the undone roast out of the oven, wrapped it in foil and tried to finish it in the ashes. We dipped the water from the backs of the toilets to drink, and gathered snow to melt for washing. The sewer problem seemed insurmountable. For the time being we followed the drought adage (If it's brown, flush it down, if it's yellow, let it mellow.)

After we had fed our family as best we could, Vic and I walked downtown to see if we could get my car. The National Guard wouldn't let us get near it. Someone returned it to us the next day. On the way, we were fascinated by a ten-foot deep hole on L Street near Eighth. We walked over to look down into it, not realizing that we were walking out on a huge ledge of frozen ground. As we neared the edge, the ledge broke off and began tilting into the hole. Although we ran back to safety, we had no emotional reaction except a mild interest. "Oh, look at that!" There was no fear because we had no adrenaline left.

We had invited the next-door neighbors, with their two tiny children, to spend the night in front of our fireplace. In preparation, I began to pick up the broken glass from the fish bowl. As I touched it, the goldfish flopped. We put him and some of our precious clean water into a mixing bowl. He lived for years.

III- Getting the Airline Running

After a few days PNA announced they would bring a plane in from Seattle, the first flight to try landing here, so I returned to work. The reservations office in the terminal at Anchorage International Airport was wrecked, along with much of the building. We went in to get some supplies and found it very spooky. The ceiling and walls were being stripped down to iron, so sounds reverberated through the unlit, dusty interior. The restrooms were roped off because the sewer and water lines were broken.

We found the reference books and reservations records we needed and crowded into the cargo office, a small redwood building next door. It would serve as headquarters, all internal functions and check-in terminal for weeks. That first day we had two phone lines and three instruments. They never stopped ringing. We felt we had to honor preexisting reservations for the flight back, but expected many or all no-shows, so we accepted a very long wait list. People who couldn't get through by phone came out, pounding on the desks their urgent need to get one of those fifty-odd seats. One man became so insistent he threatened to paste the mild mannered senior agent, who broke his cool at last. "We've been here since six this morning, have no water, nothing to eat, no communications, and WE DO NOT KNOW when or IF the plane will get here or whether you will get on it." The man backed away and left. An hour later he was back. He had opened his store and brought us a case of soft drinks, a jug of water, coffee and two dozen fresh ham sandwiches. We gobbled them up while we worked, but food and drink raised another personal problem. So the ground crew taxied up a "Connie" (a fifty-seven passenger Lockheed Constellation airplane) and parked it nearby to serve as our "facility."

When the plane from Seattle arrived, it brought a gift from PNA's owner, Art Woodley, dozens of doughnuts. Like many Alaskans, most of us were concerned that our Outside families must be frantic with worry. One of the pilots on that flight (Chuck Davis) discovered that fact, so he took as much information we had available there at the airport (mostly just names and cities) took it back to Seattle and sat up all night locating and calling our families.

A week after the earthquake, civil flight operations had been repaired sufficiently to permit resumption of our intra-Alaska flights. One afternoon we watched sadly, as they flew our toilet away to Kodiak, but relaxed an hour or so later when an emissary from the main terminal announced that we could now use the restrooms over there. It was the beginning of getting back to normal.

Val Pace

Why Did We Save Material Things?

I have always been thankful to God that the earthquake didn't happen during the time school was in session. I was a teacher at Government Hill Elementary School at the time and our school was destroyed. It would have been devastating if school had been in session.

I was at home with my husband Les and we both protected material things. Les held his stereo that he had spent months working on and I held the cupboard shut so dishes that I had purchased in Denmark didn't fall out. We laughed about it afterward, as we were newlyweds and were surprised we didn't just grab each other.

I also remember how difficult it was to contact our relatives, we tried to call but we couldn't get through to them. We sent postcards and the first they heard from us was the postcard.

Louise Paisley

Don't Knock the House Down!

I've been through earthquakes most of my life because I was raised in Western Washington. I can remember once mother had bruises all over her shoulders because she got tossed down the hall from side to side.

I was getting dinner in our house on Jewel Lake Road. I saw my husband Don driving into the garage in his pickup truck. As he came through the people door and pulled it shut, the quake struck. I yelled at him angrily, "For Christ's Sake, you don't have to knock the house down!" I thought it was going to fall down.

He never did get all the way into the house. Our son, Kim, was watching the TV. (How many children were watching that puppet show?) All of a sudden the console television traveled across the floor on the carpet. I ran over and unhooked it; I guess I was worried about something blowing up. I grabbed him by the hand and told him to go stand by your dad. Don was trying to grab me as I flew by. I was trying to close the cupboard doors, and the refrigerator door. The frying pan was in the dishwater soaking. I ran over and let all the water out of the sink but not before it splashed. I had the biggest mess and no way to clean it up.

I like to take two showers a day, and I couldn't do that. I had a small portable radio and that was the only way I got any news. I was bothered that we knew it was a good shaker, but didn't know how much damage had been done. I let some folks take my son to drive around and see. Then I wondered why I let him go. I was so glad to get him back. I just didn't realize how serious it was.

We had to clean up and re-pour the garage floor because it was all cracked up. My sewing machine never did work right after the earthquake.

Gabriel "Gabby" Pereira

St Anthony's

In ancient times when an earthquake hits an area in any part of the world, tradition tells us all that the good Lord above is telling us we must change our ways of sin and start living a better life.

As for me personally, I, Gabriel (Gabby) Pereira, now seventy-six years of age, remember that earth shattering force of nature at 5:36 PM. It is still today the strongest ever recorded in the North American continent.

Now I am retired, but then Northern Commercial Caterpillar employed me at Fifth and H Streets, downtown Anchorage, as a parts clerk in the cardex (records) department. We worked daily 8 AM to 5 PM.

After work, my wife Juanita, and I, with our two sons, were heading for St. Anthony's Catholic Church for the Good Friday services. We had our cocker spaniel Pepe in the GMC truck and we pulled up at 825 Klevin Street.

I dropped my wife and two-year old son, Richard, at the door and continued around to the parking lot. I was standing with our one-year old son Robert in my arms between the small St. Anthony's church and the rectory.

At precisely 5:36 PM that evening a severe rolling earthquake hit the Anchorage area. I steadied myself. The cement brick chimney on the rectory was swinging left and right, like the pendulum on a grandfather's clock. I was watching the dirt road; should it open wide, ready to jump to safety. Crowds of people, including Juanita and Richard, streamed out of the front entrance of the church. The ground continued to shake every few seconds and must have lasted one to two minutes or more. At the time we felt helpless. After services ended we got into our truck and went home to 611 N. Park Street in N. Mountain View.

Damages to our home were slight, but during the night repeated tremors and after shocks kept us awake. The miracle of this disaster was the relatively small number of lives lost, considering the nearly complete destruction in many areas.

Kathryn Peters

In Kodiak

My husband, Bill and I and fourteen month old Sam were living in Kodiak right down by the Breakers liquor store by the beach, and across from the new boat harbor. We went grocery shopping at Kraft's and then stopped off at Sully's for a drink just as the quake hit. Everything just rattled and rolled. It was really something. Things started falling, and then settled down; there wasn't a lot of destruction then. We went home and I tended a neighbor's child while she went to find her husband. She was pretty well shaken up. After she came back I took Sam and went down to the boat harbor to join Bill and check on the boat. It was okay so we went back to the house where we heard on the radio that Valdez had been hit with a tidal wave. Bill suggested we go up the hill, because we might have one of those. The dog sure wanted to go; he nosed us up the hill. Down below, the dock was full of people; they had heard that a tidal wave might come, but they just stood there.

As we climbed up Pillar Mountain, a friend stopped and gave us a ride. By that time more people were headed up. All of a sudden you could hear all these timbers cracking, all the log houses and things. It was eerie. You could see boats going end for end and oil tanks and things washing between Kodiak and the other island. When the wave first hit, it went right up into the schoolyard, and came back down and set everything right back down where they had been. Then it was like a bathtub, sloshing back and forth, higher and higher. There was a wall of water, and then it went back up the channel, leaving the channel completely dry at one time.

It was quite a night. When we took off I didn't take anything with us; I had nothing to put on my child. We came down the hill about 2 AM. My husband went to the boat and I went to the school. A friend took care of my child, and I started making sandwiches for the crew that was working. Like many people, we had no home and stayed in the schoolhouse for quite a while until a friend, who still had one, took us in.

On Saturday, my husband went looking for our boat. He eventually found it across from Kodiak, beached on the island across

Kodiak suffered little damage from the actual earthquake. The damage there was from the seismic sea wave, which left high water marks on these buildings.

the channel. It was a shallow draft boat, and it just sat right up there. Some of the others were pretty well smashed. He couldn't get back until Sunday because the military, afraid of looting, wouldn't let anyone back into the town. He had to go way around to get back to us.

When they let us go back to our house, we found one of the crab-processing boats had washed in and sat up on part of our house. I had an elk roast in the oven before I left: when I went back it was still there, but unusable, soaked in salt water. The back porch where I had my new freezer had been destroyed. The freezer washed away and we never saw it again. (Sears wrote our loan off completely.) In the house, I found about 50 pairs shoes, just one of each pair. I think it was what was left of a display.

There was a lot of stuff floating. The next weekend they asked any one with a boat to go out and try to pick up anything they could. We snagged quite a few boats in the water. I will never forget those big oil tanks. They had just gone end for end down that channel. All the boats had lights on them and nobody can figure out how the lights got there.

We lost everything except the boat. The government wanted to loan us some money, but they wanted papers on the boat, so we just started completely over. The next year I lost my husband to a cerebral hemorrhage, and I think it was from the stress. But Sam and I survived.

The tide is what caused the destruction in Kodiak. The earthquake itself wasn't that bad. We lost so many of our friends, people on boats, that they never found anything of, not even the boats. I remember one who radioed, "All I can see is rock." That was his last message.

Leo Powell

Peter's Creek

When the 1964 earthquake occurred, I lived in Peter's Creek in a little log house with my wife and six kids, the youngest just a baby. We had just sat down to supper when the house began to shake. I said, "Well don't worry about it it'll stop pretty soon," and it shook some more, and I said, "Don't worry it'll stop pretty soon."

Then we all decided we'd go outside. It was just five minutes or so, but it seemed like an hour and a half. I remember putting the baby and one of the little kids in the car. I can remember looking at that station wagon; it was sort of looking under your armpits or something. It would roll up and you could see the shocks, and it would settle down, and it would roll up and you could see the shocks. It didn't actually go anywhere; it just stayed right where it was.

Finally we chanced going back in the house, and in the living room most all the books had come off of one bookshelf, which also held a little bowl of goldfish. That slid almost to the edge, but didn't fall off. The kids were pretty tickled to have their pets. That was sort of a little incidental thing, but they still remember when they were little kids that the goldfish didn't get killed in the earthquake.

Later that night a family came to stay with us. Wesley Steel and his wife and some kids. He had been a mail carrier out at the Anchorage International Airport and he saw the tower go down at the airport with some men in it, and it really shook him up. So he rushed home as soon as he could and picked up his wife and kids and came out to our house. They were just going to stay all night and ended up they stayed a couple of weeks

That top part of that tower that went over is still near Palmer on the Butte Road. You could see it if you went there today; that little part of the tower is still there.

Susana Ramones

Frightening

I had only been here three months when the earthquake came. My daughter started to wash clothes down in the basement. All of a sudden the house was shaking. My husband was holding the baby (the first baby born in America; we were from the Philippines originally.) My daughter came up.

I understood it was an earthquake, but it was the first earthquake I had experienced. I was cooking octopus because we cannot eat meat on Fridays. All the pots were moving. I was cooking many things before we could go to church at 3. I was living on Mountain View Drive in a second floor apartment. I grabbed the refrigerator, which was smaller than the freezer, but I didn't want to go down the back stairs; they were shaking. I could feel the ground was moving. The pots were still shaking. I tried to pick up the octopus and put it back on the sink. Then I grabbed my baby, and looked under the table. I prayed to God, I said, "We cannot die" and I looked around, and I said, "Where is my son?" I have a son, about twelve, and I saw him running. I opened my window a little and looked out. I see the ground open in front of my house, crack open in front of my house. I started moving toward the door to go out.

It was really an earthquake, a bad one. The movement of the earthquake. You can feel that something is going to happen. And you can feel that you are going to lose your children. But what will happen if we go for good? What will happen to the kids? "God, if you are going to take me, I'm ready, but I want you to make sure my kids are with me when I go, who will take care of them? If I go for good I want my kids to be with me." I didn't want them to be left behind. It was frightening.

My husband was called to go back to work after the quake stopped. The military was giving water to the dependents, and I was one of those. My phone was not working at all, everything stopped.

It wasn't that bad at the time, but later, remembering, it is much worse. I wanted to go home, to the Philippines, but my husband was hurt, and didn't want me to go, so we stayed.

As the ground moved out from under them houses tipped from newly created cliff area onto the jumbled mass below.

Victoria Rearick

Is This Another One?

We had a mild winter that year. The snow was almost gone. It would be a nice Easter.

The children were home that day because it was Good Friday. My husband Jim and I had seven children, aged from thirteen and a half to three and a half years, two girls and five boys.

Dinner was on the table. The eleven and a half year old was delivering papers. The rest were watching TV, *Fireball XL5*. They really liked this show and hoped their father wouldn't get home until it was over. He came home.

While he was washing up they all took their places at the table. Chow Mien was dinner that evening. As my husband sat down the house started to shake.

He said, "Feel the earthquake. You always say you never feel them." The shaking did not stop, but the conversation did. The shaking accelerated. Things were falling.

The ten year old was trying to put the books back in the bookcase as they fell out. Jim seemed to be trying to hold up our house and save our new TV. I picked up the baby and headed to the dining room. My eldest grabbed the next youngest and we headed for the door. The thought was to get them all in the car.

We had to push the washer and dryer out of the doorway where they had literally walked away from the wall.

It was quite a feat to get in the car with it rolling back and forth. It was like a great wind bending the trees. The electric wires were snapping and crackling.

The shaking stopped and we went back in the house. My husband went in the cellar to turn off the fuel. Then it started shaking again. Jim ran up the stairs. As he came up it stopped. The youngest child always remembers that at that time he thought his Dad had actually stopped the quake.

Our eldest son was still on his paper route. It was getting dark. I wanted to go look for my son. He was only eleven and a half. My husband said, "No, we must clean up this mess and decide what to do for the night." I put my feelings aside and agreed. So, we all started to work.

March in Alaska, without lights, fuel or water may be rough going. My son finally came home. I was so relieved. He had a story to tell. He had five papers left to deliver. He was heading down the street. He looked down the street and it was rolling up and down. Then two houses lost their chimneys.

When he started down a steep hill he heard a noise behind him. He glanced behind him. He was teetering on the edge of a deep crevice. He couldn't see the bottom. He must step forward, but was frozen.

The house next to the street cracked in two. He was fascinated by the crack, and as he looked into the deep blackness the earth all of a sudden closed up again. He had two more papers left. He continued on.

As he approached an apartment building people were running out and screaming. One lady came out with a baby. She fell on her back and the baby went flying in the snow. All he could say was that the people sure acted strange.

We gathered next door. They had a fireplace so we had heat that night. The children slept on the floor. We had a camp stove to cook on. I can't remember how many nights we stayed there. Then Jim said, "It's time to go home." It took a while to get the electricity back on, so we could have lights, heat and water.

My kids didn't want to go to bed. Especially the twelve year old. I coerced him into going to bed. Then we got a huge aftershock. He was out of the bed, dressed with coat, hat, mittens and boots. I finally told him I would stay up and stay awake if he would go to sleep. He finally went to sleep with his coat, hat, mittens and boots on.

The aftershocks were scarier than the earthquake itself because you kept thinking, "is this another one?"

We survived with only a small damage to the house, but a big mess to clean up. And our family was all safe, but a little on the nervous side as aftershocks continued to plague us.

Diane A. Rediske

We Moved Into the Hallway

As I poured myself a fresh cup of coffee, the house began to shake.

Earthquakes were no unusual occurrence in Anchorage, Alaska. You could be confident they wouldn't last long. My reaction was usual and automatic. First: be sure where each child is. Second: don't get overly excited. Third: prepare to move everyone into the hallway, if it should continue or intensify.

On this Good Friday, we moved into the hallway!

The house was shaking, jumping, and twisting so wildly it was necessary to lean into a corner to remain standing. My three children, our cat, and I occupied about one square foot of space in that corner. One child asked, "Mom, isn't it going to stop?" My reply was, "I don't know." It seemed an eternity before it did stop.

The house was a shambles; but I was thankful it was standing. The horror was far from over. Amid continuing shakes, we slowly received news of the calamity wrought by the quake. We were among the fortunate.

A quake now brings the same immediate thought to all who experienced Alaska's big one ... "Is it going to get worse?"

Vernice Reid

Little Dried Fish

I was in Penney's with my mother who was visiting from Fairbanks. We were there to see the first escalator in Alaska. There was a big display of beautiful potted Easter Lilies, and I was buying one for my mother. While I was writing the check, the earthquake started, and kept going. It was absolutely horrifying. Incredible. It lasted so long. The building jumped off of its foundation. The sky was open between the first floor and the top floors. You could see daylight.

I had a cut across the back of the neck. It was not serious. There were not many people in the building; they were screaming and yelling. You could see the commotion on the street. Telephone poles were dipping to the ground and returning back up. Mother said, "Oh, it's going to be alright." She dropped the lily. Then the curtain wall fell and it became dark. A man was trying to get into his car when the curtain wall came down. The pillars of the building were swaying and breaking. We stood there with no place to go. When the movement stopped we headed to the back of the building to the parking lot. We made it out the door. Everyone was polite — not hysterical. A lot of people were milling about the parking lot, looking for cars. There was a woman unconscious on the ground. It was terrible to look at her. Her face was red. A woman wanted permission to get a blanket from a car to cover the woman. I got the blanket and said, "There's my permission."

We got to the car. "C" street was gravel at that time. We drove out and got up Sixth Avenue onto "C" street. We then drove to Spenard and turned off the gas in the rentals on Doris Place. (I lived at the top of O'Malley on the Lake.) I began looking for my kids. I found my daughter, Diane Rediske at her house on Tudor and Easy Street.

She was okay. I went to Import Auto where my son Daryl Methvin was working and he was okay.

My older son, Mike, was in the National Guard. I stopped at the Spenard home of his friend Carl Dumman, who was also in the Guard, to get information about their whereabouts. Mrs. Vernie Dumman had not heard from Carl. She was sitting her family down to dinner. Her way of dealing with the panic was to carry on as usual. She said, "Come in, we're just having dinner. Come in and eat with us. We're having stew." The stew was full of coffee grounds. Her well-trained children didn't say anything.

We went up to O'Malley and made it to the house. We had a battery radio. It talked about bridges out on Rabbit Creek and people stranded. They were looking for places for people to stay. Five or six people stayed with us, one pregnant. It was chaos. We took the beds apart to make more bed space on the springs. We had to dodge the glass from the china closet, which completely smashed. We had an eight-foot wall, which had fish tanks all along it. They were emptied. The tanks bounced the fish across the room onto the wall. For days we were finding little dried fish in cracks in the wall.

Daryl and stepdaughter Joanie, both fifteen, had been in an automobile. She thought they had four flat tires. They were so calm, and went about doing what needed to be done, without being asked. They got wood for the fireplace. They got ice from Hidden Lake to melt.

My daughter, Jackie Burns, was in Bremerton, Washington, with her husband and three children and pregnant. They couldn't get any reports so they packed up the car and kids and came up the Alaska Highway. It took them; I think it was two and a half days. I was shocked when I saw her at the door. All our chicks were in one basket, except Mike. We didn't hear from him for three days. They were on rescue missions.

Robert Renkert

Fifteenth and L

I had just returned from a business trip to Juneau that afternoon. The weather was mild. We lived on West Fifteenth Avenue just west of L Street. Our family included my wife Millie, and our three sons, Charles, thirteen, Andy, eleven, and Jim, three.

We were looking forward to some of the activities of Easter Week-

Bagoy Florists at 117 East Fourth Avenue.

end. It was not to be. Just as we were about to begin dinner the house suddenly began to shake violently. It was an earthquake! We took cover under an oak table and in the doorway. Thomas, our cat, ran out the door. I did not remember this, but Jim says he recalls his mother saying, "This is it! This is it!" It left a lasting impression on him.

Suddenly the shaking stopped. We were safe! A cherry pie fell off the counter. Now what to do. I filled the bathtub with water. We had power. We checked our neighbors. Next door our neighbor's carport collapsed soon after he parked. We could see cars moving toward Spenard on Minnesota Drive.

In emergencies you think of communication, which at this time was radio. KENI radio was on the air with Jeannie Chance reporting. Later KFQD came on the air.

People in our area were advised to move further inland in the event of a tsunami. Our older sons were helpful in loading the car with sleeping bags, etc. We drove the dark streets with occasional wide pavement breaks to the home of friends in Grandview Gardens where we spent the night. They had two boys near the ages of our older boys.

We drove home the next morning to bright sunshine and fresh snow. We had a fireplace and some neighbors joined us to enjoy the warmth from it. We learned that the Four Seasons, a new apartment building nearly ready for occupancy, had collapsed.

At the time of the earthquake I represented a photographic company and had merchandise, including a number of Wollensak tape recorders, in the basement of the Bagoy's Florists building which was damaged beyond repair. This company was one of the few with earthquake insurance.

Our Lions Club meeting the following Friday was at the flagpole on the City Hall lawn as our regular meeting place was destroyed. Ham radio operators performed invaluable service in getting messages to the lower forty-eight. A friend traveling to Seattle phoned our relatives that we were safe.

Our cat came back!

Doris Rhodes

The Calm Box Boy

I had just checked out my groceries in the Spenard Safeway store. They were in the basket near the door when suddenly there were loud rumbles and the building was bucking. The ceiling tiles were falling and the merchandise was cascading off shelves into the aisles. Light fixtures were dangling from the ceilings, swinging with each shock. My first thought was, "I paid for these and I better get them outside." The next instant I gave up on the groceries and staggered out the door to the parking lot. I wondered, "How far out from the building do I have to be before the front wall won't fall on me?" I joined four ladies and a box boy in the parking lot. We could not stand alone so we all joined hands. I remember reaching out to steady myself on a car and it walked away from me. The parking lot was full of cars, and it was acting like someone was shaking a big rug, which went up and down, cars and all. It seemed like nearly a foot high. I could smell natural gas, which alarmed me, because I had left my daughter, Sue, home with my four-year-old son, Mark. Would she think to turn off the gas? Someone said, "I've never been in a quake this bad." Another one said, "Neither have I and I've been here fifty years." We were bordering on hysteria, but that boy said, "It will be all right." He was the calmest one of all and I have never forgotten how helpful he was.

After some shaking subsided I decided I had paid for the groceries and I needed them, so I braved going back inside to locate my cart. A pregnant lady was screaming in the back of the store by the dairy section. I never did hear if she had a baby there or not. With all the aisles full of debris she couldn't get out alone. The checkers were asked to stand by the check stands to prevent theft. I was lucky my groceries had all been checked.

We live about a mile east and with no electricity there was no street light working. I remember wondering if cracks in the street would be big enough for the car to fall into. They weren't. People were very good at the intersections about taking turns.

At home, Sue sat on the living room floor with Mark in her lap while the house hopped around like a rabbit. My husband, Glen, had been home, too. A gold fish bowl sat on the drain board with two fish in it ready for me to change the water. Glen kept it from crashing to the floor but a lot of water slopped out. Later both fish died from the chlorine in the water I had to add.

I was working then on Elmendorf AFB with electronic engineers who were HAM operators. Some of them were up two full days and nights sending messages to families outside. Our older daughter, Glenda, was away at college in Oregon, and people down there called her for news of us. The TV and newspaper gave locations of the most damage and she realized our new house was not in a risk zone and rightly assumed we were all OK.

Karen Sue was a senior at West High School, one of only two high schools then. West sustained major damage and after a week school resumed on double shift at East. Sue said as they entered late shift at East there was a big sign saying "Welcome to East." The next morning East was greeted with a big sign saying, "Welcome to West Annex." They spent six weeks until school was out. Then, where to have graduation? The Elmendorf base commander invited the kids to graduate on base in a big hangar. Each school had something like 500 graduates. We had one of the schools crossing the stage to receive diplomas in one direction while the other school crossed in the opposite direction.

At home we had a newly finished basement rental unit that was unoccupied. We lined up for shots and while waiting in line I saw friends who I knew lived in Turnagain. They had lost their home, so I said, "Well, I have a unit. It has no heat but you are welcome to it." In two hours they moved in plus took in another couple that had also lost their home. Upstairs we had a fireplace but no water, toilet, electricity or heat. The man upstairs worked in Mountain View Sports Center and he came home with a portable camp stove, a folding potty with plastic sacks, and flashlights and batteries. I can't remember where he got diapers, but we had all we needed.

Bev Ridder

Rescued the Ivy

My husband, Jim, left for work on Elmendorf. Our three girls were in the house and Barb had gone to the neighbors to get me some sugar. I had planned to go to Penney's and have my hair fixed for Easter weekend but thank God I changed my mind.

Suddenly our dog, Muffin, started barking and running in circles, and pretty soon the house started to shake. Dishes came flying out of the kitchen, I tried to get the front door open to get Barb from outside but it was stuck. When I got it open, I grabbed the girls, started outside, looked back and saw my beautiful ivy plant on the table so I ran and set it on the floor. Funny how you do dumb things.

Later that evening we went to the Turnagain area to help people who were hurt and lost their homes.

We had no heat or lights for several days. Had to get shots so we wouldn't get sick. That's a day we will never forget and pray to God I don't see another one.

Dale Riley

"Please Dear God"

Letter written to my sister April 8, 1964.
I lived at 1824 Logan Street in City View.

"Sorry I was a little shook over the phone but second quake last Friday unnerved most of us for a couple of days again. I'm fine now! As I mentioned, I will relate the events of March 27th.

I was enjoying a three-day Easter vacation, as I didn't baby-sit that Friday. The house was shiny clean and so was I from head to toe, the children started to watch their favorite TV program *Fireball XL5*. The paper had arrived; I had poured a small glass of wine and was just relaxing before preparing dinner. I was standing in the living room when a gentle roll began — these we have had before — no cause for alarm — the quake was stronger, the TV went off — I grabbed both children to me as they were becoming alarmed — the quake grew stronger — dishes and glasses were crashing in the kitchen — the house is moving violently — what to do — stand under the strongest part of the house — "Mark, get away from the window!" Cindy is screaming for her Dad — I am praying, "Please dear God" — Mark asked "is God doing this — must calm his fears — "No dear — the earth is shifting and it is making it shake — now quietly I prayed again — "Please God, don't let this be the end." We were standing by the door and it flung open. I closed it and seemed to be trying to hold the walls up and yet in another moment I would have grabbed the children up and reached outside. We were on our knees as it was impossible to stand. This must be the reason I didn't get outside. That and the fact for my first hesitation was Cindy was still running a fever from a badly infected ear. It had been lanced Tuesday, and I hadn't allowed her to play outside. The noise from the twisting of the house and the crashing inside was tremendous. Then the quake subsided — and silence! All utilities were off. The kitchen was covered with broken glass.

My thoughts were also on Jerry hoping he wasn't in a liquor store doing display work, a bad place to be. I thought of Leah and Margo, wondering if they were at home on the ninth floor of the "L" Street Apartments. I knew that and the McKinley Building must have swayed violently but was sure they would withstand the shock. I had to get that broken glass up while it was still light out. Catsup and honey spilled on the floor — no water to clean it up. Cindy still kept crying for her Daddy. A few minutes later Jerry came home, very much unnerved. He was at the Traveler's Inn having a drink with a customer when the quake hit. As soon as he realized this was a big one he said, "Let's get out of here," as glasses were already crashing to the floor. They stood in the parking lot and he said the cars were bouncing up and down and sideways and all ways. Why they weren't all smashed, he doesn't know. He was greatly relieved to find us okay. He told us to get ready to go to his bosses place as they had a fireplace and we could be warm. Cindy said, "We're not coming back to this house are we — it shakes!"

By this time radio station KFQD was transmitting on emergency power and we picked them up on our transistor. We knew downtown Anchorage was a mess and the Penney's building in shambles — our thoughts were on the last minute Easter shoppers. How many casualties? We still didn't know about the Turnagain area. We put blankets and medicine in the car and took off for the Harts. They had more breakage than we did — they had a good deal more to break! Jerry helped clean up the glass and built a most welcome fire. We found the candles and were sitting on the edge of our chairs when the house started to move again. We grabbed the kids and coats and started out the door when it stopped. Our hearts were pounding in our mouths — we didn't know if another big quake would come — the radio station was in touch with Civil Defense and they alerted us to be ready to vacate our homes and go to our cars and drive a safe distance from falling debris but to stay off the highways. All the children looked like scared rabbits and any tremble would set them off. By now other people were coming over to the Hart home. One couple and their young teenage boy had been in Penney's just getting ready to leave when the quake hit. They couldn't go out the door as the outer wall had already started to fall. The husband threw himself over his family to guard them from falling debris. He did get hit in the leg and received a beautiful bruise. They were lucky.

Another salesman with Jerry's company and his wife (newly mar-

ried) came over. They were living on the top floor of the Hillside
Manor Apartments. (Sixteenth and H.) Someone knocked on the
door and told them to "get out". Pat said he opened the door to the
hall — and there he was, looking over the City of Anchorage.

We kept listening to that very vital contact with events, KFQD.
Now we learned of the disaster at Turnagain. No news of Kodiak

**Entire west wall of the Hillside Manor Apartments, at Sixteenth
and H Streets, crumbled and fell away. The building was sheared
in an east-west direction at the third floor level on the south
side and the lower two stories on the north side. The building
was occupied but no one was seriously hurt. It was damaged
beyond repair and was demolished.**

— Seward — Valdez. How much more, we wondered. About ten
o'clock our time a ham operator from Seattle was in touch with
KFQD. Now we were horrified with the reports you were receiving
in the Lower 48. We ourselves didn't know what had all happened,
or what was to happen. We all had fear of fire. Each tremor would
hold for the unknown. Now we heard reports of a tidal wave in the
South 48 and it was rumored it was coming our way. All low areas
were alerted to evacuate. We, at the Hart's, felt we were high enough
in our area to remain put.

Then about 11 PM the lights came on — we were momentarily stunned. Jerry went home to check and see if we had lights and heat. The water was also working. Now it was reported a fire had started in the terminal yards. Alaska Distributor has their warehouse and office there, so Joe Hart wanted to check on that fire. The children and I went home and Jerry and Joe drove to the yards. I managed to get Cindy to bed, but Mark wouldn't leave my side. The lights and heat had gone out again. About an hour later Jerry came home. He had seen a considerable amount of the downtown area — it was unbelievable. We decided we might as well get some rest. We kept the blankets in the car and coats handy. Mark slept with us. We had some pretty good tremors that night — my heart was beating wildly. The night passed. Very considerately, the electricity came on and I cooked breakfast — then off it went. By now we were advised not to drink water unless boiled or Clorox added to it. We were checking on our neighbors when another strong tremor hit. We grabbed the children and dashed outdoors. I looked at Jerry and he was as white as a sheet. We were all trembling. The lights would come on for a while then off. This apparently was just in our area. The rest waited days before they had lights and heat. We boiled water most of Saturday afternoon, as we didn't know how long we would have electricity. We were constantly glued to the radio, wondering about friends, but couldn't use the telephone for a week as the Civil Defense constantly pleaded for people to stay off the lines except for emergencies only. The radio stations did a tremendous job on keeping us informed. Beth Riley called us Saturday morning to see how we were. Their rented home was destroyed. We told them to come and stay with us.

Saturday afternoon Mark and I colored Easter eggs. It was so very important to get back to normalcy as quickly as possible. The first part of the week the businesses that could, started to clean up and open to the public.

Saturday afternoon the children and I received our typhoid shots. Dick was at the house when we returned. He was in a Spenard cocktail lounge when the quake hit. He didn't waste any time getting out of there. He, too, reported cars bouncing like crazy.

The market near us was open so I decided we had better get a few items we would need. Some aisles you couldn't walk down because of the breakage. A real cute box boy ran all over that store for me — even insisted upon getting items right in front of my face!

Other people were helping themselves and I was being waited on like the Queen of Sheba!

The city worked night and day to restore order out of chaos. Monumental feats were performed. We were all settling down to pre-earthquake tasks, reading mail from loved ones, getting mail off. Friday your card arrived, we all got a kick out of it. Then the house started to roll, dishes started to rattle. Cindy crying. "Grab the kids and let's get out." By the time we reached the door the quake stopped. Cindy said, "I told you Mommy, this house shakes." We were completely unnerved again. Jerry arrived home shaking. It took two days to get over this. Up until this time it didn't appear people were leaving. True, planes had been full, but mostly with people who had lost their homes and husbands were sending families out until things settled down. After the quake Friday I understand there was quite an exodus.

What is to happen now, we don't know. We have all taken an economical loss. My own babysitting is at a minimum. I had so hoped to get a car this summer. Cindy needs swimming classes for therapy, and I just don't have transportation and can't get her there.

How greatly this has set Alaska and Anchorage back, time will tell. We are optimistic, but doubts do creep in. I wouldn't want to leave now as I might miss something. We certainly hope for a "bigger and better Alaska." This certainly is not the time for job seekers to come to Alaska. They would only cause an unnecessary hardship by being added to the unemployed, unfed, and unhoused. In a few months we should have a clearer picture.

Thanks to you all for your concern. All Alaska knows the rest of the nation was deeply moved. We are glad that most of the fears have been calmed. Our hearts go out to those who have suffered so."

James H. Roberts

Cordova

We had most of our stuff packed and were getting ready to leave the next morning for a vacation in the Lower 48. My wife had a skillet full of hot oil on the stove getting ready to deep-fry shrimp for supper. There was a deep-throated rumble that had no origin and then everything started shaking with a roaring sound like none I have ever heard before. It was all around us. It was impossible to stand, so we sat on the kitchen floor holding the skillet of hot oil in an attempt to keep it from spilling and burning us.

After about five minutes, that seemed to be an hour, most of the shaking stopped and just the deep-throated rumble continued. One friend said he saw the mountains in the Heney Range gallop from end to end like someone was shaking out a giant towel or blanket by holding onto one end of it and flipping it in the air.

About 10:30 PM my boss, Don Everly, who lived up on the hill, phoned and told us to get up to his place. He had heard on the radio station from Anchorage, that we would be getting a thirty foot tidal wave. The radio was also reporting that Cordova was on fire and the whole business district was gone. We didn't have any fires in Cordova that night and watched Orca Inlet for the tidal wave, which never happened. We did get an extremely high tide, which lifted the dock off the top of the pilings and set it down displaced so all the piling came up through the dock.

The small boat harbor went dry at low tide due to the level of the land raising an average of six feet as a result of the quake. We heard the next day that the US Coast Guard Cutter, *Sedge*, heading up the channel to get to deeper water, ran aground where the charts showed at least thirty feet of water even at lowest tides!

On Saturday we found that the road to the airport was impassable. It was a mess, with shear lines up to a foot wide at the top, some running hundreds of feet down the road in a crooked line with a difference in height of a foot or more between the two sides. The bridge pilings, made of railroad steel, were sheared straight across. The bridge surfaces were sheared just like the road, although made of reinforced concrete.

I was an employee of PNA (Pacific Northern Airlines.) We did not have any long distance communications either by telephone or Teletype, and, with the road out, I was selected to fly to the airport with Jim Smith , a pilot for Cordova Airlines, in a Cessna 180 to help handle any flights that came in.

We flew over the Million Dollar Bridge on the Copper River Highway and saw that it was no longer usable. Apparently the quake had sheared the four-inch bolts that fastened the span to the abutment and dropped the end of the span in the water of the Copper River.

On Sunday we got on a PNA Constellation and went to Anchorage where we saw some of the devastation, including the remains of the control tower. A PNA plane was sitting on the ramp hooked up to a power unit; the FAA was using it as a control tower. We flew on to Seattle where my wife, who was a former long-distance telephone operator for ACS, sat down in a phone booth, contacted an operator for the Seattle telephone service and placed calls throughout the country for people in Cordova to let their families know that they were all okay.

Warren Roberts

Abbot Loop

It seemed like a pretty ordinary day up until 5:36 PM when I began to wonder if the world was coming to an end and I was on my way to meet my Maker. I was on crutches because of a broken ankle and about 5:15 I went outside to check our oil supply. My car was parked nearby and I was hobbling past it when the ground began to shake. I dropped my crutches and grabbed the big tail fin on my car, but it started jumping and bucking so bad I dropped to my hands and knees in the snow to keep from falling over. I could see over the treetops, waving like grain, toward Anchorage about seven miles away. Every so often I heard a big clap sound, and each time a big cloud of dust would come up from the road in a fan shape.

We had a house on a daylight basement on a little hill beside Abbott LoopRoad (which became East 68th Street.) A crack or a fault came across the yard, hit my nice new fireplace in the basement, demolishing it, and continued diagonally across the floor and out through a door making a big crack in the foundation and threshold, and tilting the corner section of the floor. It raised the slab at the fireplace by about four inches and lowered it at the door by about that much. Upstairs, some furniture looked like they had been playing musical chairs.

Out from the house a ways was another fault about ten inches wide, I tied a weight on a rope and lowered it twenty feet and no bottom. When I dropped rocks into it I couldn't hear them hit bottom.

About that time, my wife Edna got home from the store, where a big pyramid stack of canned goods tumbled, some of it knocking her down and falling on top of her. She was so excited and scared she didn't remember driving across another great ditch in the road to the house.

I had a front-end loader, so it didn't take long to fill in the cracks, but I would sure like to be somewhere else if something happens again.

Louis Roger

Ride Em, Cowboy

We were in the kitchen, just sitting down for dinner when the quake started. The kids, four and five, were in highchairs. My wife and I jumped up and tried to hold the cupboard doors shut. I yelled to the kids "Ride those horses! Now come on!" They screamed with delight as the highchairs bounced around.

They laughed through the whole thing and never knew anything was wrong.

During demolition of earthquake destroyed buildings on Fourth Avenue, between C and D Streets.

Claude E. Rogers

Maintenance Superintendent
Division of Highways, Anchorage, Alaska

Excerpts from a 1964 Report

I was home at 1328 H Street, cleaning up in the bathroom. The house started to rock gently and I thought, "My, my. Another earthquake." Gently at first, but increasing in intensity until the floor lamps started to fall over. I staggered out of the house and hung onto the breezeway door. Across the street the cars facing north and south were rocking to the east and west, but not rolling back and forth. I thought at the time the force must be from the east and west. Another thought that I clearly recall, "How can a house live through this?"

In spite of the damage in my house I did not realize the magnitude of the damage in Anchorage. I swept up the glassware, picked up the flowerpots (one had conveniently dumped itself into the garbage can) and decided to check the Highway Department buildings because the power was off and also the water. I picked up Ben Peterson and we started through town. We ran into a lot of traffic and were detoured by guards that had already been set up. As we approached the east end of Fourth Avenue, water was gushing from a broken main. The roadway had sunk. When we drove into our own yard, water was gushing from a broken main there. The shop building had been shaken apart; large metal panes containing glass on both sides of the shop were out. In other words, it was a concrete structure with most of the sides gone.

On the radio in my car we heard a request for all Highway Department employees to report to the main buildings. My orders? "Go ahead and do whatever is required."

We had already instructed our foremen to find tractors and start south along the Seward Highway and north on the Glenn Highway to determine what our damage was — if we had any roads left. We found that there was a big break about three miles North. We immediately started hauling gravel into it. We also knew that there were large snow slides down on Turnagain Arm.

Ben Peterson rounded up two light plants, one hooked up to the shop building where we got our main radios on the air and the other to the service station so that we could pump gas and keep equipment going.

There were many conflicting reports. We heard that Knik River Bridge was out, but also learned that our crews in Palmer were checking on it. Our stations at Girdwood and Silvertip came on the air; they were badly shaken up. We learned that there were many people stranded there because of snow slides and bridges being out.

Highway Department employees were wonderful. We found that among our Engineering personnel there were operators and many other people who could be of assistance. However, at the moment there was no clear course of action except to start south clearing the Seward Highway and to check the Glenn Highway to the north. The Army loaned tractors. From the south, a foreman reported that due to the fog and darkness, it would be dangerous to fight the snow slides on the Arm, especially since there might be bodies in them. We advised him to wait until they could see to start work.

Information being broadcast on commercial radio was rather incomplete and, in some cases, inaccurate. There was a report of a tidal wave that was to come into Anchorage. Elevation of our shop buildings is 80 feet, most of the town higher. It would take quite a tidal wave to get to them.

About two o'clock in the morning, we heard a request for all agency heads to attend a Civil Defense meeting at 3 AM. Mr. Steen and I attended, as did most city and state officials and department heads, as well as the military. The City led off, assessing the damages and what the immediate needs were. Others followed. Others present immediately promised many needs, such as steam thawing boilers and thawing points. General Reeve said that there were airplanes standing by in San Francisco to bring any aid needed to Alaska. We were able to report that the road had been cleared of slides between Anchorage and Palmer and thence to the South 48. The Knik River Bridge was damaged, but was still carrying traffic.

Some of our employees had obtained water and made coffee. Most, like myself, had not yet had dinner at the time of the quake and had begun to get quite hungry. None of the stores or restaurants was open. Army rations began to show up here and there, so all those who had been constantly on the job, finally had a bit of something to eat.

Later that morning Mr. Steen and I surveyed to the south by helicopter. There were many snow slides and, with two tractors, our crews were only as far as Bird Flats. At Girdwood, I picked up a volunteer cat skinner, flew him back to the middle of the snow slides where we had a D8 dozer parked, and started him working his way toward Anchorage. Two tractors at Girdwood were taken across the railroad bridge and started north clearing slides. The Civil Defense people there had a list of people stranded in Girdwood, which we took back to Anchorage for broadcast.

As we continued toward Portage, bridge damage was evident. The concrete deck of the Twenty Mile River Bridge was paving the bottom of the stream. We landed at Portage, where many were completely isolated with no communications of any kind. The huge cracks in the ground were awe-inspiring, although we did not know at that time that the ground had sunk from six to eight feet.

By this time, we knew that there could be no immediate restoration of traffic around Turnagain Arm. However, with five tractors working, the road was open by about 4:30 PM. People stranded at Girdwood were able to return to Anchorage before nightfall.

Today it is May 23. Last night for the first time the road was open between the Kenai Peninsula and the outside world. We will be able to get traffic around Turnagain for the rest of the season on a basis of two hours a day except during high tides, when the road is flooded.

Eugene G. "Gene" Roguszka

The Red Paint Was Not To Be

The red paint was not meant to be. I had been working on the construction of an addition to the house, an office area and, along side, a darkroom consisting of a developing cubicle and a print room. This project was several weeks in the making.

The immediate task was to paint some sliding doors on the cabinets, which were to be of various colors. The first to be painted the color red.

I took out the bucket of red paint, opened the lid and started to stir the contents. That's when I began to feel Mother Nature giving me a hand. This was the big one. And it didn't stop. I managed to get the top back on the can of paint, and then got out of the house.

I wasn't concerned about the house. It was primarily a log building with frame additions. I had confidence in my construction work.

But I was immediately drawn to the plight of our five cocker/springer dogs, little guys in the 20-pound range. They were telling me, in dog language, that something catastrophic was happening. I took them outside. None of us could really stand up easily. I was the worst, having only two legs to keep me upright. Those little "people" were doing much better on their four legs each.

Their faces asked something else as we stood outside in the yard. I vividly recall holding onto a ladder which rested against the house while the little guys stood around me in a circle, shaking, and their eyes asking me 'what's happening".

I could see the driveway, some five hundred feet of gravel surface flowing with waves, which seemed to be a foot high. Cracks opened and closed. That scenario repeated itself several times. I could see the spruce trees, some 30 to 35 feet, bending. To this day, I swear those treetops almost touched the ground as they swayed back and forth.

And I can see, to this day, our little friends looking at me very curious and sorely frightened. They emitted no sounds, just the penetrating looks. The memory is unforgettable.

Finally, the shaking, rolling and rumbling stopped after what was indeed an eternity. Soon, Dolores drove in to tell me of her experience in the quake. She had stopped the car two miles from home on O'Malley Road, just off the Seward Highway. Together we entered the house.

Structurally, we suffered little damage. Sure, the chimney was bent out of position; mortar chips were wedged between the wall of the house and the chimney so that it was necessary to ultimately tear down that chimney (it served the fireplace). The chimney, which served the house heating system, survived intact.

Structural damage was minimal in the home of Gene and Dolores Roguszka on O'Malley Road. Chimneys and fireplace facings came tumbling down.

But inside the house the view was a mess. Dishes were thrown out of the kitchen cupboards, some debris of glassware, but thank goodness for Melmac. It bounced when it dropped.

The stairway leading to the basement level where our living room was located, as well as the office/photo lab under construction was truly a mess. The stairwell also housed storage cabinets for canned goods. Jars of cranberry sauce and mint jelly were smashed on the stairs. It took a long time to clean, especially since our water supply was now a five-gallon bucket. (Without power our well was useless.)

The downstairs living room was basically sound, except that the facing to the fireplace was now on the floor and atop the two cushioned chairs positioned on either side.

The office/photo lab addition was not as bad. The four-inch jointer had 4 steel, somewhat pointed, legs. At each leg concrete chips were evident; the shaking and wave motion of the earthquake had caused the jointer to rise and fall with such force that the steel legs dug into the hardened concrete floor.

For days after the earthquake, the aftershocks were quickly announced by one or all five of our little dogs. They ran to the door and moments afterward we felt the jolt or heard the rumble of the shock.

Believe me, we respected their warnings every time.

One chimney at the Roguszka home was pulled away from log cabin wall and had to be replaced. Another one was destroyed. Log structure received no damage.

Evelyn Rush

Tidal Wave Scare

We were preparing to go to church when we felt the first tremors. It often takes a moment to distinguish a minor tremor from the firing of heavy artillery from the military range. However, in this case it was soon apparent that this was not a minor tremor and I encouraged the children to run outside. I held Clark around the stomach with one arm and with the other I clung to our fence, as did Cathy and John. We could watch our house rock back and forth and vibrate and quiver. My neighbor came out her front door fighting to keep her balance. She was thrown into the snow on her hands and knees where she remained throughout the quake.

At this point I began to wonder, "Will it ever never stop?" If it didn't, surely the buildings could not endure. Thankfully it subsided and then we became aware of our stocking feet. The quake had lasted almost five minutes. Compare this with the ten seconds, which a bronco rider must stay on his horse. (I am sorry to realize too late that I might have been a rodeo competitor.)

Inside the house we found broken and topsy-turvy belongings. The piano had been moved ten inches from the wall. The kitchen light fixture, which hangs on a chain, was swinging back and forth like a pendulum. This became our indicator, our homemade Richter Scale.

I put warm clothing on the children in case we had to flee again, and began to clean up. I glanced out the window and discovered to my horror that the house directly across the Park Strip from us was in a crumpled heap. This was my first inkling that the earthquake had been far worse than I thought. (I was to learn later that the house had actually fallen into a chasm, which had opened, and all I could see above the level of the ground was the roof.) The tennis courts and the skating rink on the Park Strip now were in the bottom of the chasm, which was half a block wide and about thirty feet deep. It angled away from us to the northeast taking every-thing in its path and reached downtown.

There were unconfirmed reports that a tidal wave was approaching Anchorage. We were advised to stay tuned in. We listened fearfully. After ten PM a radio announcer, voice clearly shaking, announced, "This is a confirmed report! This is a confirmed report! A tidal wave is approaching Anchorage. It will arrive in approximately fifteen min-utes. All residents between N Street and the inlet are advised to evacu-ate immediately." I rushed the children out carrying sleeping bags, radio, etc. Because snow was heaped in the middle of the streets for removal, I couldn't turn my car around until I reached an intersection, so I had to travel toward the inlet, toward the tidal wave, before I could begin to travel away from it. The fire department arrived with a sound truck to warn the residents to leave. I drove away as fast as I could, aware that my fifteen minutes had just about run out. We fled to the drugstore parking lot, where we remained in the car until about 4 AM when we decided that the wave was probably not coming.

Saturday our terror seemed to increase rather than diminish. Trem-ors continued; reports of possible tidal waves continued. We were told that the oil storage tanks at the port were leaking and that we should take every precaution against fire, as Anchorage had no water. We continue resting, hardly sleeping, in the living room with all our clothing on, even boots until Wednesday.

Nerves were getting raw from lack of sleep, proper food (we had plenty, but all cold.) Sanitation for human waste consisted of fifty gallon barrels strategically located throughout each block, marked with a large yellow "X". Into these we deposited our plastic or paper bags. The honey buckets were disposed of and replaced daily by the honey wagon. Typhoid clinics were established at all the schools. The military brought water into town to the schools, where we went to get it, and we melted snow to wash our hands. The drinking water had to be treated with Clorox, or, if you had something on which to cook, boiled. On Monday evening we were warned not to use our fireplace, because the Inlet was covered with a layer of gas and oil from leaking tanks.

On Wednesday morning, the day of days, water was restored to our area. We instituted a "back to normal day." Sleeping bags were rolled up and put away, dishes washed, children bathed. John said, "Mother I think the earthquake is over now." He spoke too soon. On Friday we had another quake which, while comparatively minor, nevertheless destroyed our recently reacquired peace-of-mind.

Colleen Rutledge

Fifteenth and H

My nieces and I were decorating Easter eggs at my parent's house at the corner of Fifteenth and H Streets. When the earthquake began, mom said, "Get in a doorway" and nine of us crowded into her doorway. As soon as it was over we turned on the radio and the announcer reassuringly said we'd had a quake, but it was minor and nothing to worry about. God love him! However, we could look out the south window and see a cement block apartment building on the bluff at Sixteenth and H with all three entrances crumpled in on itself. The building had to be torn down. At the time Fifteenth Avenue was a major road out of town and there was a steady stream of cars on Fifteenth with smiling passengers who still didn't know the extent of the damage.

My dad was at his trap line at Judd/Telachulitna Lakes area and my husband was working on the railroad in Healy. Somehow my husband got a ride to Anchorage with Don Sheldon within the next few days. It was several days before we could get a plane out to pick up Dad. We were worried that they'd sustained more damage at the trap line than we had in Anchorage; but that was not the case.

Securing water was a problem but there was a man two doors down who had a friend with an artesian well. He kept our block supplied with a 50-gallon drum of water. We had no heat, so we all went to my sister's who had a fireplace. She lived very close to Turnagain, and for several hours that night we listened to people with megaphones going up and down the street advising people to leave the area because of expected tidal waves.

It's hard to explain the real damage the earthquake did unless you'd gone through it. When the earth beneath your feet is not safe, what is? It left me uncomfortable in tall buildings; enclosed places, such as elevators; underground or in tunnels; in large crowds and many other places. I don't let my gas tank get too low and I store water under the house.

Florence Schlegel

A Journal

We lived in a small home in City View. I had been raised in the Black Hills of South Dakota where I had experienced cyclones, hailstorms, cloud bursts and even been struck by lightening, and I had lived in California where I experienced earthquakes, but never anything of this magnitude.

Pamela (aged six) had no Kindergarten this Good Friday and when the quaking began she and four-year-old Bonnie were napping on the daveno. I was lifting baby Billy Joe out of his crib in the bedroom and it took awhile for me to realize that this one was different and I needed to get to my crying girls in the living room. With Billy Joe in my arms, I walked down the narrow hall. It was like being on a ship tossed from side to side. As I reached the girls I could no longer stand up so I sat on the floor between them. They were crying from fright. The lamp had fallen and the shade had hit Bonnie. From where I was sitting I could see out the window where Fire Chief Bernasconi's wife, son, daughter, and maid were sitting on a pile of snow in their front yard.

We had little damage in our home, but canned goods, dishes and jars of jams and jellies fell and broke and the glass imbedded itself in the tile floor making a sticky, dangerous mess. With darkness setting in, we chose not to clean it up, but laid many layers of newspaper down so we could get into the kitchen. In other parts of the house we found a fallen dresser, knickknacks on the floor, perfume, bottles of medicines, liniment and other chemicals broken on the floor, softening the tile and taking the design.

There was an earth fissure that snaked between our house and the one next door going across the street and under some homes cracking the cement.

The electricity went off immediately after the quake and our homestead battery radio was useless for a while as all the stations were knocked off the air, but about 30 minutes later KFQD came on with their own generator and later KENI came on. It was *Mukluk Telegraph* without end, interspersed with emergency messages. For a while we were completely cut off from the outside world with house-radios and phones useless. Car radios and the Civil Defense stations were the only means of communication.

The following are some entries from a journal I kept.

March 28:

I drew five gallons of water and chlorinated it with one-teaspoon household bleach. We were told we would be notified when the tap water is safe for drinking. If in doubt about the water we should continue boiling it.

They aren't sure if the water or waste disposal lines are broken, we can't flush our toilet, so we put plastic bags in the toilet bowl and, after use, tie them shut and place them on the snow in the back yard to freeze for later disposal.

The radio stations are running on a 24-hour emergency basis. The broadcasters are very tired. They eat sandwiches, C-rations and peanut butter, which make their mouth dry but they continue talking and have added new words to their vocabulary such as "chasms," "crevasses," "faults," "fissures" and others. They have made several appeals to the Air Force to stop flights of big planes from flying over the city as the vibrations are causing downtown buildings to shake making it dangerous for the wrecking crews.

March 29

Easter and the Resurrection took on an added meaning this year. We prayed for parts of our city and state to be resurrected from the devastation. This was our happiest Easter ever for our family to be alive and together, but our little Bonnie couldn't understand why the Easter Bunny could not jump over the cracks and find our house.

The downtown area is blocked off and patrolled by troops.

The children and I went to Airport Heights School and we all received typhoid shots.

March 30

We received delivery of the first paper, an *Anchorage Times* extra, Easter Sunday evening. (The Daily News published yesterday, also.)

Except that all schools are closed for inspections until further notice, this area of our city appears to be getting back to near normal.

Bill spent the weekend doing volunteer work and returned to his regular job today with ATU.

Mail delivery has resumed to all but the worst devastated areas. It is almost like Christmas with so many letters from family and friends who are concerned about our safety and offer messages of hope, prayers or assistance. Many said they tried calling Alaska long distance but only heard a recording stating, "Due to an Earthquake in Alaska your call has been delayed indefinitely." Some wrote they tried to reach us through the Red Cross. HAM operators were able to get through.

We were told to try our sewer by flushing. They don't know how much pollution could result from broken sewers so, when possible, we are to limit flushing toilets to once a day.

I find myself hesitant to get involved with a shower or bathing the children.

We are trying to get our lives back to normal and finally boiled and decorated eggs for a fun family project.

A *Quake Town Directory* was published in the paper listing temporary addresses and telephone numbers of locally displaced firms and also if the firms have Full or Limited Service.

Governor Egan's office urged workers from outside not to come up, influx would be an economic burden; despite all the warnings many people are coming, some with only an airplane ticket to their names.

April 13

Yesterday, Bill, as president of the Mt. McKinley Lions Club, and a party of 19 Lions, members of the press, etc. flew on Northern Consolidated Airlines to Afognak Island to assess damage done by tidal waves. They met with the Afognak Village Council, BIA and others and pledged support of a relocation of the village to higher, safer ground. (By May some donated and some purchased supplies of tools, machinery, generators, construction equipment, home supplies, food and much more were sent to establish this new million dollar project of the 49th District of Lions International which later became known as Port Lions.)

Mid May

The demolitions operations in downtown area of Anchorage are almost done. It's a relief to many since the blasting of some buildings added fright as well as the aftershocks.

Undated

We decided to take a break and get out of town for a change of scenery for a few days and chose Halibut Cove. We loaded up the Scout and with our family of five drove out of town. All went well until we got past Portage, and found a sign. "Travel at your Own Risk" The land had sunk and the tide was just starting to run over the highway. We started across but the tide was coming in faster and stronger than we anticipated and we found ourselves in the Scout starting to drift down stream and Bill fighting the steering wheel. Finally the tires touched the ground enabling us to continue on. "What a scare!"

At high tide we arrived by plane at Halibut Cove. Found the land there had also dropped and, with our friend's home on pilings, we were feeling the aftershocks more than ever. Water would come into the lower level of their home and pulleys around the bed were used to raise it up. And to think we made this trip to relax!

Dr. Ruth A. M. Schmidt

Portage Lake

We were on Portage Lake, three geology students, a young man from the U.S. Forest Service and I, measuring the depth of the lake that weekend. We were near the center (534 feet deep topped by four feet of ice and some snow) when, briefly, the ice rumbled and shook. For a moment I thought the glacier, about a mile away, had broken and fallen on the lake, but the ice creaked and we heard loud rumbles of rock falling in the distance. We stayed together in the center, put all the equipment on the Arctic Cat and the sled and headed off toward the lodge at the end of the lake where we were staying (with permission.)

As we neared the lake's edge, we noticed some cracks, so we left the heavy equipment and tried for the shore. (I kept my skis on, the better to span any sudden cracks.) However, the ice was oscillating, moving up and down about five feet. It had broken up all along the shore, forming a pressure ridge with open water beyond. We reconnoitered and finally, just as it began to get dark, found an old moraine on the opposite (North) shore where we could get off the lake. We were cut off from the lodge, so we made for the railroad tracks, where we eventually found the home of a young couple whose job it was to watch the railroad tunnel. There we spent the night, and learned for the first time how serious the quake had been.

The next day a helicopter, out inspecting the railroad, landed. We gave them messages for our families. About the same time, the man from whom we had rented the Arctic Cat appeared. Concerned about us, he had hiked the seven miles from Portage to the lake the night before. When he saw our equipment, he assumed we were probably all right and spent the night at the lodge. In the morning, he got the Cat and then followed our tracks to us.

The small helicopter flew us back to the lodge, where we packed up and spent the second night at the trailer of our helpful Cat man. On Sunday, about noon, the Army H21 (banana) helicopter picked us up and flew us back to Anchorage.

After photographing the mess in my house, I checked on friends and learned of a radio request for all geologists to meet at 8 AM on Monday. At that meeting, I was appointed coordinator of a group to map the landslide area as soon as possible. By 10 AM we had geology passes (signed by me for the police chief.) The entire area needed to be surveyed, maps drawn, test holes drilled, recommendations made, reports written and defended. We met and worked and worked and met. By April 13th we had the first draft maps available. During those first hectic two weeks I had my dinners with the Hillmans. It was a blessing because I didn't have to worry about meals and hilarious, too, as each day brought different dinner guests and new earthquake stories.

By May 17th I was able to write to my family "The town is back almost to normal in activities, though they say it has sunk three feet from the weight of incoming geologists."

Vern Schulte

McKinley Building

We moved into the McKinley Building (later called the McKay Building) in 1952 while they were still finishing the interiors of the tenth floor on up.

I was off duty from the Anchorage Fire Department sitting in the Blue Mirror cocktail lounge on the street level. It was kind of a neighborhood bar and several people were in the lounge.

When the earthquake struck initially it was like a ripple. We didn't pay much attention. Then all of a sudden it was no longer a ripple. It was like a giant pile driver. I asked people to stand in the doorway, which is supposed to be the safest, and we all did. This building was going up and down like a giant pile driver; bottles were crashing onto the floor. A real big pinball machine was standing inside the room. It finally crashed out onto the sidewalk through a plate glass window. Chunks of concrete were popping off the building. This thing went on and on. Finally three of the fellows in the building panicked and ran out into the street. After what seemed like a long long time it finally stopped.

Being on the Fire Department at that time I knew that the building had just been converted to natural gas. Knowing about the gas line I immediately ran around to the furnace room to shut off the valve, not knowing if the main valve on the line going out of town was going to function as it was supposed to. The furnace room door was locked, but fortunately some maintenance people were still there, and I located and asked one of them to unlock the door. We shut off the valve. I rounded up a couple of flashlights and organized a search and rescue up through the stairwells and on each floor. At that time it was a big apartment building. We went all fourteen floors up the stairwells, and half way down each floor, and looked in the apartments.

There was hardly any clear floor space in any of them because of broken dishes. Amazingly enough every once in a while I would see a knickknack shelf with little figurines on it amid the mess all around it.

Fortunately, at that time of day, people were not home yet. To the few people that were there, I told, "Please meet across the street in the parking lot." I got back from the fourteenth floor and across the street to the parking lot. This was the first opportunity I had away from the building to see what the building looked like from a little distance.

It was tilted very noticeably about 10 to 15 feet out of plumb. It was like a leaning tower. Then somebody said, "I don't see an invalid from seven something," and somebody else said, "I don't see somebody from eleven something." After having seen the tilt of the building I really didn't want to go back in the building, but I did, and fortunately those people weren't there. Then I got back down and immediately walked down to the main fire station.

They announced there had been a severe after shock. Later on I found out that it had straightened the building.

Rosie Selk

We Enjoyed Ice Cream Before it Thawed

I lived in Spenard and cleaned homes while my husband worked at the city shop as a mechanic. I had just gotten home from a house near Turnagain Arm when the earthquake started. My oldest daughter had macaroni cooked and dished plates for the children. The plates were on the counter and started sliding around.

I told all the kids to go outside and hang on to the fence. As I went out after them the garage doors were opening. My car was going out in jumps. We went back in, but kept getting after shocks.

The cupboards with the drinking glasses were all over the floor and the food with plates was there too. In the two-car garage we had a barrel wood stove. We built a fire in it. I told the kids not to run the water because we needed it for drinking. The kids had taken a bath and didn't drain the tub so we used the water to flush the toilets.

We had gas lamps and kerosene lamps on hand because the electricity would be off pretty often. I called the neighbors over and since we had a barrel stove going, they came over to keep warm. We all enjoyed ice cream before it thawed out. We set up a camp stove to cook on and later that evening we put mattresses from the kid's rooms on the floor. No one wanted to be alone, because the after shocks would scare us thinking we may have to rush out again.

Bruno and Martha Seppi

Sand Lake

We lived on Sand Lake Road, now the Southwest ramp at Dimond and Minnesota Drive.

I was a registered nurse working in the nursery at the new Providence Hospital. Another nurse and I went to first lunch, so we were in the cafeteria when the shaking started. The electricity went off quickly, all that were in the cafeteria went outside via sliding glass doors. The five-story building was convulsing violently as if it were made of toy blocks. Trees were whipping back and forth in the woods, and the earth was rolling like big waves. As the earth cracked open, puffs of soil spewed forth on top of the snow on the ground.

When it quieted down, we all returned to our stations. The twelve to fifteen babies were all fine; bassinets were strewn around like a setting sun. Pediatrician Dr. Helen Whaley came quickly to check the babies. She offered to come back after she made her rounds, as she said she was sure I would be worried about my children at home. Radio appeals brought in plenty of nurses to relieve us, so I went home about ten PM.

Bruno was on his way home from work at Elmendorf AFB, and stopped at Carr's grocery on Seward Highway and Thirteenth St. (I believe it was the only Carr's then.) When he stopped in the parking lot, he thought someone was jumping on his car until he saw the electric lines rolling like jumping ropes between the poles. Stucco was falling off the building. The store was without power, and burglar and fire alarms were on, but no cash registers, so he proceeded home.

Good Samaritans had already placed planks spanning the large cracks on the road, so he did get home, and was relieved to see the house still standing and the children safe. A large crack had gone across Sand Lake Road, up our hill and across the front of our daylight basement, severing water, sewer and power lines.

The interior of the house was messy. The refrigerator door had flung open, and contents spilled onto the floor. It then closed up again. Books had fallen off shelves, but no major damage.

Fortunately, we had a fireplace in the basement, as well as a woodpile, so we could keep warm. Some neighbors without heat came to spend the night. Our house trembled most of the night. No phone or electricity, but we had a few candles.

Next day we went to Spenard to check on friends. They were okay. We saw much damage on roads, buildings and especially the high rise apartment buildings.

Pressure ridges and cracks along the north side of O'Malley Road. This area was referred to as Shannon Hill. Note the drive coming in from the right, just beyond the railing. The hill was cut down substantially during the next improvement project. This is now the intersection of Lake Otis and O'Malley Road.

Trucks with free bread were in various locations, for which we were thankful.

The Good Friday earthquake was an experience we shall never forget.

Sylvia Short

Happiness is a Shower With a Friend

We escaped the Earthquake! A friend, Marian Bell, was housesitting for us, a warm, friendly, delightful person. The house was apparently undamaged, and there was a good supply of firewood for our fireplace. Since there was warmth and lots of room, our friend invited a number of others in less fortunate circumstances to join her with their sleeping bags, camp stoves, food and liquid supplies. A jolly group was thus assembled, and it wasn't remarkable when, glancing out the front window, she saw a fire truck drive up. She went out to see whom she had invited this time, and it was then that she discovered that while burning everything up in the fireplace they had inadvertently set the roof afire! It was soon put out, and the firemen were invited to join them for a taste and a laugh!

The assorted group fared adequately, but bathing was sorely missed. Thus, when the transistor radio announced that there would be water for washing for a short time the next day, they drew straws, and two ladies who knew each other well shared the "shower." Marian said the motto for the day was "Happiness is a shower with a friend."

The extent of the news about the Great Alaska Earthquake didn't manifest itself to us right away. While it was publicized all over the reading and listening world, there are fairly frequent calamities around this sphere, which claim similar news headlines which don't engage public attention for more than a day or two.

Nevertheless, in 1970, a full six years after the Earthquake, while my husband and I were traveling in our brand new motor home all over the South 48 we ran into this contradiction.

We were proudly sporting our Alaska license plates, because both the motor home and people from Alaska were sources of interest to those outsiders. As our travels took us through the southernmost parts of our country, we noted signs that some kind of disturbance had been in the area. There was a group of new houses along the roadside, apparently just built, with bricks for their fireplaces strewn all over one side of each yard. I remarked to my husband that it seemed strange that they didn't build the fireplaces till last, and he sagely reminded me that we were in "twister" country and that this area had apparently just been visited by one.

Shortly thereafter we stopped for gasoline at a service station, and because the 80-plus gallons took some time to pump I wandered a bit around the area. Right in back of the station was the wreckage of the roof of a house sitting on the ground. A good roof, fairly new with shingles, and nothing underneath it but weeds.

I rushed breathlessly back to the motor home to ask the attendant (they had them, then) what had happened, only to be forestalled by his remark "So you're from Alaska. They have terrible earthquakes up there, don't they?"

Fourth Avenue between B and C Streets just prior to demolition project.

Vera Specking

Hope

Excerpts from a letter written in Hope on March 29th

Everybody in Hope is okay from the earthquake. It was a lulu and then some! We all got outside the house. After I got thrown off my feet three times in a row, I stayed down in the snow.

Now, we are still dodging high tides, tidal waves, or whatever they are. This morning it was all over our driveway and up in the woodshed out back. Twaits are moved out, DeFrances are out, the water is in their house three feet deep when tide is high. It has been across the road from your fence. What a time! We went 48 hours without sleep, but got a little last night.

Just came back in the house (had another sharp shake.) So far we have had forty-five to sixty shakes since the big one, some pretty rough.

I went over and checked your house. Your chimneys are intact and what pictures were down fell on something soft. Everything else breakable I put down either on the floor or the bed or sofa. There was less damage in your house than in any other in the community. The barn was not in a mess.

Just got a report on high waves in Seward — it's evacuated. We are evacuating to Clark's to be on the safe side during ever-higher water.

Food supplies not too bad but not too good here. It is rationed. There are bridges and roads out everywhere. The roads may be out three to six weeks or even longer. I suggest you stay there until things settle down a bit and we find out what is what. We don't worry. The water was two feet deep in our barn and within twenty-five feet of Thorn's new house so far. Hope it doesn't get any higher! A helicopter came in to see if we were in trouble. We are on the highway radio system, so we are not completely isolated but I don't know how they can get any mail to us. Just wanted to have this ready in case I get a chance to send it.

The post office is okay. It moved the safe about a foot and made a mess. The library is strictly in the middle of the floor. Little Dipper Inn and Post Office at Girdwood burned down. We were very fortunate — no fires, no injuries.

Beached boats rested in sections of the downtown Kodiak business area following the seismic sea waves. These waves reached a height of twenty-nine to thirty feet above the mean low water.

Betty Stark

City View

I was having coffee at a neighbors. We sat there looking at each other saying "another tremor". And then it started to really shake. Suddenly I decided it was time to get home and see if my daughter and her friend were all right. Later, the neighbors said that I had trouble running home, what with the land waving and the cars bouncing around, but I didn't remember any of that.

In all the old movies they always ran out in the streets so the building would not fall on you. (That was before there were any electric poles.) So there the two girls and I were standing outside along with the two dogs. In the meantime my sons were sleighing over at Airport Height School, and could not figure out why the cars were having such a time driving on the road.

My neighbor's husband was in the Reserve and was called to help down town, so she, a daughter and two sons came over to stay with us. That made the total of ten of us. Thank goodness we had a fireplace to do what cooking we could. We pooled our food so had plenty to eat.

We didn't think we were in shock but that evening, but when everyone had to find a place to sleep, no one wanted to go in the bedrooms. So I stripped all the beds for blankets to use in the living room, and only then recalled I had ten sleeping bags in the boy's room under a bed. That also turned out to be where our two cats were hiding.

We did not have much damage to the house, just things thrown around. The boys had a three-gallon fish bowl in their room on a dresser, which bounced around so that it was in front of the door. Even after we pushed the dresser away so we could get in, to my surprise there wasn't any water on the floor.

When it comes down to it we were very lucky as none of us were hurt. The kids thought it was a big party, and then, to make it better, there wasn't any school.

278

A. Evelyn Stevens

Earthquake Flu

I was at Lake Otis Parkway near Twentieth when the quake hit. My friend and I managed to stagger across the small room to grab speakers and the TV and leaned against the wall near a large front window (not very smart). A Volkswagen bus heading north on Lake Otis Parkway bounced across the road into the opposite lane and pressed against the far curb. The poor driver climbed out in apparent shock and tried to check his tires. As I watched the telephone poles bend, I kept thinking, "How can that be happening?"

It was all-unreal as the time went by. The sound of the house screaming and screeching as it rocked and squirmed. Supplies, and heavy objects fell out of all the cupboards from roughly east and west and crashed to the floor, dumping everything breakable, covering the entire kitchen floor.

I watched large heavy recording equipment on the north wall of the room. The part of the system on top of the center leaped off from east to west. The heavy tape deck leaped out from the inside of the cabinet from north to south at the same time. There was large picture on the wall which was literally spinning around and around against the wall on its a thin wire. It ended up crooked but never fell off. At the same time the newly made martini in a martini glass shivered and rattled on a ceramic table nearby but never moved an inch nor splashed out a drop.

As the minutes went by, an eternity, reality began to set in. Suddenly, I thought we were going to die. My four children were downtown in our home with their father, Joe. Fortunately, even through the damaged roads, we were able to get to them. We were all blessed. Little did we know how much damage there was only a few blocks away from my home. My little Corvair, under repair on Second Avenue, was thrown off the carrack. (It ran okay later.)

The Earthquake Flu. For days after the first quake the earth was moving all the time. This caused problems for those, like me, who had a propensity to nausea. About all we could do was take motion sickness medication. Not much fun!

The "second big quake" which hit the following Friday was even more frightening to many because it started the same way and hit hard. I don't recall how long it lasted but I was afraid it wouldn't end. I was at work on the top floor of the Elmendorf Headquarters Building. When it hit so hard, a fellow worker and I stepped into a doorframe and held on. Many were running to the stairs. My heart sank, as I knew some of the stairways had collapsed the week before. We were as safe as we could be in that doorframe.

One corner apartment completely destroyed in apartment house at 8th and M Streets.

Adeline Stoskopf

God Did Protect Us

My husband, Bill, and I were in our kitchen when we felt the quake begin. I was making chow mien for dinner. In a matter of seconds our dinner was on the floor, along with our one set of dishes, pots, pans, etc. I remember telling Bill, "We only have one set of dishes and now they are gone, too."

Our children, Crag and Janelle were not at home when the quake hit, they were up the street playing with their friends. When they came home they had to jump over the holes in the street, but they were not afraid. Oh to be a child! We were really worried about them when they weren't home with us.

Our living room was a disaster. The mirror above the fireplace fell down, our bookcase tipped over, etc.

The neighbor's big truck kept going back and forth in their driveway, we were afraid it would hit our car parked in our driveway, but luckily it didn't.

Our neighbor, Mary Brandt, was sitting in her car across from the Hill Building and when she came home she came over to our house right away. She had been thinking she wouldn't see us again, because we lived in a cinder block house! Mary sat up with me all night (Bill had been called to work at Elmendorf AFB.) Every time Mary and I felt a tremor we would run to the door, and stand there. Craig and Janelle slept through the night. They slept on the daveno.

We spent the next week living with the Brandt's. They had heat and water and we didn't. The following week we had that "30 second quake" and it started out like the big quake, so everyone was shaken again.

It was an experience I wouldn't care to go through again, but God did protect us.

Helen Strusz

Fifth and Barrow

Friday was always payday at Brady's Floor Covering at 145 East Fifth Avenue, and our slogan was "Under the arrow at Fifth and Barrow." The ceiling and floor covering installers were at the store to receive their checks. My husband, Clarence, a carpet installer was with the group.

The owner, George Paulson and store manager Jack Lee, Ted Millette and Pat Millette had just come in. Ted was a salesman; Norman Burgess was also there. Alice Alyward White, our credit manager, had left at five PM, but I was working until six.

We all agreed it was an earthquake when it started at 5:36, and grew with extreme intensity the next few minutes.

All of us were standing around our big "L" shaped counter as cans of floor paste and glue fell. Our own product, "KemKlean," sold in glass gallon jugs came out of the shelves under the counter and crashed on the floor. The gallons of carpet shampoo made a very slippery mess to walk through.

I stood in the office with my back to the wall that enclosed a staircase up to two small apartments.

It was very scary as I watched our big storefront window and saw the window starting to break in the upper right hand corner. As each wave came, more of the front window broke into pieces.

The entry door was to the right of that window and it was lined with linoleum standing on end on display. Those rolls of linoleum toppled crisscross like matchsticks. No getting out that door.

Our store manager crawled under his desk. Another employee crawled under another desk.

In the meantime the carpeting was falling off the racks that were mounted on the east wall. Rolls of carpets were also mounted on a rack with wheels and were moving all over the floor. There were three racks of that type. It was chaos.

As the shaking finally stopped we proceeded to get out. Norman Burgess offered his hand to me and we walked through soupy carpet shampoo. We tried to walk over the mess on the floor of carpet samples and other items in that area.

As we got to Fifth Avenue in front, I looked down Fifth and saw tremendous dust still in the air from the outside wall of J C Penney that had crashed to the sidewalk.

All the people who were in the buildings along Fifth Avenue were in the street. Some were crying, yelling, hysterical, hyperventilating from the terrifying, terrible experience.

Our car was parked in Brady's lot behind the store. My husband and I hurried home to check on our little house we rented from Ora and Ivan Stewart located on the corner of Seventh and A where the Federal Building is now located.

We traveled the alley to Barrow Street, into Fourth Avenue, and down to the corner of Fourth and A where Howard's Chevron station was located. We could not have gone farther up Fourth as one half of the street had sunk.

We saw that the Denali Theater marquee on the north side of Fourth Avenue had dropped to ground level.

We turned left on A Street to Seventh, and our little home was standing. Outwardly the only damage was the outside chimney. It had fallen off and crushed the high fence that housed Starlet the Stewart's reindeer.

In the house the TV on a stand had tipped over, pictures were crooked, and it was a mess, as to be expected. In the kitchen my little apartment size gas stove had wiggled out to the middle of the floor. The coffee percolator with grounds was on the floor. Things were out of the cupboards. My good dishes stored in the cupboard had all come out and were upside down in the sink, as were the old dishes.

We knew we could not stay in the house that night as the gas was off and no heat.

Friends, a military family living in Willow Park, asked us to come and stay with them. The government owned this and I felt with so many people affected, somebody would be there to repair and get them heat and electricity as soon as possible.

That night we slept on the floor with our clothes on. We had a radio on and we felt we might have to get out that night again because of all the after shocks we were experiencing. We stayed with them until the following Thursday.

On the Thursday after the quake my husband was having lunch at the house when the phone rang. It was the Red Cross calling telling us our son, who was in Florida on vacation, was coming in on Wednesday night by plane, and we should meet him.

The airport tower was down from the quake, so we were told to come out and turn on car lights so the plane could see the runway. The plane landed safely, and to find our son was a real task. We had flashlights to look for him. I do not recall how he claimed his luggage. Probably the next day when it got light.

I was pretty numb for a couple days but did return to work that next Tuesday and our gas was turned on by the end of that week. We were able to go back to our home to live.

The next Friday we had another quake and everyone remembered how fast to get out of the store taking the back door to Barrow Street. I was wearing heels to work during that time and of course I had them on, but I could not run fast enough in the heels to suit me and I swore I'd never wear heels again to work.

Emard Packing Company, Ocean Dock Road, Anchorage.

Arliss Sturgulewski

Anchor Park

Some events we witness are so dramatic that we retain a series of images in our minds. The images are as real and clear as a set of photographs. Such is my recollection of the Great Alaska Earthquake of March 27, 1964.

My late husband, Sturge, was a supervisory engineer with the Alaska District Corps of Engineers. He traveled to job sites in remote Alaska locations and was often gone from our Anchorage home for long periods of time. This was during the time of DEW line and White Alice Communications System construction as well as the military buildup for the Vietnam War. Our time together was always so very special.

Fortunately, Sturge was home when the earthquake struck. Our young son, Roe, was at a neighbor's house playing with friends. Sturge and I were standing in our kitchen dining room of our modest home in Anchor Park. The construction was wood frame on a concrete slab in an area of good soils. And how lucky that turned out to be.

We were enjoying our favorite end of the week drink of old-fashioneds. With the beginning of the quake, we watched in fascination as a boiling pot of king size Alaska prawns danced off the stove. Just behind us the doors on our hutch popped open and our wedding crystal cascaded out, crashing in tiny bits as it hit the concrete floor.

Our first thought was for the safety of our son. Our neighbors' home was just a block away from our home. I remember running and stumbling over heaving ground, which was undergoing severe seismic shockwaves. Upon reaching our neighbors' home, we found the five Bennett children and our son seated on the living room floor next to the wall. They had been watching *Fireball XL5* on television and wished the earthquake could happen again because it was so exciting.

Our friends, Gene Bennett, and his wife, Rene, had known what to do and made sure the kids were safe. Gene was then with the Anchorage Fire Department and what a wonderful person to have on hand for the Big One.

As we returned home, we found chaos. Our water heater had danced out of location and we were without electricity and heat. Our black cat, Miss Pris, was missing — later to be found between the blankets and sheets in our son's room. Never did quite understand how she got there — poor thing was terrified.

My wonderful husband determined that we must get the car gassed (we had no idea of just how bad things were — we just knew something very frightening had happened) and buy white gas so we could cook using our camping gear. Off he drove to a nearby garage and wouldn't you know, he was involved in a collision just a few blocks from our home. No doubt he hit or was hit by someone else out for his or her own response to the big event. No one was hurt but our car ended up in the shop for some weeks, marooning me while my husband carpooled to work (without his contribution of our car!).

We were without real news of the magnitude of what happened until a good friend of ours made it to our home around 1:30 AM the next morning. His apartment in the Turnagain Arms — just due north across Third Avenue from the Anchorage Hilton — was trashed by the quake. His tale of streets torn up — buildings on Fourth Avenue destroyed was so frightening. The reality of the devastation began to hit home.

Only later did we realize some of the blessings of that day. Most children were at home with their families when the quake struck. Many of the downtown office buildings were empty of workers. Tragically, lives were lost, including some friends, but considering the intensity of the quake it is a miracle that lives lost and property damage wasn't much higher.

Our lives were affected in many ways by that day but we felt so very lucky we escaped injury and other serious ramifications. But believe me when I say I am not ready for a rerun of that quake. It doesn't take more than a mere tremor of a small earthquake to cause my heart to race and my feet to move.

Evan Swensen

Montgomery Wards

"Mr. Swensen, you go to hell" Vera Stribling shouted back. The eighteen foot high divider wall of the Montgomery Wards store on Gambell Street was threatening to come loose of its anchors on the ceiling beams. The store floor was undulating like the back of a big snake, forcing the wall to buckle and bow — pieces of sheet rock were falling on the floor around Vera each time the wall twisted and turned with the pressure. I thought the wall was going to collapse on her where she crouched underneath her desk.

Stan Marquiss was standing between two rows of filing cabinets in the Credit Department. With each roll of the quake one side of the row of the cabinet drawers would slide out. Stan would run down the row pushing them back in, just in time to repeat the action on the other row. He wouldn't get them all back in before the other side of the row's cabinet drawers would slide out. He was loosing the battle. Finally he looked up at me standing in the doorway. He shrugged his shoulders, gave a what's-the-use look and walked away. As he did the filing cabinet drawers slid far enough to cause the cabinets to crash over into the isle — credit records flying everywhere.

I could hear breaking glass falling out of the front store windows and could only imagine the destruction going on in the showroom at the front of the store. I could see the racks of customer's orders buckling and breaking and crashing into heaps of chaos on the warehouse floor.

I remember the noise — it seemed the store was falling apart. I couldn't see any other store employees, except Stan and Vera and speculated in my mind that some of them would be seriously hurt. And then the noise and shaking quit. There was a moment of deafening silence. I could hear employees asking each other if they were all right. As each answered, it was soon discovered that we had experienced the same kind of miracle that we were to learn happened all over town — no one was hurt — at all. The store was in shambles — it looked like an explosion had occurred — but not even a cut or bruise to anyone.

I told everyone to take the money out of their cash drawers and put it in the safe and go home and check on their families. Of course it was immediately discovered that the phones were out. I asked each one to come to the store the following morning and let me know how their families were and if they needed anything. Almost all offered to stay and help do something with the store. I told them to just go home and check on their families and let me know tomorrow.

In just a few minutes I was left alone, wondering about my own family, but feeling some responsibility, as the store manager, to protect what was left of the store. I was also concerned about the people in the other two stores — one store in Spenard, and the Downtown store next to J C Penney.

A couple of large plate glass windows in the front of the store facing Gambell Street had broken. Large pieces of glass had fallen and imbedded themselves into the floor. Had anyone been hit by them there would have been serious damage, judging by what the glass had done to the tile and wooden floor. I don't know why we had plywood in the store, but we had a few pieces — just enough to board up the store front. By the time I got the plywood and tools ready someone showed up and helped me put up the plywood — then they were gone.

About this time, someone from the Downtown and Spenard stores came by on their way home and told me that the Downtown store was destroyed, but everyone was okay. That's when I first learned of the amount of destruction in downtown Anchorage. They told me that everything was as secure as they could get it at the Downtown store, but all the windows in the Spenard store were broken out and the store was wide open.

All the while we were putting up the plywood I could hear sirens screaming down Gambell Street. It was awful. When I was left alone again, I remembered that I didn't have a car. My wife had kept it to go shopping. As I was wondering how I could get home, she pulled up with all the children in the car. Yes, we had some damage in our house, but everyone was okay. I got in the car and we headed down Gambell Street toward home. By now it was beginning to get dark. The road was almost void of traffic. It was an eerie feeling driving down Gambell with no other cars on the road and no lights — anywhere.

On our way to our home we stopped by the Spenard store and arrived there just as the landlord pulled up with a pickup truck full of plywood. It only took a few minutes to board up the store and we left for home.

When we arrived home there was no heat and no lights and no phone. But we had camping gear and a fireplace and we made do. We were just grateful that everyone was okay. It was a long night; however, as I worried about the 40 employees and their families.

When morning came I returned to the Gambell Street store. I had intended to just get reports from everyone about their families, but instead, upon learning that all were okay — and after hearing many of the individual miracles each person related about their family's safety — the employees wanted to go to work. So we did. We worked throughout the day and put the store back in some sense of order. The employees from the Spenard and Downtown stores hauled all the customer orders to the Gambell Street store. By day's end we were ready for business and on Monday morning we were open, almost as usual.

Radio stations announced that people could pick their packages up beginning Monday morning. Among the customer orders were many items that they needed to get their lives back to normal. Within just a few days nearly all the orders were picked up — and new orders were placed.

When communication was established with my superiors I learned that ten rail cars of boats and motor were on the way to Alaska, but could be diverted to other stores. We were a catalog store, but unique in the Montgomery Wards system. We also did a great amount of retail — and boat and motors was an experiment. Top management wanted to divert the ten rail cars to other stores and take their losses. I insisted that they keep the boats coming. I remember my boss's forceful response, "we'll keep them coming, but if they don't sell, it's your job." I told him I'd take the chance. As it turned out we had to order another three car loads of boats and motors. Alaskans had a lot of work to do after the earthquake, but they also had money, and they wanted to recreate. We sold all our boats and motors and a huge amount of recreation and outdoor gear from the catalog. It didn't cost me my job. As it were, I kind of became a hero with the company. We had the best year of any Wards store — anywhere — ever.

But the miracle of it all was that none of our employees or friends or their families were injured. I've never know better people than those who worked for me at Montgomery Wards when the 64 Great Alaska Earthquake shock the city. They were real Alaskans — everyone.

Vera always enjoyed telling the story that she had told her boss to go to hell and she didn't get fired for it.

View from the Travelodge on Third Avenue to small, broken homes across the street.

Audrey J. Tait

API

It was after hours. Doctor had asked me to stay to get a report done. I was typing away to the drum of the Dictaphone at the Alaska Psychiatric Institute when a SHUDDER rocked the building. Back and forth, in a horizontal motion. On and on it went. Ceiling tile, pieces, and dust came down. I made it to the doorway of the office and anchored myself "as one" with the doorjamb — BOTH SIDES.

I "knew" I was the only one in the whole wing of the hospital. I looked down the long, silent, wide hallway past the doctors' offices to the big double doors at the end of the hallway, beyond which was the front lobby and escape to the outside. But I was confident where I was. The long hallway would be too hard to stay upright. I was good where I was. On the right side of the hall a door burst open. Two people flew out, running the other way to the double doors. One lost her shoe and came back to get it. I got out of there. There was no way I was going to stay.

Next thing I know I was in the lobby. There were bunches of people, patients, standing there, silent and motionless. I went outside to the far side of the drive where there were more people. I turned back around facing the hospital. There were two people in a car at the curb with the motor running and a light pole DIRECTLY above them swinging violently. I walked over there and said, "You better get away from the light pole. It's right above you SWING-ING." I went back to my spot. They didn't move. At some point I remember seeing the car drive down the driveway. I don't know when but they turned around and came back.

My next memory is driving west, down Northern Lights Boulevard in the area of the Bun Drive In. And I was able to do so. No impediment, nothing, in my way to getting to 3904 Arctic Boulevard. My daughters and husband were fine. My precious daughters, two and a half and eight years old rode out the quake in the big recliner opposite the TV. The recliner had shipped back and forth, side to side, in the small alcove in the wall. Miraculously they stayed safe. Husband was balancing the Coldspot refrigerator, as it was "walking across the floor." He had just made a dish of Jello and put it in the fridge. I have no memory of Cookie the dog, but I know she was fine.

The house survived, the Coldspot refrigerator was replaced in 1992-3, still running. Arctic Boulevard several feet to the south of our house received a crevice across it, 6 to 7" wide.

Even though there was such a great scare Anchorage remains my home.

Prior to the earthquake, the entry at the Alaska State Bank, 5ᵗʰ and E Streets, was even with the sidewalk. The building was thrust upward, leaving a definite "Step Up" in place.

Carol Theodore

Bread and Butter Stuck to the Side of the Counter

I was ten years old and lived in Spenard at the end of an alley. My cousins lived just next door, and some down the street. We played, fought, and tattled on one another. We walked to school. Other than that we weren't allowed to cross the street, so we all pretty much lived down that alley. It was almost all family and friends. A parent would go to the store and left the kids to play with the cousins in the alley.

One day our foster sister Rosie made us spaghetti for dinner, and afterward we lay down in front of the TV to watch cartoons. Mom had gotten home from work and fixed herself a plate of spaghetti and bread and butter. Dad was still at work. The phone rang. Mom answered it. The person on the other end said, "Earthquake."

Mom yelled, "Earthquake!" and we all scrambled outside as the earth began to shake. Mom held onto a pole and the dog. We stood in the doorway on the side of the garage. Telephone poles swung back and forth almost touching the ground and the garage door popped up. Out rolled Mom's car shimmying and shaking out of the garage and down the driveway, pulling the tool chest with it. Rosie's boyfriend's car rolled down the street.

When everything stopped shaking we went back inside. All the glassware had fallen out of the cabinets and shattered. Stuff that wouldn't have broken if it had fallen out remained safely in the cupboards. In Mom's room the gigantic glass piggy bank in the corner shelf had fallen down and shattered. There were pennies everywhere. The oddest thing was Mom's dinner. The spaghetti was upside down on the floor, and the bread and butter were stuck to the side of the counter.

For a few days we stayed in our double car garage. Not just us, but the rest of our family as well. It probably had something to do with having no heat except for the wood stove in the garage and the fact that pipes in our aunt's house had burst and flooded the basement. We didn't care, we were kids and we got to have a sleep over with our cousins. All the ice cream we could eat and hot cocoa made over the wood stove seemed like fun to us. Looking back on it, it probably wasn't much fun for the adults. Two families, both with four kids camping out in the garage, a mess to clean up, tsunami warnings to listen for, and aftershocks to endure.

Shattered glass from windows of the Market Basket food store at 530 E Street.

June Thompson

Iliamna Avenue

My husband and I and seven kids were living in Turnagain By the Sea on Iliamna Avenue when the earthquake shattered our lives. I was at the stove cooking dinner and my husband was in the living room reading the paper. Since it was Good Friday, the kids were home from school. If they had been in school, Terri, the next to the oldest girl, might have been killed as the room she would have been in was demolished. The two oldest boys were at a friend's house on the street behind us—McCollie—and when they saw the house behind the one they were in go down, sliding into the inlet, they came running home with a neighbor boy, no caps, coats or boots although it was snowing.

When the first jolt hit, I thought the kids were jumping off their beds but when a heavy ceramic jug above me came down, just missing me, I yelled, "EARTHQUAKE!" We had lived in Seattle, Juneau and Fairbanks and had experienced earthquakes.

When I yelled, "EARTHQUAKE!" my husband yelled at us all to get under the doorway but when it continued to shake, he told us to go outside on the patio.

The camper was swaying back and forth in the driveway and the trees were doubled over. The electricity was off and we couldn't get the car out of the garage so we all piled into the camper with me grabbing our dinner off the stove to take along. We drove downtown to see if my husband's office was okay. (Later a friend in Tacoma said she saw our camper on TV). The office was okay so we drove to a friend's who had a mobile home where we combined our dinners.

A tsunami wave was expected about 11 PM so we left three of the kids there and went home to check on the house. Good thing, as guards had already surrounded the area. We had no heat, no electricity and no water. A friend who had baby sat for me when we lived in Airport Heights and whose husband had a "sideband radio," called (still had telephone) and offered to get a message out to our families. I asked her to send it to Helena, Montana as I thought it would be a better chance for someone there to have a radio. They got the message to my mother-in-law, asking her to send word to my Mom in Wolf Point, MT but Mom never got it. I wrote a letter that Saturday, but with no electricity it didn't get postmarked here but in San Francisco. My mother wondered what I was doing in San Francisco. She had tried to find out if we were okay through Red Cross , but they were no help at all.

The tsunami never happened so we stayed in the house that first night—slept in the living room with sleeping bags and had a fireplace for warmth. Coats, boots, and caps were all beside the door along with important papers just in case we had to evacuate again.

We had a Coleman lantern and stove so we had light and could cook. The next day my husband took the camper to get gas and a permit tag to come and go. Then he took the car and did the same. (All during the time we were under guard, a guard member would follow anyone in who came to see us—this wasn't very popular with our teenage girls!)

The grocery stores were a mess but they let people in one at a time to get what foodstuff each family was allowed. The army had set up a guard at each entrance to Turnagain and they also furnished portable toilets and barrels out front for disposing of waste.

My husband was able to go to work in his office but then the city had him helping check out damaged buildings for safety since he was an architect.

The office had water so he would bring home a couple of gallons of water for drinking each day and I melted snow for doing dishes. A month or so later irrigation pipes were brought up from California and water was piped into our house. I took the camper oneday and drove to a friend's house that had water and electricity to wash clothes and bathe the kids.

The morning after the quake, we walked to the street behind us and found the side of McCollie on the Inlet was almost gone—a little later some of the houses did go down. The street sign was level with the ground. The whole area around our house sunk three to four inches. A deep crack in the back yard had opened up—you could drop a pebble down but not hear it hit bottom. A hole in our front yard sunk down about two feet but eventually closed up again.

We had about $12,000 damage to our house. We had to replace one wall in the basement and seal cracks in the floor, and one wall in the living room. However, we were lucky, I didn't lose any dishes even though plants toppled off the shelves on the divider between the living room and the dining room. Our dog took off for several days, but eventually returned.

It was a memorable experience but it was also an awakening that material possessions mean very little when you realize your family is the most important possession you have.

Aerial view, from north, looking south, of the Fourth Avenue demolition project.

June Timmerman

The Lord Bless You Real Good

My three sons and I had just returned to our home on Arkansas Drive in Spenard from town. We had been shopping for a suit for our oldest son, Paul, who was graduating in May. We bought the suit at Koslosky's and left it there for alterations. We drove home on exactly the streets that were hit hardest by the quake and had been home about fifteen minutes when it hit. My husband was on his way home, and he said he at first thought he had a flat tire or that someone was trying to push him, and he put his brakes on. Nothing happened so he pushed a little harder on the brakes, and by that time he knew what was going on so pulled over to the side of the road and waited it out.

Just before the quake, there was a roar that sounded like an angry sea or a rumble similar to a fleet of Army tanks all going across country at the same time. I was preparing potatoes to cook, and my phone rang. It was a friend from our church whose husband was in the Philippines building homes and a church for our Missionary work there. We were discussing whether Art would be back Saturday or Sunday or Monday. Suddenly Sheila said, "Feel that, it's an earthquake!"

I said, "Oh well, it'll pass," and our line went dead.

The boys and a friend of theirs, Ben, came rushing upstairs and said, "Let's get out of here, earthquake!"

I wasn't excited, just thought, "Why bother?" But all at once I discovered I hardly could walk across the floor, the house was heaving and bucking. It was the same feeling of turning yourself around and around, making yourself so dizzy you can't stand up. I started out the front door and down the sidewalk, and the ground came up to meet me. Ben reached out a helping hand and I took hold of it and then I reached out to my number two son, fourteen year old Kenny, and there we all stood in a circle holding hands in the middle of the driveway, trying desperately to keep our balance. There was a huge log house across the street from us and I kept thinking, if that log house breaks up, we've had it because I know the construction that went into that home, and log houses are hard to tear down. I remember thinking, why doesn't the earth open up, and actually waited for it to start dividing because I didn't see how anything that powerful could happen without some horrible results.

The fact that it was Good Friday went through my mind, and how on the same day almost two thousand years ago Christ was crucified, and how the earth went dark, and God sent the earthquake then, I thought, God is tired of fooling around with these people in Anchorage and is showing them who is boss.

I suddenly stopped thinking and started listening. The three boys were praying (my youngest, David, was next door playing) and one look at their faces told me they were horrified. People all up and down our street were screaming and running from their homes, windows and dishes were clanking, breaking into millions of pieces. The telephone and electric wires looked as though someone was playing jump rope with them. The poles were heaving and trembling like you would shake your finger at someone. I tried to console the boys and told them not to be frightened and not to panic, that it would be over soon. I was silently praying all the time.

Finally the earth came to a rolling stop, and to my amazement all the houses were still standing intact. The neighbors started joking across their fences and "staggering' over to talk to each other. We all dreaded looking inside our homes. When I finally got enough nerve to peek into ours, I wanted to leave home and let someone else clean the mess up. All our canned goods were on the floor; everything that was breakable was broken. The biggest mess was the catsup and two half-gallon of pickles, mustard, strawberry jam, honey, all mixed up together with cocoa, powdered sugar, instant coffee, etc. We couldn't get across the floor. The beds were overturned, chests out in the floor, relieved of their drawers and contents, potted flowers and dirt everywhere, piano out in the middle of the floor. I thought, "Help! Where do I start?" About that time my dear husband walked in the door. I have hardly mentioned him. You know why?

I wasn't the least bit worried about him. I knew that wherever he was, he was with God and God with him, dead or alive. But it was good to see him, I tell you! He started cleaning up the floor, and I, gathering courage from him, started helping. Of course the power was off, so we had no water, no lights, no heat. With about two quarts of water, after scooping up the mess from the floor, we tried to wipe up the sticky goo.

Some good comes out of everything. One instance that I know of is, my mother was converted. She is now living for the Lord and I'm sure there are many others who made the same decision because of the quake. We have friends who now live in Hamburg, N.Y. He used to say nearly every time he left us, "The Lord bless you real good," and when I got the message off to them on Monday after the earthquake, I simply stated that our Wesleyan Methodist Church, which they helped pioneer, and Church Family were all well and that "The Lord bless us real good." Across the miles I could see them smile and say a prayerful "Amen."

'Copter flying over tennis courts torn asunder by the fault that ran down fourth Avenue, L Street, and across Ninth Avenue.

Bonnie Tisler

I Knew Anchorage Would Survive

I didn't experience the ground shaking of the '64 quake but I have vivid memories of it. I was a Navy wife at the time, based in San Diego, Calif. My husband had deployed on the carrier Bennington bound for Vietnam. I had a four-month-old daughter and my first son on the way. I had considered coming home to Anchorage during the deployment but we had purchased a home and I decided to wait there.

We had visited friends through the evening and came home tired and went to bed. At 3 AM the phone rang. My sister-in-law was calling from Illinois. She asked how my parents were. "Just fine, how is your family?" "There has been an earthquake in Alaska." "Really, we have them all the time. What are your summer plans?" "I don't mean to alarm you but they say the gas lines have ruptured and Anchorage is going up in flames." "That is ridiculous." "Let us know when you hear from them." "I will, but I'm sure they are fine." I went back to sleep.

The news reports the next morning were alarming. I called the Red Cross to see if they needed help or could get word about my family. They said the airport was closed so no help could be sent and communication was disrupted. I prepared for a long wait. The Ship was just crossing the date line and expecting a Tsunami. Actually it did happen but it was only about one foot high.

Ten days later I received an Air Mail letter from Mother. She detailed the damage to our home and the sad news about the Mead boys. A high school classmate had been their nanny and I knew them as young children. One of my high school teachers was badly injured and indeed did not survive. Our family was fine. Uncle Emmett had stood in line for hours to send a message to his son in Los Angeles. He didn't relay the message to me. I haven't spoken to him since.

I knew my parents could easily handle any emergency. I knew that Anchorage would survive.

Pauline Lee Titus

H and Eighth

I had just come home from work and cooked my dinner when the quake hit. It was all I could do to hang onto the doorknob to keep from falling down, while part of my dinner slid from the stovetop onto the floor. It felt like I was on a ship on a rolling sea.

After the quake subsided, I ate what I could salvage of my dinner, and began to straighten things up. A few items fell from the kitchen cupboard, and the door to the bedroom slammed shut. The chest of drawers fell across it and I had a hard time getting that door opened. The electricity went off and there was no heat. I put on my down clothing and got out the sleeping bag and spent a cozy night.

The next day the electricity came back on, but we still did not have the central heat. My landlady said to use the oven. There wasn't much to do, so I went around downtown to see what had happened. Not many people around except the military guards. At the time I didn't know that the downtown was off limits at Ninth Avenue. (I was living within the downtown area.) I walked around and took some pictures and found that the block where my car had been parked earlier that Friday had sunk down about twenty feet.

We had one strong aftershock. For the better part of the following month, I felt a slight dizziness due to the many small aftershocks. It was said that women were more sensitive to these than men.

Robert W. Tompkins

Getting Home from Elmendorf
I worked on Elmendorf AFB.

After the quake started, three of us went outside and watched power poles swaying and tried to hold on to each other because the ground shook violently. I started on my way home toward the power plant and was met by a vehicle coming toward me at a very fast rate. I didn't know why, but discovered later the road was damaged. I thought that the power plant would explode so I reversed direction and went down Post Road. At Third Avenue, I saw dirt being blown into the air and thought it was a gas line break. Rather than pass this area I took a road to the right that led to the Alaska Native Service Hospital. There was a road there before but now it was only a cliff! I had to return to Post Road and pass the gas line break. Nothing happened, fortunately. Went south on Gambell Street. All traffic signals were out. On multiple roads there were transverse cracks and differential elevations of two inches or more in the roads. Made it home without incident.

March 29, 1964

We are all fine and very fortunate. At the time of the earthquake I happened to be at work, since I planned to work overtime that night. I was talking with two other employees when suddenly the building started to shake and the light fixtures began to sway. Immediately I said "Lets get outside." We had difficulty getting out because the earth was shaking so violently. Once outside we had difficulty standing up. The power poles and power lines were swaying to the point I thought they would all snap. My automobile and another one parked along side rocked like a boat in a rough sea. I thought they would be tossed over. It was the most harrowing experience I have ever had and I truly thought it was the end of the world.

Hep and the family meanwhile were all home eating dinner and they were interrupted by the quake. They had difficulty getting outside because of the building movement. Trudy and her oldest baby, who were struck by a falling candleholder, suffered the only injury. All the dishes foodstuffs, etc. fell out of the kitchen cabinets and quite a few objects were broken. The glass jars on the shelves in the basement were tossed on the workbench and the floor and made an awful mess.

The first night we did not have power and water, consequently my heating system was not working. I waited until the next day and took the gun out of the furnace, closed the front, opened the back and took off a portion with the firebrick. Then I fabricated a metal door so I could feed wood into the fireplace from there. I built a small fire and kept it going all day. I could not keep it too high because the water in my heating system had siphoned back into the water supply system and I only had a little water in the boiler. I managed to maintain a temperature of sixty-two degrees although it had been down to fifty-seven degrees. Last night we let the fire go out and this morning it was down to fifty-two degrees in the house and ten degrees outside. We received electric power back Saturday afternoon and water late in the evening. Today I reconnected my furnace and we are back in operation again. We used a bucket for our toilet and boiled snow for water to wash dishes. Fortunately we had about four gallons of water that we keep for emergency purposes. We now have water but have to boil it. Today I had my first shower since the quake.

The first and second nights we slept in shifts with our clothes on. We kept the cars parked outside with blankets and food, water etc. handy in case we had to evacuate. We are very fortunate since the house suffered no structural damage and both cars are okay.

On my way home from work I crossed many open fissures in the road and it took me much longer than usual to get home because of the traffic. I did not see the major damaged areas since I went on alternate routes and now these areas are all blocked off so you cannot get into them to see what it looks like.

When I went back into the office to get my belongings all the bookcases and files were strewn around the office. The grills on the bottom of the light fixtures were off and the vending machines were down and broken. What a mess! I must go to work tomorrow and I imagine we will have a crash program to repair all the damaged property on the base.

Nick Tonkin

Long Distance Service

My wife, two children and I lived near Dowling and Old Seward Highway. I was home, my wife, Babe, was preparing dinner, my two children were watching the TV Program *Fireball XL5*. When the tremors began, it seemed like another of the many quakes I'd experienced. However, in seconds I could no longer stand up, wife and children screaming, kitchen ware and food stuffs pouring from cupboards, TV and buffet falling over. My wife was on the floor. The children and I hung onto the couch for dear life. It felt as if we were riding a bucking rodeo bronco. Our dachshund was thrown around the floor like a stuffed toy.

When it stopped after a couple of minutes we hurried outside and into our automobile. I thought it would be a great idea on this pleasant March evening to see what happened downtown. We drove out on Dowling and turned onto the Seward Highway (there wasn't any traffic!) I noticed the yellow line was broken and offset by pavement cracks but this didn't deter me. When I turned off onto Fifth Avenue, I was shocked to see a cement block building heavily damaged. At an intersection I looked north to an unbelievable scene. I finally realized that I was looking at the marquee of the Denali Theater resting on the sidewalk, the lower part of the building mysteriously gone. Bagoy Florists was a wreck and what I could see of the rest of Fourth Avenue beyond belief.

I raced out of downtown and back to my home. We were all in shock. I then began to think about us being engulfed by a seismic wave, but figured we must be a hundred feet above sea level.

A short while later, when local telephones came back; I was able to reach my place of work. I was Assistant Plant Supervisor at Alaska Communication System Toll Building (now AT&T) on Government

Hill. Luckily several supervisory personnel had been nearby at the Anchor Bowl and were able to help restore basic long distance communications to the States. While close to forty tons of batteries powering the equipment had been destroyed by the quake; we were back on the air in an hour and twenty-one minutes.

We employed one hundred sixty telephone operators. Most of these brave women came to work. We strung telephone wire to our stairwell, foyer, and the parking lot. If people were able to get to Government Hill they could call anywhere, for free, to let friends and relatives know they were alive.

The Corps of Engineers initially condemned the toll building but these brave ACS people still showed up for work.

The Salvation Army's response was wonderful. They showed up with food and drinks within a day or two. Many of us worked as long as we could stay awake repairing the destruction.

The beginning of the Fourth Avenue demolition project. Anchorage-Westward Hotel in background.

Elizabeth A. Tower, M.D.

Wieners in the Fireplace

The Tower family was crosscountry skiing on the old Forest Park Golf Course when the earthquake struck. Since we had two cars, John took his and immediately headed for Providence Hospital. I loaded the three children and our Collie dog into the Land Rover and drove to our Second Avenue home. Surprisingly there was not much evidence of damage along the route that I took. At home I had some broken glass to clean up so I told the two older kids to stay out doors. They wandered up to Fourth Avenue and ran back to report the extensive damage there.

After doing what I could to clean up the house while it was still light, I went next door to check on our elderly neighbor, the artist Mildred Hamill. I found Mildred and her friend, Sally Manserud, sitting comfortably in front of a roaring fire. They were curious to find out more about the damage in town, so I went back to get my battery radio, the kids, and some wieners to roast over their fire, since we had no electricity to cook dinner. The last gasp of the battery radio informed me that all medical personnel were to report to Providence Hospital. Everybody was comfortable for the time being so Mildred and Sally agreed that I should take the car to report to the hospital and in the meantime get more information on the earthquake damage on the car radio.

When I checked into the hospital, I found that far more medical personnel than patients had checked in. I returned to Second Avenue and learned that the area had been evacuated for fear of a tidal wave. I checked the emergency centers in the downtown area, but could find no information about the whereabouts of Mildred, Sally, and my children. When I returned to the hospital to tell John that I had lost the kids, he informed me that Sally had decided to go to her home in the Rabbit Creek area with Mildred and wanted to know what to do with the kids. He suggested they take them to the Moerlein's home at the top of O'Malley Road.

When I reached the Moerlein's at about midnight I found that about fifty people in addition to our children had ended up there in search of high ground. About half the crowd, including Judy Moerlein who had her leg in a cast, was camping out on the lawn because aftershocks were still rocking the house.

We returned home the next day and did what we could to be comfortable without water or electricity. We still had the wieners to roast in the freestanding fireplace and the army was dispensing water.

On Easter Sunday we went to church to give thanks for our survival, but found, when attempting to return home, that the Second Avenue area had been evacuated again. Unable to get home, the whole family retreated to John's office at 825 L Street to help clean up broken glass. Molly Stigum, the business manager, was there and she suggested that the Tower family stay with her in the Cheney Lake area where they had electricity and water. We all spent a week with the Stigums until the power was restored downtown. The Collie dog had the run of the house on Second Avenue and slept in every bed.

John C. Tower, M.D.

Medical Disaster Drill

It was my day off from office duty at Anchorage Pediatric Group at 825 L Street. I drove from the office out to the Forest Park Golf Club (now the site of the Atwood estate) and joined my wife, Betsy, and our three children for an afternoon of crosscountry skiing. The snow cover, although wind blown, was adequate and the temperature mild. We had just made the turn from the lower hole to the next which was a straightaway pasture boarded by a line of birches on the left when the "shake" started abruptly with accompanying low pitched groaning and moaning from the snow underfoot. With recollection of previous earthquakes experienced in our second floor bedroom abutting an ancient brick chimney, I barely had time to comment to Betsy, "At last an earthquake where nothing can fall on us!" when all five of us were precipitated from upright skiing on the level to prone. The to-and-fro motion was so violent that our vision was hazy although I was aware that three-foot birches were being bent, in unison, striking the ground on either side. The violent shaking kept up an indeterminate time, estimated at five minutes, accompanied by screaming from the nearby Turnagain subdivision. That solid ground could open up into deep grabens did not occur to me despite the tracery of cracks in the snow by my nose.

The major quake finally settled down to aftershocks and I set off for the "new" Providence Hospital on the outskirts of Anchorage at that time, finding considerable disarray and only two doctors, Milo Fritz and Perry Mead there. Emergency power was on.

I went to the ER and attended a crush-injured man who died before I could establish an IV.

Within minutes there was a great rush of physicians, nurses, ancillary medical personnel and volunteers from all directions and

from the town's other hospitals, Presbyterian, Alaska Native Health Hospital, Alaska Psychiatric Hospital, and the Elmendorf 5005 military hospital, evacuated because of gas leaks and structural damage. Immediate transport to Providence of the critically ill was under way.

What followed that evening and over the next several days was the greatest emergency medical disaster drill I could envision with the Nuns of the Providence Order supervising and shifts of doctors, nurses, dieticians, maintenance personnel, and pastors bustling about caring for patients in the aisles, hallways and even in the subsurface tunnels.

Besides my pediatric work with an epidemic of bronchiolitis I chiefly was preoccupied with seizures in adults and children from typhoid shots.

Many structures suffered only minor cracks in concrete floors. The Travellodge Inn, on 3rd and A Streets found floor, wall, and ceiling cracks as well as cracks around windows.

Henrietta Roberts Vaden

The Birthday Cake was Fine

I was living with my husband, Doug and our four children at the family home at 1903 36th Avenue in Spenard. School was out for the day, Good Friday. It was also Doug's birthday, so Sylvia Sue was making a cake for her daddy. We didn't have enough sugar to finish the icing so she had gone down the street to borrow some. Then came the big earthquake! The cake slid off of the counter to the floor but landed right side up still on the platter. Dishes came out of the cupboard and slid on the floor. The birthday cake was fine! I looked out and saw trees moving, ground rolling and I ran out to look for the mushroom cloud rising. I was sure that Cuba had dropped the Atomic Bomb on us. Cynthia Ann and Beth were fine and Sue finally came back with the sugar. Doug and Tom came in so all of the family was accounted for.

Doug and Tom put a stovepipe up through where the fireplace chimney had been and hooked up a barrel stove. They hooked up the kitchen stove to a propane gas bottle and we had heat and cooking and we also had water; we were fortunate.

Tom helped Pastor Aubrey Short and his wife of the Faith Baptist Church get wood, build a fire in their fireplace, and help them manage through the period that followed.

One of my brothers called me from Muskogee, Oklahoma to make sure that we were all right.

Now, forty years later, I am still living in the old house.

Nina Van Huss

The Milk Plant

I remember it only too well. I was office manager for Arden Farms on Mountain View Drive and was alone in the office except for some of the deliverymen coming and going. I was finishing the bank deposit to be dropped off at the bank downtown. One of the men asked, as a favor, if I could help write up his delivery tickets for Saturday. I agreed and went to a file cabinet to put the deposit away. Suddenly the cabinet tipped forward but I thought I had done it when I opened the drawer. It went back against the wall with a lot of force. Then the Sales Manager, who was new to Anchorage, came into my office and asked if there were railroad tracks close. He said he heard a train. By the time we could answer him the whole building was shaking and there was a horrible din from the plant. Later, we found most of the noise was coming from the Cold Room where milk ready for delivery was stored. There were dozens of the big containers, each consisting of a plastic bag inside a cardboard carton. They were making a loud bang as they hit the floor and exploded. I never did find out how many fell or were broken but there was milk running from under the door and out into the hall.

The lights went out and the only route out of the building, without going through the plant, was through a long dark hallway. It was really black in there and someone was holding on to my arms above the elbows. I think he thought he was helping me but he was so scared he was just hanging on to anything he could. Later he told my husband that he had "saved" me.

Out in front of the building we watched my little T-bird go dancing across the parking lot right up to the side of a big tanker loaded with milk. I had to shut my eyes because I was just sure I was going to have a mashed flat T-bird. My car gave two more little hops in the other direction and away from the tanker as if it had a mind of its own.

If I hadn't helped the deliveryman, my usual route would have taken me right down Fourth Avenue to the night deposit on the side of the National Bank of Anchorage and I would have been in the worst part of the quake. Instead, I went directly home, driving over sparking electric lines without a thought of danger. I wanted to see if my house, little dog and two cats were all right.

Kodiak's small boat harbor was completely destroyed by seismic sea waves, as was a good portion of the downtown business area. Dozens of fishing boats were lost.

Nez A. Vecera

Midtown

My name is Nez Alice Vecera. I arrived in Alaska (then a territory) in 1955 as a new bride. My husband, Venzy H. Vecera, was a math teacher at West High School.

We were all at home when the earthquake struck. My husband and I and our five children, ranging in ages from six months to seven years old, all huddled together in the middle of the living room floor. Our house, located in midtown, was swaying back and forth.

It felt like we were on a roller coaster. I was afraid that the house was going to collapse. I could also see the house across from us swaying back and forth. There were dishes on the floor, water swishing in the bathroom and the fireplace doors opening. I was screaming.

There were aftershocks and aftershocks and people would panic, as we didn't know what was going to happen.

Our six-month-old daughter was sick with pneumonia. Our three-year-old daughter was very scared and couldn't sleep. We closed all the bedroom doors and stayed together in the living room.

About two days later, when it was safe, my husband built a fire in the fireplace to keep us warm. We had no electricity, water, heat nor phone.

Venzy went to the Spenard Fire Station for water. He melted snow for other uses. It was several days before all utilities were restored. The gas company went from house to house to light the furnaces.

West High School, my husband's place of employment was a two story building before the earthquake. After the earthquake, it was heavily damaged and it became a one-story building. West High School double shifted with East High School.

Through the night, we could hear the ambulance sirens transporting injured people to the hospitals. We kept up with the news with a battery-operated radio.

It was a terrifying experience and I hope I don't have to go through it again. We were not hurt and our house did not sustain damages.

Harry Walker

Journey to the Epicenter

A short time after the 1964 earthquake I moved our mobile home to Anchorage from Moose Creek. I had a new teaching contract and I had also signed on for temporary work with Alaska Dept. of Fish and Game. What I found was astounding. Anchorage was in shambles — buildings flattened, broken in half, slides, faults, roads cut off, drop offs, etc. It was amazing even more people were not killed or buildings destroyed. Did I really want to bring my family to such a place? The spirit of the people I met in that short stay made that an easy decision.

Mother Nature would show me much more of her abilities in a month or so as my job with Fish and Game moved me throughout Prince William Sound — the epicenter. My education is Earth Sciences, but reading texts, lectures and labs are all mundane comparisons when facing the real presence.

Across the bay from Coghill River, there is glacier miles long, and a mile or more wide. It struck me as odd that a great portion of the east side was debris covered and the west side clear. There is a high sharp peak on the west side, rising above the glacier. Most of the front and top of that mountain was gone and fresh scars indicated a massive slide, but no debris was evident at the base of the mountain. The only possible way for the debris to have reached the east side of the glacier was for the quake to have thrown all that rock across it. Not likely, but it happened.

Much of the land around the Sound had sunk or been heaved up from the quake. In some places, at high tide, only the treetops showed while at other places the tides couldn't reach the old shoreline — in some places it would be over a hundred feet below the old high-tide line. Swells and waves over the outer bars (which had been changed, submerged or hidden) behaved in unpredictable fashion. Those waters have always been treacherous with huge swells coming unimpeded off the Pacific Ocean forming dangerous Breakers. This year was much worse. There were several boats lost, but only one life as I recall. Not all the topographic changes from earthquakes are obvious; some of the most severe are subtly hidden.

Someplace near Columbia Glacier, along the shore it was obvious that seismic waves had really worked over the trees up to several hundred feet from shore. Trees, at least fifty feet above the shoreline and two or more feet in diameter, had all been snapped near the base of the trunk, and large barnacle covered boulders were littered in with the debris. It appeared the boulders had been dredged up by the big seismic waves and had cut the trees off at the base.

At the lower end of Port Wells we stopped at what was left of a mine. Everything was down. There had been a house, some sheds, and a large flat roofed structure, probably a big shop or bunkhouse. That was completely flattened. The roof was sixty by seventy-five feet or more and spread on the ground, covering everything like a blanket with ripples and humps like a quilt thrown over a bed. But the oddity was that there was not a single tear or break in all that tarpaper, except for a few square holes chopped through by search crews. The whole structure had collapsed to two or three feet thickness. Nothing protruded through the roof or anywhere around the perimeter. It had to have come straight down as if someone had stepped on it or it had been picked up and dropped straight down and collapsed. Some of the few people who had been very near the heart of the epicenter reported, "the ground jumped!" Maybe that building had been tossed up and fell on itself.

The mine portal was open and did not show much damage. We did not enter but a few feet. A large tractor and truck did not look disturbed. Fifty yards below close to the beach there was a small, undisturbed cabin. Someone had scratched a note on the wall that all was okay and a man was going to try and walk out to Whittier. Below that tacked to the wall a scrap of paper from an Army helicopter pilot dated a few days later and after the quake, said they searched, and found no one. I don't know what happened to those people.

These are a few of my memories of visiting and working in Prince William Sound a short time after the 1964 earthquake. Times were chaotic, money short, and protocol absent in that immediate post earthquake period. People everywhere saw what needed to be done and did it. No quibbling, no squabbling. Alaska was very much different than today.

Jackie Weatherly

"Help Yourself!"

When the big one hit I was working as a clerk in the liquor store at Piggly Wiggly grocery in Spenard. The windows that were on three sides floor to ceiling started popping out, glass flying everywhere. Bottles were falling to the floor and breaking. The smell was terrible. I ran out the side door to join the people from the grocery store who were in a line holding each other up. One of the bakers grabbed me. He held me up until the shaking stopped. I returned to the very broken store. Many people came in asking if they could have a drink. I said, "Help yourself." I took the cash box and headed for home to check on my family. There was a large crack across Arctic Blvd. Two men came with boards for us to drive across. Everyone was okay at home.

One week later I was at the beauty shop. My head was on the sink. I heard another quake coming, and I ran out the front door yelling I don't know what. Everyone thought I was nuts, but just as I got to my car the next big one hit. All of a sudden everyone was outside with me.

I don't want to ever go through that again.

Catherine Weimer

There Goes My Lenox

It started as the day devoted to moving back into the kitchen. I had just painted it, cupboards and all. I was finishing the task a little after five PM.

Bob came home then from our potato farm in the Sand Lake area. I asked him to take out the trash. I would warm the leftovers and we would have dinner.

As he was walking through the back yard, he thought he heard water running in our vacant little rental. In the house, I heard a loud rumbling, which sounded like a lowboy moving a dozer. Suddenly there was a big jolt. An earthquake!!

Bob turned around and I moved toward the back door. As I grabbed the doorknob, the second jolt hit. I flung open the door and thought "My God! The carport is going down!" I went right out under it. Bob came back toward me. When we met, I was knocked off my feet but Bob stood like in an open dory, like the fisherman that he was. He was amazed! As we watched the young trees across the street to the west whipping back and forth, he kept saying, "Watch the 1200 L. It's not moving a bit!" I sat and watched the lawn heave. The car in the carport was bouncing crazily. We could see our poor parakeet, who always had an open cage, flying frantically about. Dishes were smashing down from the cupboard shelves. Later, Bob teased me by telling people that I kept wailing, "There goes my Lenox plates!" The quake seemed to roll across the lawn like waves coming ashore. Still the 1200 L didn't move a bit. Bob kept saying, "Boy, this is a long one."

When we came into the kitchen, it was a mess. Glass was all over the floor from the stack of glass dessert plates. My dozen Lenox plates on the shelf were leaning drunkenly but okay. The glass cover from the electric frying pan was smashed. The cherished green cut glass vase from the top shelf was without a chip on it. In the basement, our domestic hot water was heated from coils in the boiler of our furnace. The stand on the water tank was broken from the weight of the tank pounding on the cement floor. It was hanging from the water pipes. Bob shut off the water until we could get a new stand. Basically, that was the only damage to our home.

The first thing Bob did was go to the neighborhood grocery store (one of his farm customers). He found they were trying to serve customers by candlelight. He came home and got a Coleman lantern and took it over for their use. Incidentally, we had some of them that we had used for light in the rootcellar before Chugach Electric electrified our farm. We were hunters and campers so we had Coleman stoves too. I used one atop my electric stove to warm up those leftovers.

Our neighbor who had a business downtown, popped in to see how we fared. He told us about Penney's and how bad things were downtown. So after dinner we went to sightsee. By that time, the National Guard had sealed the downtown. They had just finished an encampment.

We then went west on Ninth Avenue and saw the newly built Four Seasons was a pile of rubble. There was a yawning graben just past Ninth Avenue and L St. We turned on L to Eleventh. I'm not sure if we got down to our friends' home then, but when we did get there, their home was not badly damaged.

It got quite cold after the quake. Some places where water mains were broken, irrigation pipes were laid along the streets to bring water to some homes. Of course they froze and burst. In our neighborhood we got potable water from a tank on the Park Strip. We had five-gallon jerry cans (again used on our farm), which we shared.

The first thing we did after sightseeing was to light the fireplace for warmth. I took my big washtub out and filled it with snow. I brought it in to melt by the fireplace, water for flushing. One does have to think of everything!

One week after the quake, I was in City Hall (the old building on Fourth Ave.). We had a stiff aftershock. The clerk was very excited and ran out. Her children were at home. I noticed when the shaking stopped that I was sitting right under a heavy light fixture.

When the snow melted that spring, I noticed the dry lawn grass looked like it was cut with a knife. The frozen ground had stretched from the wave action.

One vivid memory of the whole experience was how the people behaved. One couldn't go down the street without total strangers asking how you fared. Did you have damage? Did you need anything? They really cared. People opened their homes to others to come bathe or do their laundry. Many acts of kindness. Rarely heard whining, just gratitude that things were not worse.

Deep fissures line this street in Turnagain By the Sea. Some fissures were only a few feet deep. Others grew into bottomless crevasses. Men in this photo are geologists inspecting the area. It was feared that aftershocks could send more homes tumbling into Cook Inlet.

Max and Betty Wells

Valdez

We thought we were living quite a normal, fairly successful life. The kids were doing fine in school. Business has been better for Wells Commercial Company than in the previous year. Teddy and Tammy (his niece) were a constant source of entertainment. Grace and David were busy in scout work and school. In all, life seemed quite wonderful, until—

Max had just come back from picking up a group of high school kids who had been skiing six miles from town. I had suggested Max take Ted along for the ride. Laurie and Crickett were playing under the apartment, in the warehouse. Grandma Wells (who had celebrated her 80th birthday on March 24th) was writing letters in her cozy new apartment. Grace and Jeannie were tending store for Max. So we were all home—nine of us.

Then we felt the first tremor, Max sort of laughed, for we knew what it was — but it got harder and harder. Max ran down the hall for he knew that Laurie and David and Gram were down underneath us. Jason grabbed Teddy up and ran down the stairs, barefooted, as he had just taken off his ski boots. I followed Max, after first turning off the gas stove, where Jay had been heating water for tea, and also the furnace. The warehouse doors had flung open, so Laurie and David ran outside. By the time I started downstairs, the walls of the stairs were fairly hitting my shoulders. I heard the metal siding tear as the building shook back and forth. Max was standing by the car (which was fortunately headed up the street) herding the kids into the car. I watched fascinated at the huge Alaska Steamship *Chena* raring up and down by the dock. We could see its propeller way out of the water. The earth was cracking and heaving all around us. Wires were snapping off the poles.

Max says he saw the concrete slab the store is built on rare up and he could see twenty feet back beneath it. Jean and Grace jumped a crevasse to get out of the store. A teacher friend of ours, Scott, ran back in to get Gram out of her apartment. The building ripped apart just as they passed that section.

Max saw the docks go down and the *Chena* go out of sight. He realized there would be a wave coming. There was water in the street partially from broken mains but mostly from the pump action underneath the ground. We drove up part of the block, turned up an alley, and around a corner. Max was trying to get us to higher ground. Our neighbor's fuel truck was stopped by a crevasse, so Max knew we couldn't drive further. He threw Crickett up on top the tanker, and helped Grace try to get up. Jay climbed up, holding Teddy. Grace didn't get a good hold, and hung just by her hands. We watched her bumping over the fissures. She lost her shoes in the muddy, churning water. Max, carrying Laurie like a sack of sugar, Gram, Jean and I started wading up the road, holding hands, so when one slipped in a crevasse, the others helped pull him up. Max and Gram fell in one large fissure, and were wet up over their waists. We did get to higher ground. Max glanced back one time and saw a thirty-foot wave coming toward us. It fell back before it hit us. Jean, Laurie and I sat in a pickup with another girl and her two other people. Gram stayed in town with some friends, until the fire started that evening.

We came back into town about 9 PM and stayed at the Huddleston's home, along with about thirty-five others. Jeanette had made coffee from some of the precious water, and fed everyone who felt like eating. Sally, her daughter, found dry clothes for those of us who were wet. All of this time, I did not know where the rest of our kids were, though I was sure that they were all okay. Jason had brought Teddy to me. It was hard not to have Max and Jerry with us, but we knew someone had to look for survivors from the dock area.

About 11 PM the lights started going out, and we had another bad shake. The children, who were by now in bed, started screaming. Max came back to tell us to get out of town, that the Union Oil Company tanks were afire, and fire was spreading all along the water front, and coming in on the high tide. It was at this time that the highest tidal wave occurred. The sirens started wailing for the town to evacuate. By flashlight, we gathered some bedding from Jeanette's house, and diapers and food and the cars started out of town. We went as far as 35 Mile Roadhouse, where about 150 people were gathered. This place was to become a very overworked place those next few weeks. Max and others went back into town about 4 in the morning. It was getting daylight. What a terrible scene of devastation it must have been - the docks were gone, and some thirty friends and neighbors with them. The hotel, plumbing shop, cafe, transfer and cold storage places were all burned to the ground — our store building and apartment warehouse were still standing, not touched by the fire all around them. The windows were broken out of the store, and most of our nice, spring stock, some of which we had never unpacked, was floated out the window or ruined by the salt water. The area had sunk about 6 feet, so that now normal high tides come in about two or three feet on the floor. About 600 feet of the dock area slid into the bay when the docks went down. There was not one boat left intact in the harbor, but one pleasure boat, which had been stored up in the top story of a cannery, was found way down the bay, floating without a scratch on it. Not one trace of the *Heather Dee* was ever found. Our dear old dog, Dart, was electrocuted. It could have easily been one of us.

Yes, we lost our business, home, store, and a few personal things, and the *Heather Dee*, but we know that material things are not important. Our greatest loss was the many friends who were on the dock.

Margarete L. Wike

Army Wife

As a young army wife, I was shopping in the commissary when everything started to shake. I grabbed my purse, left my groceries, and rushed out to the parking lot. I made a mistake. I ran between two cars parked nose to nose and only room for me to stand between with a hand on each one. I could have had both legs crushed, as the earth continued to shake more violently. That is when I learned to pray.

When the shaking stopped, I drove home to Mountain View. My husband, Bob, my son Bobby, and houseguests were waiting. I went into the house and they handed me a rum and coke to calm my nerves. Everyone was safe, and that was all that mattered. I was very relieved that they were all right. A house can be repaired, but not a family member. Total damage was three garbage cans of broken dishes, and minor damage to the house.

Although I did not bring any groceries home, no problem. I had a six-month supply of staples in the basement. I lived in Wurzburg, Germany during WWII. When the allies were doing some of their heaviest bombing I spent three weeks in the woods. Something like that helps prepare you for emergencies.

It took me at least a year before I could get into an elevator, and no department store for a long time. My first trip through the tunnel to Whittier, many years later, was a nightmare.

I have a sewing box that Bob gave me that was slightly damaged, and I have not had it repaired. I have that as a reminder that things can change in a hurry.

Frances Wilson

In Church in Mountain View

It was a quiet balmy day with little snow. I took the youngest daughter to church at St. Patrick's Church in Mountain View. The service started at 5:30. Several relatives and priests were there. The service had been underway for six minutes when there was a whispering noise. My sister said, "What is it?" I said, "I think it's an earthquake." The chandeliers were swinging. Statues and candles fell. A few people went out the back, but a priest held out his hands and people sat down.

People thought the world was coming to an end. A child said, "Mom, are we going to die?" I said, "Can you think of a better place?" The bible shook. The curtain of the temple shook. We expected fire engines. The priest put the candles back and continued with the service until after six PM.

There were cracks in the buildings there, but home in the East side on Old Harbor Avenue there was less damage. My husband, Merrill, was at home. A few things were broken and there were cracks in the sidewalk. We had a power radio, which ordered, "Anybody who can't help, stay home." We couldn't contact our daughter on the other side of town, but our son-in-law, in the Air National Guard helped.

You could get a little nausea from the after shocks.

Esther C. Wunnicke

We're Tough

This earthquake story was written to friends and family on April 8, 1964.

Bill left his office at five o'clock and stopped at the bank and the dry cleaners. I had the children all dressed except for their coats ready to go to six o'clock Good Friday services with Bill as soon as he got home. I intended to go back upstairs as soon as he came, put on my hose and get one year old Amy's coat and hat that were laid out on the bed. Paul, age three, Amy and I were all downstairs when Bill walked in, and Paul was playing with his fire truck and had on his fire hat.

Bill had just walked in the door, hung up the cleaning on the coat rack on the stairs and hadn't even taken off his overcoat (it had been snowing all that day) when the first tremor came. I looked at Bill and said, "Earthquake! This is one I can tell June I felt." And sat down in a chair with Amy on my lap. Then the tremors came faster and with increasing force and intensity and the house began to shake, groan and roll. Bill picked up Paul, I kept Amy in my arms, and we all knelt in the stairwell with the children under us. Both of them were frightened and we both kept saying to them, "It's all right. It's all right. It's nothing to be frightened about." And we really weren't frightened during the quake. The speaker doors on our stereo that was hung by brackets to the north wall of the living room were flapping like anguished birds, and I do remember thinking that we were going to get that stereo on the head any minute. So we edged a bit farther into the stairwell. I could see part of the kitchen from where I was kneeling, and one of my mental "pictures" is of the three dozen Easter eggs I had just boiled flying through the air like missiles. We just had no realization of the magnitude of what had happened until we went outside after the quake subsided. As we were going out the door Paul began to cry when he saw my ill-starred philodendron uprooted on the floor. I remember saying to him, "Oh, Paul, don't get excited. This place doesn't look any worse than when your sister has been turned loose in it for a few hours!" She had just uprooted the philodendron a week or so before. (We have that plant with us in the trailer and think it deserves to live — battered as it is, because it's the one that traveled for six weeks all the way from New Mexico in the bottom of a wastebasket.)

When we walked outside the first thing I saw was the house across the street from us on the east in a hole with the upstairs balcony resting on the ground. Then my eyes traveled in a half-circle and I saw the crevasse across Seventh Ave., the house diagonally across L Street from us tipped crazily into it, and beside it the Bachner apartments broken in two with the west half in the crevasse. The dust was still rising from its fall. On the corner we saw Mr. and Mrs. Erickson standing with a woman who was screaming and crying. She had been in the Bachner apartments and had gotten out just in time. Then we went to make sure the Gilcreases were all right. They were standing in front of their house. Lois put her arms around me and said, "I'm going back to New Mexico!" Art said something that made me think that, working with the missile tracking station he knew something that we didn't know, and it was an atomic bomb. I remember saying, "Oh, no, Art, that was an earthquake." As though I had ever been in one before and was an expert! Then we ran to where we could get a view of the 14-story L Street Apartments and saw that it was still standing. In so doing we saw the new Four Seasons Apartment a pile of rubble at Eighth and M, and bit by bit the enormity of it all began to soak in. Bill had overheard the Soysters and Lintons making plans to meet to celebrate Mr. Soyster's 72nd birthday that evening, so he was sure that they were all in the Soysters' apartment on the fourteenth floor of L Street Apartments. All during the quake Bill kept saying, "I know the Lintons are at the Soysters. Poor June, she'll be terrified. Poor June." So our next thought was to see about them. Bill went back in the house, got the steel box with our important papers in it, Amy's bottle, some more coats and we got in the car and left. There were minor cracks to the South and West of our house too, and since further tremors, fire or tidal wave were the next possibilities, it was not a safe place to stay. We probably would have stayed longer to get more clothes out of the house, if we hadn't been so concerned about Bill and June and the Soysters.

We couldn't go south on L because of the crevasse, so we worked our way around through the main portion of downtown Anchorage. Then in wave after wave the shock of the destruction began to come to us as we saw buildings crumbled, with walls gone, tipped into crevasses, windows shattered. But not once from then on, except for the woman from the Bachner apartments, did we hear anyone even raise their voices. There was an uncanny quiet, as though one were walking through a silent movie. People were running, but they were not running in panic, and we saw nothing but calmness and courage demonstrated by the people of Anchorage.

When we came to a street that wasn't there we would back up and try to find another way. As we neared Holy Family Church at Fifth and H, we got out of the car, because we wanted to go in and tell Him "thank you." They wouldn't let us in the building, although from the outside it looked untouched. (Since then it has been checked out and Masses resumed on a regular schedule April 5.) We had immediately turned on the car radio. There was nothing on the emergency channels and we could only get three stations. One was a "skip" with someone exhorting everyone to return to God, one was a Japanese station on which we could not understand one word, and the other was KENI operating on auxiliary power, still not knowing what had taken place except that the power was off, and playing rock and roll! As Bill drove, I kept turning the radio dial trying to find out what had happened, what instructions one should follow, or anything!

We finally got on Fifteenth St. and when we drove up in front of Bill and June's house we saw their car. What a blessed relief! We thought that they must have changed their minds and decided to celebrate Mr. Soyster's birthday at their house. We hadn't realized how long it had taken us to get there (Bill later estimated that it was about forty minutes). It took us a long time after we went in to fully comprehend that they HAD been at L Street, had come down, and before coming to look for us had hurried home to dress June's leg which was badly cut. Where they had been was a terrifying place to be. Mr. Soyster had been knocked down in the kitchen, Bill and June made it to the hall, and Alice Soyster made it to the doorway of their apartment leading into the hall and stayed there clinging to the doorjamb and trying to keep the door from slamming so that Merwin would not be trapped inside. Bill and June wrapped their arms around each other as they were thrown to the floor and were rocketed back and forth and up and down the hall like a human bowling ball. I can only imagine, and I have a pretty vivid imagination, the terror of knowing that one could not escape from the building, that it might come crashing down at any moment, and the awful swaying, rocking movement. I don't know who the architect and builder of that building was, but he, and Almighty God, have all our fervent thanks for their safety.

There was no power, fortunately, so Anchorage was spared fire. The three men took turns going out to listen to the car radio, and we then began to get reports of the damage in Turnagain where the houses fell into the Inlet, damage to Kodiak and Seward and warnings of tidal wave, and the first-exaggerated estimates of casualties in Anchorage. We bedded down on the floor in our clothes, pressed June's dishtowels into service as diapers for Amy and waited out the night without heat, lights or water. Paul thought that coffee can was great stuff and even after we had sewer facilities he wanted his coffee can! There were a number of aftershocks, but none of any great intensity. I believe that there have been some 50 or 60 aftershocks altogether since the initial quake, the hardest one coming last Friday (April 3) at 12: PM and another sharp one yesterday morning (April 6) about 9:30 AM. Everyone's sense of balance seemed to be affected, so we often felt a "wave or quake" when there was no visible evidence of one.

We went back to our house at Seventh and L early Saturday morning. It was all barricaded off and we followed a military jeep in through the barricade. Stationed at the corner near our house were two Eskimo National Guardsmen. They are small people, but to us they looked eight feet tall! There had been no looting, thanks to the character of the people involved, and the quick action of the military and National Guard in stationing guards at damaged sites. In fact, one of the Assistant DA's who lived in the apartment next to us told me they had fewer incidents of crime than they did during normal times. We were amazed that morning to see how our house had stood and how little actual damage we had. The fact that the ground broke just east and South of us probably relieved us of a lot of the reverberations from the quake. We got our typhoid shots that day and worried most about getting word out to our loved ones.

We heard on the radio that some mail was going to go out, so we wrote hurried notes and mailed them. At Linton's that afternoon we had electricity and heat, but still no water or sewer. At our home there were no utilities. We spent the day bringing food from our house to theirs, going to the distribution centers for water, etc. and all the business of surviving and keeping the children cared for and feeling secure. All of this under the tension of waiting for each new aftershocks and worrying about you worrying! The men went to see about their office in the Cordova Building, which had been badly damaged but was still standing and to do what they could about saving the USGS records. We stayed glued to the radio, tried to get in touch with other friends in Anchorage, told "fairy tales" to the children, and marveled over and over again at the miraculously few casualties and our own safety.

Sunday we went to Mass unbathed, unshaved, and certainly without any new Easter bonnet. Mass was said in the Catholic Junior High School which had sustained only minor damage, and it was as we were leaving that we heard on the car radio that they would now begin to take personal telegraph messages. It was about 1 o'clock that we got our wires filed.

Monday morning while the men were working at the office building, I went back to the house for more clothes for the children, and was sitting there in the car when our regular mailman, with his regular smile, came swinging down the street. There were letters written after the news of the quake from friends and family. I cried then for the first time, and I needed to. We all returned to the house that evening and fully intended to stay there. Bill and the children slept well that night, but I didn't. I prowled the house all night, and it was an eerie place to be. The next day Bill went to work and I cleaned up most of the mess as best I could. We melted snow water for cleaning. Then Mrs. Culver, our landlady, came and told us that Civil Defense had asked her to move from her home on Romig Hill, another bluff area. When she told them her plan to bring sleeping bags for her and her children down to her office at the back of the house at Seventh and L, they told her "not to bother" because that was the next worst area. It had been thawing rapidly that day and new cracks in the ground were appearing. So, we packed up again — a bit more organized this time — and went back to the Linton Refugee Station. Their landlord knew of a trailer available, so we came right on out here that night and arranged for it. There was no heat or electricity in the trailer, so we stayed that night with Lintons and moved in here about 9 o'clock Wednesday night. It looked like a palace to me! And it still does.

There are many stories of tragedy and near tragedy, of courage and miraculous escape, and now we are hearing some of the funny ones too. My favorite is of the roaring drunk in one of the Fourth Avenue bars. This drunk fell off the bar stool just as the quake began and after it was over came crawling out the door of the bar, which had slid off the bluff, to the feet of a policeman. The drunk kept saying, "I'm shorry, offisher, I'm shorry, I didn't mean to do it!"

But this is our story, prosaic as it is, and we are all doing fine. I have my scraggly philodendron. Bill is still eating sourdough pancakes every morning. Paul has his fire hat, and Amy's dimple has returned to her cheek.

You know that no letter from me would be complete without a bit of bragging on our kids, so I'll just add these. The next morning after the quake Amy got up and walked completely across the living room to Bill Linton. We guessed that she thought if she were going to have to run for her life, she had better be learning how. And a few days ago when Bill and I were talking about some friends who were leaving Alaska now, Paul said, "But we're not going. We're tough!" To our knowledge he had never heard anyone say this, but he was right. We are Alaskans now for better or for worse.

Jackie Young

Bootlegger's Cove

Were you really in Alaska during the big earthquake? How many tourists over the years at the Captain Cook Athletic Club have asked me this?

My firemen husband, John, was on duty at the department while my adorable Mom babysat our five children at our home in Bootlegger's Cove and I kept our store (Young and Younguns Bowling Supplies on Spenard Road) open for business. Things were slow, supposedly because of the Easter holiday, so I had decided to go to my health club. I had started my van outside to warm the engine and I was back in the building when a top female bowler came in for shoes for an approaching tournament. I had one shoe on Mary when the quake began. She shrieked and I told her the ones I felt in California appeared stronger and not to worry. Then a file cabinet toppled to the floor, two bowling balls rolled off and bowling bags began to tumble from the ceiling hooks. We were both becoming frightened so we rushed out to my running van, each of us holding onto an outside door handle. The van would carry us to the building, stop and back out almost to the street, and start in again for the building. During this time the customers at the bar across the street were screaming because all the booze landed on the floor.

When the trembling finally ceased I got into my van after locking the door to our destroyed store. I hurriedly tried to get home to my children and seemed blocked at every turn with collapsed streets. I still don't remember the streets I was able to use to get to Thirteenth and U but I do remember it seemed to take forever. I discovered I was lucky I had not gone to the Athletic Club. The women's side, which was fortunately empty, had collapsed like many other Fourth Avenue structures. National news carried pictures of nude men holding hands, forming a circle for both moral and physical support. These men had been in the men's side during the quake.

At home I found two of my small children hiding under the dining room table. Mom was holding the baby, Becky, who had been in her high chair. Mom had made up her mind that the safest place for Becky was to throw her on to a pile of snow and had been ready to do this when the quake stopped. Our house, which we had just built, was built to withstand quakes, to sway. Neighbors reported it did just that. It SWAYED!

After listening to each child's terrorizing report, my stepfather, Smitty, came in with tales of his trip from downtown Anchorage to his house at Seventh and O; so many tales that he was photographed and interviewed for the National TV news. Smitty asked me to run to his house with him to check it out. We saw considerable damage on the way but none close to our house. It was confined to the area from Tenth Avenue to Fourth Avenue. Mom and Smitty's house was gone. As we gingerly wandered through the rubble we couldn't help but notice that their beautifully decorated hutch cabinet had made many trips across the floor and not one item inside got broken. As we were examining the house, fire trucks were outside, telling all of us to move to higher ground because of the potential tsunami damage.

We ran back to my house to get Mom and the kids and took off for the City View Fire Station, where we all crowded in for the night. I was so disappointed not to see John, and the children missed their daddy, but for three days and nights he was on the fire truck scouting for people who needed help.

When we safely returned to our home the next day we began making room for Smitty and Mom to move in with us. They were pretty depressed but said many times they were grateful it was their house that was destroyed and not ours, with our five children.

Smitty and Mom got no government help because they had paid for their home; instead the government helped the banks with people with mortgages.

Also the government helped many businesses that really had only lost a small amount of inventory and gave them loans at 3%. We know now that we could have qualified for this money, but naively believed that if we didn't take the money there would be enough to fund the Smiths and others who really lost everything.

Our home suffered no real damage until six months later when the water lines up the hill from our house burst, filling the upstairs with cold water and the downstairs with hot.

The Funny Side

Many stores remained open and did their best to accommodate customers. After a time they could see some humor in all that had happened and signs began to appear in store windows. The following are some examples:

Down to earth prices

Closed Due to Early Breakup
Business has dropped off.
Mac's Foto

It is not our Fault

We Intend to Stay and Grow with Anchorage

TEMPORARY QUARTERS AT SEVENTH AND G
EARTHQUAKE BRANCH
MATANUSKA VALLEY BANK

Closed for Spring Cleaning

We have to quit rocking and we are ready to roll.
Seen at Alaska Aggregate Corp.

We don't have any 'Shake' siding on Sale but do carry a good supply of other building materials.

Other sayings appeared in conversations and elsewhere.

Alaskan Twist

Never a dull moment
the place is jumping

Not terra firma, but terror firma

New disease — Alaskan twitch

You come from the
wrong side of the cracks

People didn't like their
neighbors, so they moved
their house and lot.

Not Turnagain By the Sea, but
Turnagain in the sea.

We are all eligible to belong to
the RCA (Rodeo Cowboys of
America) we rode things out.

Mother Nature went on the
move and into her wild act.

We were down,
but never OUT!

The lights went out
all over

Earthquake Songs Around Anchorage

Whole Lot of Shaking Going On
by the Earthquakes

Lights Out
by the Tidal Waves

Home on the Bay
by the Tremors

Funny How Towns Slip Away
by the Drifters

On the Sunken Side of the Street
by the Levelers

Wrecked Homes in the Sunset
by the Shifters

Standing on the Corner Watching all the Streets Divide
by the Splits

———————

There was a joke going around town about a man who was in one of the bars downtown on Fourth Avenue, and his punch line was, "All I did was just stamp my foot, and the whole town fell down."

———————

There was another story about a woman who ran out of the house with no clothes on. A man on the street asked her, "Lady, did you forget something?" So she ran back in and grabbed her purse.

———————

The tallest tale concerns a gentleman who was injured while living on the topmost floor of the apartment building on L" Street. He had just come home from work and was relaxing in a warm bath when the floor started to shake and his wife began to scream. Not bothering to dress, he jumped out of the bath and ran to the kitchen where his wife was vainly trying to staunch the stream of water erupting from the kitchen sink.

Thinking to turn the water off, he knelt in front of the sink and was trying to turn off the faucet under the sink when the family cat, apparently terrorized by the shaking and screaming, leapt up and sunk her claws into his bare buttocks.

Understandably startled, the gentleman jumped and struck his head forcibly on the bottom of the sink, knocking himself out. After the rescue workers with their stretchers were able to get to the top floor some time later, the gentleman's wife insisted they carry her husband downstairs, the elevators not working of course, as he as bleeding and still groggy from the head wound.

On the way downstairs, there was an aftershock, and one of the stretcher-bearers dropped his end and our gentleman fell out and down a flight of stairs, breaking one leg.

This gentleman is known as the person who always swallows hard when asked, "Were you hurt in the earthquake?"

I heard that a clerk at the Rexall Drugstore was waiting on some visitors from the East when the first small quake began. "What's that?" they asked. "Oh, just an earthquake;" said the clerk. We have them all the time." Then the big one hit. They left the store which was rapidly being trashed and stood in the street, watching. "How do you stand it?" asked one of the tourists.

Fault lines seemed to toy with buildings — sinking some, upending some and leaving others. Somebody said they believed some buildings must have been held together by their reputation.

One story was about a couple in an apartment on Third Avenue. She was taking a bath when the earthquake started. She couldn't get out of the tub, and called for her husband to help her. Instead of helping her out, he fell into the tub and they waved through the quake in the water.

Mike Campbell

Little Jim

Little Jim, he was a fisherman
and a good man through and through,
But when, each time, Jim docked
in port he was known to drink a few.

On the 26th day of March, back in 1964,
Little Jim tied up to the Kodiak
pier and headed for the bars on shore.
Little Jim tied up to the Kodiak
pier and headed for the bars on shore.

In the wee hours of the morning,
with a stumble in his stride,
Jim staggered back to his ship
so he could sleep through a few high tides.

His head so filled with whiskey,
in his cabin he laid down,
And slept like a babe in his mother's
arms when the earthquake hit that town.

Jim slept like a babe in his mother's
arms when the earthquake hit that town.

Oh the damage was enormous,
9.2 on the Richter Scale.
And the people cried as the buildings
shook and the sea began to boil.

All the sirens they were screaming
as the tidal wave came near,
When the water rushed out of the
harbor, every face was filled with fear.

But still Jim kept on sleeping
while his lines all broke away,
And his ship settled down in the
Kodiak mud on the bottom of Chiniak Bay.

Then the tidal wave came crashing
in with a great unearthly roar.
Scooped up Jim's ship like it was
a toy and carried it over the shore.

It skittered right down the
street crashing into cars and walls,
But Jim was used to Alaska storms
and he slept right through it all.

Little Jim was used to Alaskan storms,
he slept right through it all.

Little Jim was used to Alaska storms,
he slept right through it all.

Many ships were torn apart that
day and many lives were lost.
But Little Jim's ship was gently
placed in the middle of a parking lot.

Now several hours later
when his bladder did prevail,
Little Jim woke up to nature's
call and he stumbled to the rail.

He stared at all the damage and
his blood went cold with fear,
"Oh brother," said Jim, how could I have
been, so drunk to have driven her here.

"Oh brother," said Jim, how could
I have been, so drunk to have driven her,
drunk to have driven her,
drunk to have driven her here."

All but one dock facility in Kodiak was destroyed. Seismic sea
waves demolished more than 215 structures. Some 600 people
were left homeless.

Earthquake Quotes

I remember thinking
that it must be a war.
Patricia Garrett

On the north-south wall everything on the shelves came
crashing down. But anything on
the east-west wall stayed intact.
George Arcand

The noise was such that it
sounded as though the
walls were falling in.
Betty Arnett

I thought the Russians
had dropped a bomb!
Robert Boyer

Everyone get to higher
ground. Everyone get to
higher ground immediately,
a tsunami is coming.
Dorothy Arnold

I came to your house to tell
your wife she was a widow.
Tom Marshall

Hey man, I'm standing here
balancing glasses and I look
like I'm dancing over here.
Bud Berkin

My friend said she was
chased out of her kitchen by
a portable dishwasher.
Phyllis Allinger

I finally decided to start
crawling home because the
shaking seemed endless.
Beth Henderson

Our furniture started moving
in the bedroom and I had an
awful time getting out of there.
It kept blocking the door.
Dr. Helen Beirne

Mothers were herded out of
their beds and rushed to the
nursery where they were told
not to look for their own child
but to pick up a baby, any
baby, and to hurry outside.
Roland Bloes

By the time we got back to
our house, the place was
guarded and only those people
who could prove they lived
there were allowed in.
Helen Butcher

The ten foot window of
the building was waving.
Beverly Dalzell

Our poor old Springer
Spaniel had the shakes.
Eugene C. Smith

The office was quite small'
it contained a desk, a chair,
and three four-drawer filing
cabinets. All were moving to
and fro across the office and
I was trying to avoid...
Peter Jenkins

Suddenly we realized our
son usually crossed Campbell
Lake on the way back from
his paper route.
Les and Berneice Kelm

When the motion started I
assured my employees and
a lone customer, that it was
only an earthquake...not
to worry...!
Army Kirschbaum

Believe me when I say I
am not ready for a re-run
of that quake.
Arliss Sturgulewski

My hands that were still holding my twofer scotch-and-
waters. My hands that had
taken the glasses under the
table, out from under the table,
all around the block, into the
car and now, as I watched,
began shaking so hard they
dropped both drinks in my lap.
Jean Paal

Bill and June wrapped their
arms around each other as
they were thrown to the floor
and were rocketed back and
forth and up and down the hall
like a human bowling ball.
Esther Wunnicke

Mom had made up her
mind that the safest place
for baby Becky was to throw
her on a pile of snow....
Jackie Young

...could find no information
about the whereabouts of
Mildred, Sally and my children.
When I returned to the
hospital to tell John that
I had lost the kids....
Elizabeth Tower

Mr. Swensen, you go to hell
Vera Stribling

Index

About Janet Boylan

Janet first came to Alaska the weekend of Thanksgiving in 1968. "The days were cold and crisp and I thought it was the most beautiful country I had ever seen." She taught at Campbell School and Clark Junior High. She took a hiatus for nine years and stayed home to raise son, Bradley.

By 1996 it was time again to move on to new endeavors. Since she had always wanted to play bridge she started going to the Anchorage Senior Activity Center. After a few years of looking after family and doing what had to be done the decision was made to be active at the Center. As Chairman of fund raising for the Center, Janet knew there was always a need. She hit upon the idea of writing a book of earthquake stories to sell. It was a topic a lot of people at the Center were interested in pursuing, and she received a lot of encour-

agement. Dolores Roguszka was one of the lucky ones that volunteered to help with the editing.

Husband Don has always been very supportive, and ready to help in any way he can. He has been very patient while we have been busy on the computer, getting interviews and putting the book together.

We only hope those who read the book will get as much enjoyment out of it as we have meeting a lot of wonderful people and listening to their stories and getting those stories into print.

About Dolores Roguszka

Dolores Roguszka is a retired freelance photographer, writer and teacher. Her professional photographic experience spans forty years, and her publication credits include such periodicals as National Geographic, Audubon, New York Times, Women's Wear Daily, Alaska Sportsman, Alaska Construction and Oil Report. Ms. Roguszka began her career as an apprentice photographer in Anchorage, Alaska. That career included publication of articles and photographs Internationally.

She also taught photography through the Extension Program of The University of Los Angeles. Her book "Amphoto Guide to SLR Photography" was published during those teaching years, and was used as a textbook for her classes.

She noted "Participation in this book has been such a pleasure, particularly since the book will record a bit of history that otherwise would have been lost forever."

She first moved to Alaska in 1953, and still lives on O'Malley Road with her husband Gene.